Baptism is a big and contested topi̶c̶ ... to Old Testament circumcision, wa̶s̶ ... sprinkle or immerse, do you baptiz̶e̶ ... exegesis, lots of debates, and several p̶ ...̶.̶.̶.̶ᴍ̶a̶s̶.̶ ̶T̶h̶a̶n̶k̶f̶u̶l̶l̶y̶ Dr Deenick has provided us with an accessible and judicious analysis of the key texts. Also, with a mixture of theological acumen and pastoral sensitivity, he explains how baptism is, ultimately, a sign of the gospel for the entire family of faith. Easily one of the best books about baptism you will ever read!

Michael F. Bird
Academic Dean and Lecturer in Theology,
Ridley College, Melbourne, Australia

Deenick explains in this fascinating book that all of us need to be washed and cleansed by God, showing that true purification comes through Christ's death and resurrection. At the same time, he makes a provocative and in some respects new case for infant baptism based on his understanding of circumcision. Deenick's tone is not polemical but charitable and humble as he makes his case. As a Baptist, I remain unconvinced. Still, I encourage all to read and interact with this work, and I hope we can all agree with Deenick that we look to Jesus alone for salvation.

Thomas R. Schreiner
James Buchanan Harrison Professor of New Testament Interpretation
and Associate Dean, The Southern Baptist Theological Seminary,
Louisville, Kentucky

This book is vintage Deenick! Whatever you believe about baptism, this valuable book will give you many generous doses of biblical theology, biblical evidence, theological cohesion, and pastoral clarity. It will clean up your ideas, expectations, and practices of baptism, and also enrich your views of salvation, and of the church. It is theologically deep, and highly practical. Heartily recommended.

Peter Adam
Vicar Emeritus of St Jude's Carlton, Melbourne, Australia,
and former Principal of Ridley College, Melbourne

Can more really be said about the age-long debate over baptism? This book makes it clear that more can and should be said. Through a fascinating exploration of biblical themes like circumcision, sacrifice, washing, cleanliness, covenant, and the work of the Spirit, Karl Deenick opens up fresh angles on baptism, no matter which side of the issue you stand on. But what makes this book particularly valuable is that it not only stimulates rigorous thought about baptism in a very accessible way; it does so opening up wonderfully rich perspectives on the gospel itself – the glorious gospel that baptism points to.

MURRAY CAPILL
Dean of Ministry Development,
Reformed Theological College, Melbourne, Australia

Discussing baptism is like trench warfare: Each side of the debate is more interested in fortifying its own position than listening to the other side. Reading Deenick's book is like stepping out of a trench and climbing up an adjacent hill to view the theological landscape from a fresh point of view. Deenick weaves together a host of Biblical texts on circumcision, sacrifice, covenant, and the Spirit in order to demonstrate that, more than anything else, baptism is a sign of the gospel and of the community gathered around God's Messiah, Jesus. If you're tired of hearing the same arguments on baptism reheated and served as leftovers, this book is for you.

JOE BARNARD
Pastor, Holyrood Evangelical Church, Edinburgh
Author of *The Way Forward, Surviving the Trenches* and
Hymn Workouts: 100 Exercises to Set Your Heart Ablaze

Washed by God

THE STORY OF BAPTISM

Karl Deenick

CHRISTIAN
FOCUS

Copyright © Karl Deenick 2022

paperback ISBN 978-1-5271-0888-2
ebook ISBN 978-1-5271-0951-3

10 9 8 7 6 5 4 3 2 1

Published in 2022
by
Christian Focus Publications Ltd,
Geanies House, Fearn, Ross-shire,
IV20 1TW, Great Britain.

www.christianfocus.com

Cover design by
Pete Barnsley

Printed and bound by
Bell & Bain, Glasgow

Contents

For Keith, for his wisdom, friendship and good advice.

Preface

This book has been a long time in the making. I have been working towards it for nearly fifteen years. The journey first began at Bible college with a crisis over my view on baptism. I was brought up in a church that held to infant baptism, but as I read the arguments of people arguing for infant baptism I found myself wholly unconvinced. I was set to become a baptist. That is, until a friend of mine, knowing that I was a contrarian, wisely suggested that I read some baptists. The result was that I was dissatisfied with everything.

It was from those first struggles that this book began. The intervening years included six years of doctoral studies, amidst the throes of pastoral ministry, plus a number of other projects. But along the way I discovered many wonderful truths about God and the gospel of His Son, Jesus Christ. While it has taken many years, it has been a labour of love and, indeed, of joy. Nevertheless, to finally finish and publish this book is a great answer to prayer. I'm not foolish enough (anymore!) to believe that this book will convince everyone. But I do hope that it will bring much clarity to a frequently muddy debate. Moreover, my earnest desire is that it will not simply help people to understand baptism better but that it will help people to love God and delight in Him.

This book owes much to many. There have been countless conversations over the years and countless books and articles that have helped me. Particular thanks goes to all those who read this book in whole or in part, and in various forms, and provided feedback of one kind or another. There has been a small army from all different sides of the debate from scholars to friends: Mikey Lynch, Peter Adam, Geoff Harper, Steve Voorwinde, Steve Nicholson, Ange van Winden, Kristy Lade, my dad, my brother, Jed Matthews, Graham Poole, Anthony van Bemmel, Ollie Tweeddale, Murray Capill, and Martin Williams. Their help has made this a better book.

Finally, this book is dedicated to my dear friend, Keith, who suggested all those years ago that I read the arguments of the other side. We were studying together for ministry, but sickness prevented him from completing that journey. Nevertheless, this book would not have ever come to be without him. This book belongs to him and much else besides.

KARL DEENICK
Launceston, Tasmania

1. Introduction

Over the last few years I've found myself having the same conversation over and over. Partly that's my setting. I work in a church where about half the people hold to the practice of baptising babies (infant baptism) and the other half hold to the practice of requiring a profession of faith before a person is baptised (believer's baptism). Some of that is because of the history of this particular church. The church started long before I arrived, when a group of people who had grown up in the church grasped the gospel, some for the first time and others with a new clarity. In that kind of mini-revival context it's not unusual for an emphasis on believer's baptism to arise – people are keen to demonstrate their desire to start again or start for the first time in the Christian life.[1] But some of the confusion about baptism also lies in the fact that many couples in my church come from different traditions. As the barriers between denominations have crumbled over the last few decades, Christians with different perspectives on baptism have intermarried. When those couples have their first child a few years later, they must decide whether they'll baptise their children or not.

---

1. Justo González notes that, during the Great Awakening in America, the increased emphasis on the 'experience of conversion … raised doubts as to infant baptism. Therefore, many Congregationalists and Presbyterians, led by the Awakening's emphasis on personal experience, eventually rejected infant baptism and became Baptists. Entire congregations did so.' (Justo L. González, *The Story of Christianity: The Early Church to the Dawn of the Reformation*, vol. 1 of 2 vols. (San Francisco: HarperCollins, 1984), 229-30).

So too, the rise of non-denominational evangelicalism has led to many people finding theological models among those whose position on baptism is different from their own. I myself think of men like John Piper, D. A. Carson or C. H. Spurgeon. Someone on the baptist side might think of Tim Keller, John Frame or John Stott. All are broadly reformed evangelicals but differ on baptism. So too, many parachurch organisations remain noncommittal on aspects of baptism.[2] For instance, the Gospel Coalition's theological statement chooses not to take a position on baptism and, very wisely, when they produced booklets explaining their core theological convictions, the booklet on baptism was co-written by an infant baptist and believer's baptist.[3]

We live in an era of wonderful collaboration between evangelical Christians, which is even more encouraging given that we live in an increasingly fractious society. Yet that can leave behind an uncertainty about the undecided issues like baptism. And so, although it's not unusual to find some people who have very strong views on baptism, I generally find that most people are more confused than strident. That's true not just in my own church, but in other churches too. As I've spoken to people in lots of other churches, I've had the same conversations about baptism or heard stories of the same uncertainty.

That kind of uncertainty can lead to indifference. But baptism is not something that we can take or leave. Jesus' final charge to His disciples involved a call to baptise:

> Therefore go and make disciples of all nations, baptizing them in the name of the Father and of the Son and of the Holy Spirit, and teaching them to obey everything I have commanded you ... (Matt. 28:19-20).

As I often say to people in our church, it's not that what we think about baptism doesn't matter. There is a right answer and a wrong answer, and we should all keep pursuing the truth. It's just we don't

---

2. Generally, they remain noncommittal on the 'who' and 'how' of baptism. Or as it is often referred to, the 'recipients' and 'mode' – that is, should only believers be baptised or should children be included too, and should they be sprinkled or fully immersed?

3. Thabiti M. Anyabwile and J. Ligon Duncan, 'Baptism and the Lord's Supper,' in *The Gospel as Center: Renewing Our Faith and Forming Our Ministry Practices*, ed. D. A. Carson and Timothy Keller (Wheaton: Crossway, 2012), 231-51.

think that it matters so much that we need to separate over it. In many ways, that means we need to work even harder.

But as I've had the same conversation over and over again, I've also come to think that questions on who should be baptised and how (immersed or sprinkled, etc.) are comparatively uninteresting questions. Somewhat ironically, the reason those questions are talked about so much seems to be because the Bible says so little about them. But there's an awful lot you can say about baptism before you even say anything about who is baptised and who isn't. And indeed, the things that we can say unequivocally about baptism are incredibly rich and they drive to the very heart of the human predicament and the promise and hope of the gospel of Jesus Christ.

For me personally, thinking hard about baptism has been a deeply rewarding experience. Even before I arrived at the church where I am, gaining clarity on baptism was something of a life quest. So much so that I spent six years of my life completing doctoral work on circumcision – an Old Testament sign which is often linked with baptism.[4] You probably won't be surprised to hear that you could almost count on one hand the number of people who have done that. And yet in my efforts to discover who should be baptised and how, I've found other far more interesting things along the way. I've come to understand the glory of the gospel in a new way. It has warmed my heart and led me to praise. I've found I can explain much more clearly to people, both inside and outside the church, what the good news about Jesus really is. I've developed a new appreciation for the Old Testament and all those bizarre Old Testament ceremonies. I've developed a new love for Christ and His work. I've also found that when I've explained to people what baptism is and isn't, and how it signifies the gospel, it not only helps them fit together lots of pieces of the puzzle that never fitted before, but it also gives them a deep sense of satisfaction in the work of Christ.

I've come to think that in the confusion over who should be baptised and how, we're missing a wonderful opportunity. We're missing an opening to explain the gospel really clearly. Baptism is a God-given sign, not to obscure the gospel, but to make it clearer.

I hope that this book is not just another in the long line of books discussing who should be baptised and who shouldn't. Obviously,

---

4. That link between circumcision and baptism is, in my view, often understood quite poorly by all sides of the baptism debate. But more on that in chapter 4.

that's an important question to answer, and I'll outline a little later what I think and why. But my aim for this book is to explain and exalt the gospel, to uncover the threads that run through the Old and New Testaments, and to show how the Old Testament foreshadows Jesus and how Jesus fulfils everything in the Old Testament. I hope that in clarifying baptism it will help to clarify the gospel.

A Word on How to Read This Book

I'm a bit of a fan of mountain biking. But in mountain biking, and other sports, sometimes the one trail branches off into two sections – a 'black line' and a 'blue line'. The 'black line' is for mountain biking pros, while the 'blue line' is for people like me who are not great riders, who only ride for exercise and who just want to come home in one piece.

The same is true of this book. Debates over baptism have a very long and complicated history, one which I don't want to bore you with. For that reason, in the main body of the text you'll find the 'blue line'. It's designed to be uncomplicated. The aim is to help you get to the end in one piece.

But for the more adventurous, in the footnotes you'll find the 'black line'. That's for people who want more detail, who aren't convinced by something in the main body, or who might have some idea of the debates in the background. The 'black line' gives you a little bit of access to some of the hard work that stands behind the 'blue line'.

So my advice is to stick to the blue line. I usually do in books. And only check out the footnotes if you want more information.

2. Wash, Rinse, Repeat
Cleansing and Washing in the Old Testament

The Old Testament is maybe not the most obvious place to start looking to understand baptism.[1] If you search for the word 'baptism', you won't find any Bible verses listed in the Old Testament. In fact, the first time baptism appears in the Bible is with John the Baptist at the beginning of the Gospels. But although baptism seems to have appeared almost out of the blue with John the Baptist on the banks of the Jordan, it actually has a remarkable Old Testament pedigree.

Even though the word 'baptism' is never used in the Old Testament, the Old Testament is full of water and of concepts like cleansing and washing. The first Christians were Jews who were steeped in Old Testament practices. They performed those ceremonies day in and day out, and had done so for centuries. And while baptism is not identical to any of those Old Testament rituals, those rituals certainly laid the foundation for baptism.

In this chapter, we'll dig into those Old Testament practices and try to understand what they were pointing to and how they

---

1.   Some do begin by looking in the Old Testament, but they begin by looking at the sign of circumcision that God gave to Abraham. We'll think more about the connection between circumcision and baptism in chapter 4. Others spend a fair amount of time considering first-century Jewish conversion rituals (see chap. 5, note 2). But the most obvious background to baptism is the one provided by the cleansing rituals in the Old Testament. If you're not convinced by that idea yet, hopefully the next two chapters will help convince you.

announced the gospel beforehand. Then in the next chapter, we'll look at how Jesus and New Testament writers used the language of cleansing to describe the effects of the gospel and how it's connected with baptism.

The Purity Laws in the Old Testament

Call me strange, but if there is one thing I get excited about it's the cleansing rituals and purity laws in the Old Testament. Don't get me wrong, I'm glad I don't have to do them. But what I love about them is that they're so graphic, if not a little confronting. Leviticus, the book where most of those rituals are spelled out, is a kind of lost treasure. I often think of it as the picture book of the Old Testament. Though baffling at first, when you begin to understand it, it reveals itself not as a book of dry theology or weird ceremonies, but as one that puts deep truths in ordinary clothes. Leviticus and its ceremonies have a strange power to bring the truth to life in our imagination. In fact, few chapters in the Bible help us come to grips with God's view of the world and of our human predicament as visually as the chapters in Leviticus that deal with purity and with things being clean or unclean.

Living in a Divided World

The first regulations in Leviticus on cleanness are the regulations about clean and unclean foods in chapter 11. In those laws, God specified what the people were able to eat and what they couldn't eat, and what animals would make them unclean if they came into contact with their dead bodies. Here is a sample:

> The LORD said to Moses and Aaron, 'Say to the Israelites: "Of all the animals that live on land, these are the ones you may eat: You may eat any animal that has a divided hoof and that chews the cud.
>
> "There are some that only chew the cud or only have a divided hoof, but you must not eat them. The camel, though it chews the cud, does not have a divided hoof; it is ceremonially unclean for you. The hyrax, though it chews the cud, does not have a divided hoof; it is unclean for you. The rabbit, though it chews the cud, does not have a divided hoof; it is unclean for you. And the pig, though it has a divided hoof, does not chew the cud; it is unclean for you.

You must not eat their meat or touch their carcasses; they
are unclean for you'" (Lev. 11:1-8).

God says in verse 3 they could eat land animals that had a completely
split hoof and chewed vigorously.[2] In verse 9 He says they could
eat sea creatures that had both scales and fins. Verse 13 specifies
that there were birds they couldn't eat, such as eagles, vultures and
various owls. There were some insects that they couldn't eat and
some they could. And the list goes on. The chapter is summed up
with these words:

> These are the regulations concerning animals, birds, every
> living thing that moves about in the water and every creature
> that moves along the ground. You must distinguish between
> the unclean and the clean, between living creatures that may
> be eaten and those that may not be eaten (Lev. 11:46-47).

Now people have suggested a variety of reasons why God considered
some animals to be clean and others to be unclean. Some people say
that it was a matter of hygiene. The suggestion is that the unclean
animals were more likely to give the people diseases. Some people
say that it was a matter of avoiding animals used in the rituals of
other religions. But that doesn't really work because a lot of the
animals used for sacrifices by the Israelites were used by other
nations in sacrifices too. Some people suggest that it's a matter of
an animal's perfection or wholeness within its class. So, for instance,
a winged insect that walks around on four legs is, in a way, mixed
up: insects with wings should fly, not walk; fish should have fins and
scales. Animals that don't fit within the normal pattern of creation
should be avoided. Or so the theory goes.

It's hard to know which one is right. I think the last theory and
the hygiene theory have the most going for them. But really, it doesn't
matter that much. Although it can be worth thinking through why
one particular animal is clean and another isn't, thinking about

---

2.   The English expression 'chew the cud' is a technical description of animals
that regurgitate food to chew it again more thoroughly. Cows, for instance, do this.
But insisting that is what is meant here is probably demanding more than the phrase
in the original language means. Neither rabbits nor camels, for instance, 'chew the
cud' in this technical sense. The expression in Leviticus 11 simply refers to animals
that chew their food thoroughly. (See Gordon J. Wenham, *The Book of Leviticus*,
New International Commentary on the Old Testament (Grand Rapids: Eerdmans,
1979), 171-72).

the underlying reason for why a sheep is clean, but a camel isn't, risks missing the deeper significance of these commands. At one level, the point is relatively clear: **the world is made up of things which God views as clean and unclean, and unclean things are to be avoided.** What's more, coming into contact with unclean things means a person must be cleansed to be able to approach God.

But although Leviticus 11 is all about physical impurity, avoiding physical impurity was never the end game. Through this practice of distinguishing physical impurity, God was teaching the people about the importance of distinguishing moral and spiritual impurity. That can be seen in the rest of the Old Testament where the language of *ritual* cleanness and uncleanness is used to describe *moral* cleanness and uncleanness.[3] For instance, David says in Psalm 24:

> Who may ascend the mountain of the LORD? Who may stand in his holy place? The one who has clean hands and a pure heart, who does not trust in an idol or swear by a false god (Ps. 24:3-4).

Similarly, through Isaiah God calls the people to:

> Wash and make yourselves clean. Take your evil deeds out of my sight; stop doing wrong. Learn to do right; seek justice. Defend the oppressed. Take up the cause of the fatherless; plead the case of the widow (Isa. 1:16-17).

Christopher Wright helpfully explains the significance of the Old Testament preoccupation with cleanness and purity when he writes:

> ritual cleanness, from the kitchen to the sanctuary, was meant to symbolize God's greater requirement of moral integrity, social justice and covenant loyalty. In fact, as the prophets (and Jesus) vigorously pointed out, if these latter things were lacking, then ritual cleanness of the most scrupulous kind at every level was worthless.[4]

In fact, the symbolism is probably easier for us to get a hold of than we might realise. We still use language today that reflects the idea

---

3. For a helpful discussion, see Jay Sklar, *Leviticus: An Introduction and Commentary*, Tyndale Old Testament Commentaries 3 (Nottingham: Inter-Varsity Press, 2013), 49, 173.

4. Christopher J. H. Wright, 'Leviticus,' in *New Bible Commentary*, ed. D. A. Carson et al., 4th ed. (Downers Grove: InterVarsity Press, 1994), 139.

here in these chapters. People talk about 'moral filth' or 'pure' and 'impure' motives. In the same way, the picture in Leviticus is of a world made up of pure, right and good things, and of a world that also contains impure, wrong and bad things. When God created the world, He created it good and clean. But when Adam and Eve sinned, the world became riddled with filth – it became polluted by sin. And so the world is now a mixed place. You don't need to be a rocket scientist to work that out. There are some places where that's exceptionally clear. For example, God's words in the Bible are pure things in the world; Jesus was the only 100 per cent pure thing in the world; but the sex industry is an impure, unclean, wrong thing in the world. God wanted His people to avoid the unclean and impure and to pursue the pure. As Paul writes to the Philippians:

> Finally, brothers and sisters, whatever is true, whatever is noble, whatever is right, whatever is pure, whatever is lovely, whatever is admirable—if anything is excellent or praiseworthy—think about such things (Phil. 4:8).

God was teaching the people through these regulations that He hated impurity, and that if they wanted to enjoy His presence they had to stay well away from impurity. There is a basic division in the world between what is pure and what is impure, between what is clean and what is unclean. But the kind of impurity that God really hates is not ritual impurity but moral impurity.[5]

The Threat of Contamination

So God wanted the people to avoid impurity. The problem, however, is that keeping away from impurity is very difficult because it spreads like wildfire. Ritual uncleanness is described almost like a contagion or a spreading disease. Uncleanness from animals could be 'contracted' just by coming into contact with their dead bodies or by eating them. Similarly, when unclean skin conditions are described in Leviticus 13, the problematic ones are those that keep spreading. Verse 7 says:

---

5. It's important to grasp that uncleanness itself was not a sin, even though uncleanness not properly dealt with could become sinful and dangerous. That is, being unclean after childbirth was not a sin. Rather, uncleanness was a *symbol* of sin. It was a lived-out metaphor of the brokenness of the world in which we live. Yet, in Old Testament times, the failure to deal appropriately with that (symbolic) uncleanness constituted disobedience to what God had commanded.

But if the rash does spread in their skin after they have shown themselves to the priest to be pronounced clean, they must appear before the priest again. The priest is to examine that person, and if the rash has spread in the skin, he shall pronounce them unclean; it is a defiling skin disease (Lev. 13:7-8).

The same is true for the mould on the piece of clothing in verse 47 and following: if the mould spreads the clothing is unclean.

The threat of contamination also explains the strict quarantine restrictions for those who were infected:

Anyone with such a defiling disease must wear torn clothes, let their hair be unkempt, cover the lower part of their face and cry out, 'Unclean! Unclean!' As long as they have the disease they remain unclean. They must live alone; they must live outside the camp (Lev. 13:45-46).

This is not merely a matter of hygiene. It's a picture of the contagious nature of sin. It's not that having a skin condition was or is sinful. It's not that the person with a skin disorder had sinned in some way and God wanted everyone to see that. It wasn't that a person with a skin condition was more sinful than any other person. These laws about what is clean and unclean were broad pictures about the nature of sin – sin is like a spreading rash.

That's why it was so important for the Israelites to distinguish between what is pure and impure, because spending time with spiritual impurity would drag them into spiritual impurity as well. That is very much the repeated story of the Old Testament. The people compromised on God's instructions to remove sin from their environment and they ended up getting dragged into sin – bad company corrupts good character (1 Cor. 15:33).

Paul applies these truths to the Corinthian church when he says:

Do not be yoked together with unbelievers. For what do righteousness and wickedness have in common? Or what fellowship can light have with darkness? What harmony is there between Christ and Belial? Or what does a believer have in common with an unbeliever? What agreement is there between the temple of God and idols? For we are the temple of the living God. As God has said: 'I will live with them and walk among them, and I will be their God, and they will be my people.'

Therefore, 'Come out from them and be separate, says the Lord. *Touch no unclean thing*, and I will receive you' [emphasis added].

And, 'I will be a Father to you, and you will be my sons and daughters, says the Lord Almighty.' Therefore, since we have these promises, dear friends, *let us purify ourselves from everything that contaminates body and spirit*, perfecting holiness out of reverence for God (2 Cor. 6:14-7:1) [emphasis added].

Most of us know the corrupting effects of sin from experience. If someone is spending time with the 'wrong crowd' we worry, because we know that attitudes and behaviour rub off on people. If you spend too much time around people who are sharply critical and complain about everything, you'll end up becoming sharply critical and complaining about everything too. If you spend loads of time around people who talk about nothing else but their latest 2000-inch television or how their new smartphone has revolutionised their life, then you'll end up with a heart which is shaped and framed by the desire for those things. And once things are in our heart, they're very hard to get out.[6] It might be scenes from movies that you can't forget or conversations that you've been a part of that stay with you. They go in easily, but they don't come out easily. Such is the infectious and corrupting nature of sin.

While we no longer practice any of these specific commands with respect to skin conditions, contagious diseases remain a powerful metaphor for the problem of sin. The recent Covid-19 pandemic has reminded us that viruses are silent but effective killers that spread frighteningly easily and which can bring a world to its knees. Like

---

6. But that raises the question: how does that fit with Jesus' life in which he ate with the people that everyone else called 'sinners'? From Paul's perspective the issue is not spending time with people who don't follow Jesus, but being bound to them in some way and getting involved in their style of life. A friend of mine used to be part of a footy team. He never went to the 'mad Monday' celebrations because he knew that everyone would just be getting smashed, and he never went to the stripper nights, for obvious reasons. But he still played footy with those guys and when one guy's marriage failed, he was able to help. That is, he played for the team, but he was bound to Jesus. And his allegiance to Jesus trumped his allegiance to the team. Of course, it may come to the point where you can't spend time with a person anymore because everything they do drags you in as well. The truth is that there are no easy answers and it takes immense wisdom and prayer in every circumstance. There are no hard and fast rules except that God calls us to both love sinners and be careful about the damaging and contagious effects of sin.

Covid-19, and the black plague and flu pandemics of past centuries, sin is a virulent and powerful killer. We're not remote islands, quarantined from the toxic effects of sin. We are deeply affected by the sin in our world. If we are to be cured of the deathly disease of rebellion against God, we need a medicine that can protect us. We need to be inoculated against sin by a strength more powerful than sin itself. But more than that, we need sin to be eradicated. God's plan is to do to sin what humanity has done to smallpox – get rid of it from the world. But as the next section of Leviticus shows, we need God not only to eradicate sin *out there* in the world, we need Him to eradicate it in us.

Overflowing with Filth

The Old Testament commands surrounding ritual cleanness and purity divided the world into the clean and the unclean and encouraged people to avoid the contagious effects of impurity. But the last chapter in Leviticus on purity introduces a much deeper problem. It turns out that the biggest problem is not the pollution from others but the pollution spilling out from ourselves.

Chapter 15 is all about discharges from the body. It ties in too with chapter 12, which speaks about the uncleanness that results from having a baby. In both chapters the thing that causes uncleanness is something from inside a person coming out. It might be a man with an unnamed discharge (15:4) or an emission of semen (15:16); it might be a woman with a period (15:19); it might even be an unclean person spitting (15:8).

The shocking and deeply troubling truth which comes into focus in this chapter is that even if a person kept away from the wrong animals, even if they miraculously avoided the skin problems that others faced, they still couldn't escape uncleanness because there was an unstoppable source of defilement coming from within every person. Even if you tried very hard to avoid uncleanness, you couldn't, because at least some of the causes were involuntary. They're part of our nature.[7]

And therein lies the shocking reality. The problem is not unpleasant discharges from people's bodies – that's just the picture.

---

7. Lesley DiFransico highlights the pervasive nature of impurity in the Old Testament writing, 'ritual impurity is a predominantly unavoidable and natural state of defilement that one would expect to undergo in the course of life.' (Lesley R. DiFransico, *Washing Away Sin: An Analysis of the Metaphor in the Hebrew Bible and Its Influence*, Biblical Tools and Studies 23 (Leuven: Peeters, 2016), 22).

The problem is the stinking, vile, revolting ooze of rebellion and hatred of God that pours out from people's hearts – an unstoppable flow which is part of our very nature. There's no tap that can turn it off. There is a constant, odious stream of sin pouring out of people's hearts.

In Mark's gospel, we have a record of Jesus explaining the meaning of these regulations. He said to the crowd:

> 'Nothing outside a person can defile them by going into them. Rather, it is what comes out of a person that defiles them. ... Don't you see that nothing that enters a person from the outside can defile them? For it doesn't go into their heart but into their stomach, and then out of the body.' (In saying this, Jesus declared all foods clean.)
>
> He went on: 'What comes out of a person is what defiles them. For it is from within, out of a person's heart, that evil thoughts come – sexual immorality, theft, murder, adultery, greed, malice, deceit, lewdness, envy, slander, arrogance and folly. All these evils come from inside and defile a person' (Mark 7:15-23).[8]

Jesus says that it's not what you eat or touch that makes you unclean in God's sight. What makes you unclean is the stuff locked up in your heart that comes pouring out as rebellion against God. The problem is that out of your heart come all kinds of things like 'evil thoughts, sexual immorality, theft, murder, adultery, coveting, wickedness, deceit, sensuality, envy, slander, pride, foolishness.'[9] As C. S. Lewis so honestly and eloquently put it:

> For the first time I examined myself with a seriously practical purpose. And there I found what appalled me; a zoo of lusts; a bedlam of ambitions; a nursery of fears; a harem of fondled hatreds. My name was legion.[10]

---

8. The first century Jewish philosopher Philo held a similar view, writing, 'Furthermore they cleanse their bodies with lustrations and purifications, but they neither wash nor practise to wash off from their souls the passions by which life is defiled. They are zealous to go to the temples white-robed, attired in spotless raiment, but with a spotted heart they pass into the inmost sanctuary and are not ashamed.' (Philo, *Cherubim*, 95 [Whitaker, Loeb Classical Library]).

9. In a similar way, evil spirits are often referred to in the Gospels as 'unclean spirits' (e.g. Mark 1:23; 3:11; 5:2; 7:25). That is, they are spirits who live in settled opposition and rebellion against God.

10. C. S. Lewis, *Surprised by Joy* (1955; reprint, London: Collins, 2012), 263.

It's easy for us to reduce holiness and sin to doing and not doing the right thing. That's obviously part of it. But the laws about cleansing show us that the problem is not just this sin we committed yesterday or that sin we committed the day before; the problem is the unstoppable flow of sewage that pours out of our hearts. Deep down in our hearts lie all kinds of wrong thoughts, wrong desires and wrong loves, like lust, greed, and hatred. The problem is not just that we've lied, but that we're predisposed to lying. It's not just that we've used porn or lusted after another man or woman, but that we enjoy it. The problem is not just that we've wasted our money, but that our hearts are inextricably drawn to greed.

What is most disconcerting is that many of these feelings are involuntary. They aren't considered feelings; they are thoughts and sensations that come to us *naturally*. We might see a person and are instinctively repulsed by them. Or we catch sight across the room of someone who we've had run-ins with before and our bitterness rises automatically. Or a married man or woman might see someone who is not their spouse and, without planning it, they're aroused by them. Or for the person who struggles with same-sex attraction, they catch sight of a person of the same gender and before they even know it, they feel attracted to them.

The troubling reality is that sin is not merely what we do; it is part of us. We were born that way. It has been deeply woven into us right from the womb (Ps. 51:5). The problem is our deepest instincts and desires. The problem is that we are *by nature* objects of wrath (Eph. 2:3). And the consequence is that we not only need to be forgiven but to be rescued from a creation which is deformed and unnatural.

The problem is that our hearts are like sewage pipes: they spew out filth all day long. The messiness of every boil, every birth, every period, every emission of semen, every bit of bodily oozing is a picture of a spiritual reality. It's a picture of our hearts which overflow with rebellion against God. It's a reminder that it's not what goes into a person that makes them unclean but what comes out. Sure, these things don't make people ritually unclean anymore and they don't require people to go through the same steps to become ritually clean, but they remain God's powerful, visual, daily reminder of our human predicament.

A Beacon of Hope: Water and Blood

But, alongside all these pictures of impurity in Leviticus 11–15, there are also pictures of hope. Most causes of impurity come with a remedy. For instance, in the most minor cases, time is enough to cleanse a person. If a person came into contact with the carcass of an unclean animal, they simply had to wait until evening to become clean again (Lev. 11:24, 31). But for almost everything else, cleansing required washing and sacrifice.

If a person didn't merely touch the carcass of an unclean animal but carried it, then, as well waiting until evening, they also had to wash their clothes to become clean (Lev. 11:25). So too, after suffering from a non-spreading skin disease of some kind a person had to wash their clothes (Lev. 13:6, 34). If a garment was affected by a 'disease' that didn't spread, it could be washed, and if the affected area faded after washing then that part could be torn out and the garment kept. Otherwise, if the area didn't fade or if the 'disease' spread then the garment had to be burned (Lev. 13:47-59). For someone being cleansed after suffering from a spreading skin disease, more was required. They had to shave themselves and bathe in water, not once but twice (Lev. 14:8-9). For someone with a discharge, or even someone who came into contact with something the person with the discharge had touched, they had to wash their clothes and bathe themselves in water (Lev. 15:5-11, 13, 20-22, 27).

But in the more serious cases, cleansing also involved atonement through sacrifice. After giving birth, a woman would be unclean for a period of time. To complete her purification she would bring a burnt offering and a sin offering and the priest would make atonement for her so that she could be clean (Lev. 12:6-8). Cleansing from a spreading skin disease was quite a complicated affair. The person would bring two live clean birds, cedarwood, scarlet yarn and hyssop.[11] One of the birds would be killed over a bowl of fresh water. The live bird and the hyssop, cedarwood and scarlet yarn were then dipped into bloody water. That bird was then set free while the recovered patient was sprinkled with the bloody water. Several days later the recovered patient would bring some other animals for sacrifices. They would be slaughtered by the priest and some of the blood applied to the thumb, big toe and ear of the recovered

---

11.   Hyssop was a type of shrub. For more on hyssop, see the next section, 'A Cleaning Brush that Works on the Soul'.

patient, suggesting that the blood is effective for the whole person. Finally, the priest would offer a sin offering, burnt offering and grain offering to make atonement for that person (Lev. 14:1-20). The cleansing process for people with discharges was simpler. For normal discharges, only washing was required. But for abnormal discharges, after washing with water, the person would bring to the priest a sin offering and a burnt offering with which the priest would make atonement for the person in order to cleanse them (Lev. 15:14-15, 29-30).[12]

But the greatest connection between atonement and cleansing comes on the Day of Atonement. In Leviticus 16, immediately following on from all these cleansing rituals, is the description of one of the most important days in the Old Testament calendar. On one day of the year the high priest would go into the Most Holy Place and make atonement for God's people. The high priest would wash himself and put on special clothes before he could appear before God in the tabernacle. He then proceeded to atone for his own sins and the sins of the people by making various sacrifices and sprinkling the blood on items within the tabernacle.

The central sacrifice involved two goats. In a powerful piece of symbolism, these two goats worked together to picture the great hope for Israel. One goat was slaughtered and its blood sprinkled on the ark of the covenant within the Most Holy Place as an offering for the sins of the people.[13] The high priest would then take the other goat (often called the scapegoat), lay his hands on its head, and confess over it all the sins of the people of Israel (Lev. 16:21).

---

12. The fact that the water itself was not seen to have any power itself can be seen by a comparison with similar washing rituals in other cultures from around the same time. Jonathan Lawrence notes, 'In contrast, bathing in the Hebrew Bible involves no incantations or prayers, never mentions water as a source of life or death, offers little discussion of the nature of the water, and separates bathing from healing.' (Jonathan David Lawrence, *Washing in Water: Trajectories of Ritual Bathing in the Hebrew Bible and Second Temple Literature*, Academia Biblica 23 (Atlanta: Society of Biblical Literature, 2006), 7).

13. Leviticus 16:16 says that this sacrifice makes atonement for 'for the Most Holy Place because of the uncleanness and rebellion of the Israelites, whatever their sins have been. He is to do the same for the tent of meeting, which is among them in the midst of their uncleanness.' The idea seems to be that atonement is being made for what the Israelites have done in defiling God's 'house' by their sins. Defiling the 'house' is an offence because it is symbolic of God's presence among them. Ultimately, then, to defile the 'house' is to offend God.

That goat was then taken outside the tabernacle, outside the camp of Israel, and released into the wilderness.

There are many aspects to the Day of Atonement but the core symbolism is this: through the two goats (acting as one), Israel is ransomed from the consequences of their sin by the death of the first goat and then their sin is carried far away into the wilderness by the second goat.

The point is that pollution and defilement invite God's wrath. We ourselves are polluted and defiled, and we continually pollute and defile God's world. And God's just anger at that situation needs to be dealt with. But not only does God's wrath at our pollution of ourselves and His world need to be dealt with, we also need to be cleaned up so that we never pollute His world again.

That two-fold concern of the Day of Atonement is captured at the end of Leviticus 16 in these words:

> … because on this day atonement will be made for you, to cleanse you. Then, before the LORD, you will be clean from all your sins (Lev. 16:30).

Notice, first of all, that the Day of Atonement is not concerned with being cleansed from contact with dead animals, skin diseases or bodily emissions. The Day of Atonement is concerned with being cleansed from sin.

But also notice that the Day of Atonement is concerned with two aspects of dealing with sin: atonement *and* cleansing.[14] Atonement is about paying the penalty for sin. Sin demands death, and the blood of one goat is shed in order to ransom the people from their own death. In Leviticus 17:11 the people are told:

> For the life of a creature is in the blood, and I have given it to you to make atonement for yourselves on the altar; it is the blood that makes atonement for one's life (Lev. 17:11).

But cleansing is about bundling up all the defilement and impurities that infect the people and then carrying them away into the farthest parts of the earth. Hence goat number two.

It is important to understand that while we often talk about 'washing our guilt away', that's not the way the Bible uses that language. In the language of the Bible only the impurity within us

---

14. To put it more succinctly: atonement ransoms, cleansing purifies. (cf. Sklar, *Leviticus*, 50-54).

(that leads to guilt) is washed away,[15] while guilt itself and God's accompanying wrath is atoned for through sacrifice. Nevertheless, the two are clearly bound up together since the impurity within us leads to guilt. Moreover, the remedy to uncleanness depends on atonement. Thus, God says through Ezekiel:

> Because I tried to cleanse you but you would not be cleansed from your impurity, you will not be clean again until my wrath against you has subsided (Ezek. 24:13).

God's work of cleansing and purifying Israel awaited the exhaustion of His wrath in atonement.[16]

The Day of Atonement, as well as the other ceremonies for cleansing, provided hope that God's people could be ransomed *and* cleansed from their sin. But they only symbolised what God would do in the future. And as a result, they also left the people longing for more.

Longing for a Deeper Cleansing

It becomes clear as you read through the rest of the Old Testament that people understood the deeper *theological* significance of these ceremonies. It's also clear that people had grasped that there was a need for something that was more than external. In the next three sections we'll look at three places in the Old Testament where people used the language of cleansing to express their hope that God would do something deeper.

A Cleaning Brush that Works on the Soul

There have been few people like King David. He was a man after God's own heart (1 Sam. 13:14). He was appointed by God to lead God's people. But although his reign started out well, the sin living deep inside his own heart eventually caused him to fall and to fall catastrophically.

---

15. Consider, for example, 'Jerusalem, wash the evil from your heart and be saved. How long will you harbor wicked thoughts?' (Jer. 4:14). See also Isaiah 1:16; 4:4; Jeremiah 2:22.

16. In Ezekiel 24, God is foreshadowing judgment coming on his people because of their persistent disobedience. Nevertheless, Ezekiel 24:13 raises the possibility that cleansing would be forthcoming if God's wrath could be dealt with in another way, such as by atonement.

One day, walking about on the roof of his palace, David looks over and sees a beautiful woman by the name of Bathsheba bathing. And although he's married (and although she's married), David sends his servants to get her and he sleeps with her. As though the situation wasn't already bad enough, Bathsheba falls pregnant. Unfortunately, Bathsheba's husband, Uriah, is off fighting the king's battles. If Uriah returns to find his wife pregnant, he'll know the baby is not his and David and Bathsheba's unfaithfulness will be discovered. So, in a cunning ploy, David fetches Uriah home in the hope that Uriah would sleep with his wife and so never discover that the baby belonged to David. Unfortunately for David, Uriah is too noble and he refuses to go home to his wife while the ark of the covenant is in a tent and the army is camped in the open field. Consequently, David gets Uriah drunk in the hope that he'll abandon his principles and go home to Bathsheba. That doesn't work either. At which point David concocts his most vicious plan. He writes to Uriah's commander and tells the commander:

> Put Uriah out in front where the fighting is fiercest. Then withdraw from him so he will be struck down and die (2 Sam. 11:15).

Once Uriah is dead, David sends for Bathsheba and she becomes his wife. She gives birth to a son and David thinks he's in the clear.

But God is not so easily deceived. He sends Nathan the prophet to confront David and after telling David a little parable to soften him up before the final blow, Nathan says:

> Why did you despise the word of the LORD by doing what is evil in his eyes? You struck down Uriah the Hittite with the sword and took his wife to be your own. You killed him with the sword of the Ammonites. Now, therefore, the sword will never depart from your house, because you despised me and took the wife of Uriah the Hittite to be your own (2 Sam. 12:9-10).

It is in direct response to that situation that David writes Psalm 51. In the heading for Psalm 51 we're told:

> A psalm of David. When the prophet Nathan came to him after David had committed adultery with Bathsheba.

Psalm 51 is David's prayer after his sin with Bathsheba is exposed. It is one of the great prayers of repentance in the Bible. But what is significant is that in Psalm 51 David picks up the language of the cleansing rituals and applies them to his guilt and sin. He says in verses 1 and 2:

> Have mercy on me, O God, according to your unfailing love; according to your great compassion blot out my transgressions. Wash away all my iniquity and cleanse me from my sin (Ps. 51:1-2).

First David cries out for his sins to be blotted out. It's the language of erasing something from a book.[17] What David is asking for is for God to rub out any record of his wrongs.

We know from bitter human experience that our relationships with other people can be tarnished by our memory of the ways they've wronged and hurt us in the past. It can be something as little as a passing comment or even a passing look and the hurt stays with us for a long time. For the relationship to be restored the memory of that hurt needs to be rubbed out. It's the same with God. For our relationship with God to be restored we need Him to rub out the infinite number of things that we've done against Him.

But David also cries out to be washed and cleansed from his sin. He uses exactly the language that is used in Leviticus to describe the cleansing and washing rituals. Then, in verse 7, he refers specifically to the implements of those cleansing ceremonies:

> Cleanse me with hyssop, and I will be clean; wash me, and I will be whiter than snow (Ps. 51:7).

Hyssop was often used to sprinkle people with water or blood. No one knows exactly what plant it was but it seems it was particularly effective for holding liquids and then dispersing them. It was probably a shrub with relatively dense foliage and possibly with hairy leaves so that it would retain a fair amount of liquid after having been dipped in water and which could then be

---

17. For example, God says to Moses 'Whoever has sinned against me, I will blot out of my book' (Exod. 32:33; see also Num. 5:23; Pss. 69:29; 109:13-15). See also DiFransico, *Washing Away Sin*, 90-91. Edward Dalglish has found a similar custom in ancient Babylon, where a writing tablet would be broken to cancel its contents, such as 'in the purchase of a slave or in the return of money' (Edward R. Dalglish, *Psalm Fifty-One in the Light of Ancient Near Eastern Patternism* (Leiden: Brill, 1962), 87).

shaken or brushed over something.[18] It was basically the ancient equivalent of a brush or rudimentary sponge. It was used most famously by the Israelites to sprinkle the blood of the Passover lamb on the doorposts of their houses (Exod. 12:22). But it was also used to sprinkle water mixed with blood in the ceremony for cleansing a person who had suffered from a spreading skin disease (Lev. 14:5-6) and for sprinkling water mixed with ashes for cleansing a person who had come in contact with a dead body (Num. 19:18).

But although David is using the language and imagery of these Old Testament rituals, he clearly has something much deeper in mind than simply washing his skin. What he desires is for God to both forget the past and also to give him a 'pure' or clean 'heart':

> Hide your face from my sins and blot out all my iniquity.
> Create in me a pure heart, O God, and renew a steadfast
> spirit within me (Ps. 51:9-10).

Even though David uses the language of these ceremonies, he recognises that such an inner transformation is beyond the power of the sacrificial system:

> You do not delight in sacrifice, or I would bring it; you do
> not take pleasure in burnt offerings. My sacrifice, O God, is
> a broken spirit; a broken and contrite heart you, God, will
> not despise (Ps. 51:16-17).

These ceremonies are not the ultimate means by which God forgives and cleanses His people but merely pointers to the need of that deeper work.

David desires a brush or a sponge and water and blood that will work deeper than the surface. He wants one that can wash away the overwhelming jealousy and desire that leads to adultery and can soak up the cavernous hatred and fear that leads to murder. He desperately needs God to forgive him for the past but he also needs more than that. He, like us, needs something that can reach deep into his heart and expunge the evil that lurks there so that he might be kept from doing the same kind of evil again.

---

18. See Irene Jacob and Walter Jacob, 'Flora,' in *Anchor Bible Dictionary*, ed. David Noel Freedman, 6 vols. (New York: Doubleday, 1992), 2:812.

A Shower that Touches the Heart

What David desperately desires, God promises to accomplish. One of the most significant places where the language of cleansing is taken up in the Old Testament is in Ezekiel 36. In that chapter, God promises to do a deep cleansing work on His people that will cure them of their sin.

In Ezekiel 36, God is speaking to His people Israel after they have been sent into exile because of their sin. They have been crushed and made desolate by the surrounding nations (v. 3). God describes the problem that led to their exile using the language of impurity:

> Son of man, when the people of Israel were living in their own land, they defiled it by their conduct and their actions. Their conduct was like a woman's monthly uncleanness in my sight. So I poured out my wrath on them because they had shed blood in the land and because they had defiled it with their idols. I dispersed them among the nations, and they were scattered through the countries; I judged them according to their conduct and their actions (Ezek. 36:17-19).

The trouble was that judgment brought shame not only on the people but on God. God says:

> And wherever they went among the nations they profaned my holy name, for it was said of them, 'These are the LORD's people, and yet they had to leave his land' (Ezek. 36:20).

People would look at Israel and say to themselves, 'God can't save His own people. He's not strong enough.' So God vows to act, not because His people deserve it, but because of His great name (Ezek. 36:22-23).

God vows to bring His people back to the land that He promised them. But for that to occur, some serious internal fixing needs to happen in the hearts of His people:

> For I will take you out of the nations; I will gather you from all the countries and bring you back into your own land. I will sprinkle clean water on you, and you will be clean; I will cleanse you from all your impurities and from all your idols. I will give you a new heart and put a new spirit in you; I will remove from you your heart of stone and give you a heart of flesh. And I will put my Spirit in you and move you to

follow my decrees and be careful to keep my laws. Then you will live in the land I gave your ancestors; you will be my people, and I will be your God (Ezek. 36:24-28).

In order for God to live with His people, for them to be His people and for Him to be their God, they need to be thoroughly washed. They need to be washed from their idols: the idols that draw them away from their love for God. This 'clean water' is so powerful and reaches so deep that it accomplishes the very thing that David had prayed for – it gives people a new heart, free from the defilement of sin. It takes hearts that are so compacted with evil and so resistant to God that they are like stone and it turns those hearts into living hearts – hearts of flesh. The identity of this 'clean water' is revealed in verse 27: it is God's own Spirit that will cause this recreation when God puts His Spirit inside His people. It is the Spirit of God that will enable people to walk in God's ways and obey God's laws and so live with God and be His people and love Him as their God.

Most of us have had plenty of showers in our lives but I'm guessing that none of us have ever stepped into a shower and come out a different person. Most of us have desires that seem to be wired so deeply into us that we can't get rid of them, no matter how hard we try. They seem instinctive. But imagine if you could go into the shower with adulterous lust and come out holy. Imagine if you could go in as a person who covets every cake in the bakery window and could come out a content and thankful person. Imagine if you could go into the shower indifferent to God and come out with a heart burning with the glory and grandeur of God. That is precisely what God promises to do for His people in Ezekiel 36. God promises to put His powerful Holy Spirit into people such that they are never the same again. The work of the Spirit will be like being sprinkled and washed with clean water. It will be like stepping into a shower and coming out a new person.

A Purifying Fire and Laundry Soap

But the kind of cleansing that we need and that God promises is costly and potentially quite dangerous. In Malachi 3, God foreshadows cleansing and purification using more severe language. He promises:

'I will send my messenger, who will prepare the way before me. Then suddenly the Lord you are seeking will come to his temple; the messenger of the covenant, whom you desire, will come,' says the LORD Almighty.

But who can endure the day of his coming? Who can stand when he appears? For he will be like a refiner's fire or a launderer's soap. He will sit as a refiner and purifier of silver; he will purify the Levites and refine them like gold and silver. Then the LORD will have men who will bring offerings in righteousness … (Mal. 3:1-3).

Ever since hearing these words in Handel's *Messiah* I've loved them (even if I'm a little disappointed that Handel kept the refiner's fire but left out the soap). I've loved them because God foreshadows a day when He Himself will come among His people and cleanse them.[19] But He will cleanse them, not by sprinkling them with water, but in the way that gold is refined in a fire or 'fuller's soap' is used to wash things clean. God makes a similar promise in Isaiah 1:

I will turn my hand against you; I will thoroughly purge away your dross and remove all your impurities (Isa. 1:25).

To refine gold, silver and other precious metals they are heated to high temperatures where they become liquids, at which point the impurities either evaporate and are burned off or they separate and float to the surface. The impurities that float to the surface can then be scooped off the top, leaving the pure gold or silver behind. 'Launderer's soap', also called 'lye', refers to a cleaning product used in ancient times. It was an alkaline salt that was dissolved and then used in combination with beating and scrubbing to clean clothes.[20]

The combined impact of these two images is to convey that the stain and corruption of sin is not easily removed. Like the impurities in precious metals, sin is thoroughly mixed into our natures; it can't simply be scraped off the surface. At least, not without frightfully high temperatures. And just as for bad stains on good clothes, sometimes the only option is strong soap and vigorous scrubbing.

19. Although the purification begins with the Levites and especially the priests, verse 4 (and the broader context) shows that it moves out from there to encompass the entire nation (see Pieter A. Verhoef, *The Books of Haggai and Malachi*, New International Commentary on the Old Testament (Grand Rapids: Eerdmans, 1987), 291-92).

20. For more details, see Douglas Stuart, 'Malachi,' in *The Minor Prophets: An Exegetical and Expository Commentary*, ed. Thomas E. McComiskey (1998; reprint, Grand Rapids: Baker Academic, 2009), 1352-53.

But powerful soaps and fires aren't up to the task of cleaning away sin. In Jeremiah, God says that the people's efforts at cleansing themselves have come to nothing:

> 'Although you wash yourself with soap and use an abundance of cleansing powder, the stain of your guilt is still before me,' declares the Sovereign LORD (Jer. 2:22).[21]

They've scrubbed and scrubbed but they're still as dirty as they were before. Many of us try to use fire and scrubbing to clean up our lives and hearts, only to discover after a great deal of pain and effort that it hasn't worked. We subject ourselves to bitter torments. We punish ourselves. That was a favourite procedure in the history of the church. People would wear camel or goat hair underwear to chasten themselves (it was terribly uncomfortable and abrasive, as you might imagine!). Or they would go into a desert or live in a cave. And while the bottom has fallen out of the camel's hair underwear market, many people still employ the same kinds of schemes. People try to make themselves feel as guilty as possible and as miserable as possible in the vain hope that it will change their heart. But all these methods were, and are, surprisingly ineffective. And so, in Malachi 3, God promises to do what no soap or fire could do: clean up people's hearts and lives.

Cleansing the Entire World

Before we draw this exploration of cleansing to a close, there's one more episode that's worth considering: the flood. So far, we've seen the depth of the problem – sin lies deep in our hearts and we can't wash it out. But the flood shows the extent of the problem – it's not just some people that need cleansing, everyone needs it.

The account of the flood in Genesis 6 begins with a description of just how far humanity has fallen after the good world God created was plunged into evil by Adam and Eve. In Genesis 6 we're told:

---

21. 'Guilt' in this verse is probably better translated as 'sin'. As the context suggests, the problem with Israel is not simply her past deeds but her unreformable character. William McKane writes, 'Deeply ingrained habits have brought about an inner perversion so fundamental that repentance, a change of heart and new patterns of behaviour, would seem to be ruled out' (William McKane, *A Critical and Exegetical Commentary on Jeremiah*, 2 vols., International Critical Commentary (1986; reprint, Edinburgh: T&T Clark, 1999), 1:43). Cf. Jer. 4:4 where the language of 'washing' is again used to refer to the evil that lives in their hearts.

> The LORD saw how great the wickedness of the human race had become on the earth, and that every inclination of the thoughts of the human heart was only evil all the time. The LORD regretted that he had made human beings on the earth, and his heart was deeply troubled (Gen. 6:5-6).

This is a desperately sad indictment on humanity. Only ten generations after the world was created, we find the world torn apart by evil. As a result, God determines to destroy evil through a massive flood (Gen. 6:17). The only things that are not destroyed are those which are in Noah's ark. Although the flood is cast primarily as judgment, it is fundamentally an act of cleansing, or even, an act of recreation.

The description of the flood and its aftermath is laced with the language and themes of Genesis 1.[22] On day two of creation God had separated the waters above and the waters below (Gen. 1:6-7), but in the flood that water meets again, as water springs from the deep and rains down from the heavens (Gen. 7:11). So too, on day three of creation God had gathered the water into seas and created dry land (Gen. 3:9-11), but in the flood the waters once again flood that land. And, of course, on the dry land God had created living things (Gen. 1:24-25), but in the flood those are destroyed (Gen. 6:17). In that sense the flood 'un-creates'.[23] But, following the flood, the process of creation is unwound and the world is returned to its original 'formless' condition (Gen. 1:2). The springs of the deep close and the sky stops pouring down water (Gen. 8:2). The water and the land are separated again as the flood waters recede (Gen. 8:3, 13) and God reissues to Noah the command He had given to Adam and Eve:

> Then God blessed Noah and his sons, saying to them, 'Be fruitful and increase in number and fill the earth' (Gen. 9:1).

In other words, the flood is a kind of undoing of creation but it's also a remaking of creation. It's an opportunity to start again. And it all looks so promising. Noah is described by God like this:

---

22. See, for example, Bruce K. Waltke and Cathy J. Fredricks, *Genesis: A Commentary* (Grand Rapids: Zondervan, 2001), 128-29.

23. Victor P. Hamilton, *The Book of Genesis*, 2 vols., New International Commentary on the Old Testament (Grand Rapids: Eerdmans, 1990-1995), 1:291.

> Noah was a righteous man, blameless among the people
> of his time, and he walked faithfully with God (Gen. 6:9).

God finds the one man among all the evil who still has regard for
God. God means to start creation over again with the best man
that He can find.

But the flood waters have only just receded when it becomes
clear that everything is still not fixed. Noah gets drunk, lies naked
in his tent and Ham goes in and finds some kind of crude pleasure
in gazing at his father's naked body (Gen. 9:18-25). It turns out that
just starting again with the same old mucked up people won't make
the world a better place. And if the flood wasn't evidence enough of
that, there's plenty of other evidence too.

Some years ago, Fox produced a show called *Utopia*, where
fifteen people were taken away to begin a new society. Barely a few
days had gone by when divisions began to emerge.[24] Perhaps that's
hardly surprising for a reality TV show, given they generally thrive
on orchestrated animosity. But the idea of small groups of people
going away to begin utopian communities where everything will be
better is not the unique domain of reality TV shows. The idea is as
old as the hills – the idea that if you can just go away, if you can just
start again, everything will be okay. It's what the hippies did with
their communes. It's what the Pilgrims did in going to America. The
Pilgrims were Christians leaving England and Europe in the hope
of starting again and doing better in America. Some people try to
do it with church. They try to reboot church – church 2.0. If we can
only start again, everything will be better: a new denomination, a
new way, a new approach.

What *Utopia* promised on the social level, other reality TV shows
promise on the personal level.[25] They offer the chance to be reborn:
home makeovers, personal makeovers, relationship makeovers,
professional makeovers, celebrity makeovers. They promise a new
start, a new you, a new future.

We deceive ourselves when we think that if we can just start over
everything will be different – a new job, a new house, a new city, a

24. S. D. Kelly, 'Stranger in a Strange Land: Fox's New Reality Show "Utopia"', *The Gospel Coalition*, October 3, 2014, https://www.thegospelcoalition.org/reviews/stranger-in-a-strange-land-foxs-new-reality-show-utopia/.

25. Jon Caramanica, 'New Starts on "Live Free or Die," "Survivor" and "Utopia,"' *The New York Times*, November 21, 2014, http://www.nytimes.com/2014/11/23/arts/television/new-starts-on-live-free-or-die-survivor-and-utopia.html.

new marriage. It doesn't work because wherever we go, we take the problem with us – sin. Humanity is the same as it has ever been and we need something extraordinary to fix us up.

But the flood leaves us with a tantalising possibility: what if you could start again? What if you could find a man who really was perfect and blameless? And what if you started the society with that man? And what if that man could gather people to himself in a way that doesn't leave them as they were before? What if instead of our pollution corrupting him, his goodness could transform us? What if that one man could change people, really change people? What if that man could reach inside people's hearts and remake them; not just remake the world out there but remake the world within us? What then?

Noah was a pretty good guy but even he wasn't good enough to be the beginning of a renewed humanity. And even if he had been exceptionally righteous, how would his goodness help us? It would have remained locked up in him and the best we could do would be to look on and wish that we were the same. But he wasn't good enough and neither are we. The same disease which affected him affects us all – sin. The flood was God's response to human evil and it was a new start, but the ultimate response to human evil and the ultimate new start must lie elsewhere; in someone truly perfect, and in someone truly perfect who can bring about the kind of cleansing that the Old Testament so desperately longed for.[26]

The Meaning of Cleansing in the Old Testament

Through the cleansing rituals of the Old Testament God gave people a picture of the need for a deeper purity. He showed that sin

---

26.   In a similar way, both the crossing through the waters of the Red Sea (Exod. 14) and the crossing of the waters of the Jordan (Josh. 3–4) symbolise the same cleansing and new beginning of the flood, incorporating both judgment and deliverance – deliverance of those who passed through safely and judgment on those who did not (first the Egyptians and then the wilderness generation). In both cases, too, the events afterwards (in the wilderness after the Red Sea and in the Promised Land after the Jordan) show that something more is needed. Paul even describes the Red Sea crossing as a kind of baptism (1 Cor. 10:1-4). Fesko rightly notes some of these connections, J. V. Fesko, *Word, Water, and Spirit: A Reformed Perspective on Baptism* (Grand Rapids: Reformation Heritage, 2010), 204-14.

permeates our world, that it spreads like wildfire and that it wells up from within us. That uncleanness even affected God's own people. It affected men like King David, a man after God's own heart. But God also showed that He was prepared to do something about it. Although we can't fix ourselves, God foreshadowed through the sacrificial system that He would ransom us from our evil pasts, and provide the deep cleansing of our heart to enable us to live in His presence. Although we've not seen a lot of detail on *exactly* how God will do that (most of what we've seen is conveyed in images not precise details), we do know that it will be by God coming to His people Himself (e.g. Mal. 3:1-3) and by God pouring out His Spirit (e.g. Ezek. 36:24-28).

Of course, none of these passages take up the language of cleansing and washing in the context of baptism. Yet to ignore them on that ground is to fail to recognise how much these rituals would have shaped the people who first encountered baptism in the ministries of John the Baptist and Jesus. For the people of Israel awaiting the coming of the Messiah, these things were a daily reality. They were a kind of lived out commentary on the nature and the promise of the gospel. For those who enacted these rituals daily, the language of washing and cleansing were pregnant with meaning.

3. Streams of Water Within
Cleansing and Washing in the New Testament

The Old Testament promised cleansing. In the rituals of the Old Testament, God gave the people pictures of the good news. He showed them that one day He would clean them up and make them right with Him again. But all the rituals of the Old Testament were only skin deep. People were longing for God to do something more. And as we come to the New Testament, we find that all that language of cleansing and washing is taken up to describe what is accomplished in the work of Jesus and also the Spirit. For example:

> Husbands, love your wives, just as Christ loved the church and gave himself up for her to make her holy, *cleansing* her by the *washing with water* through the word, and to present her to himself as a radiant church, without stain or wrinkle or any other blemish, but holy and blameless (Eph. 5:25-27) [emphasis added].
>
> God, who knows the heart, showed that he accepted them by giving the Holy Spirit to them, just as he did to us. He did not discriminate between us and them, for he *purified* their hearts by faith (Acts 15:8-9) [emphasis added].
>
> Or do you not know that wrongdoers will not inherit the kingdom of God? Do not be deceived: Neither the sexually immoral nor idolaters nor adulterers nor men who have sex with men nor thieves nor the greedy nor drunkards nor slanderers nor swindlers will inherit the kingdom of God.

And that is what some of you were. But you were *washed*, you were sanctified, you were justified in the name of the Lord Jesus Christ and by the Spirit of our God (1 Cor. 6:9-11) [emphasis added].

If we claim to have fellowship with him and yet walk in the darkness, we lie and do not live out the truth. But if we walk in the light, as he is in the light, we have fellowship with one another, and the blood of Jesus, his Son, *purifies* us from all sin. If we claim to be without sin, we deceive ourselves and the truth is not in us. If we confess our sins, he is faithful and just and will forgive us our sins and *purify* us from all unrighteousness (1 John 1:6-9) [emphasis added].

These passages form some of the most beautiful and compelling pictures of the gospel. In this chapter, we are going to dig into how it is that Jesus and the Spirit accomplish that great cleansing work promised by God in the Old Testament.

The Promise of Jesus: Water and Spirit

One of the places that speaks most about the work of the Spirit in the New Testament is the Gospel of John. There Jesus often speaks about the work of the Spirit and how there is some kind of new work of the Spirit that is unleashed by His death and resurrection. Two key episodes that tie that together with cleansing are found in John chapters 3 and 7.

Born Again by the Washing of the Spirit

In John 3, one of the religious leaders, a man named Nicodemus, comes to Jesus by night. Nicodemus recognises that God is doing something through Jesus, but it appears that Nicodemus is not entirely sure what it is. What follows is, on the surface, a very strange discussion. Nicodemus says:

'Rabbi, we know that you are a teacher who has come from God. For no one could perform the signs you are doing if God were not with him.'

Jesus replied, 'Very truly I tell you, no one can see the kingdom of God unless they are born again.'

'How can someone be born when they are old?' Nicodemus asked. 'Surely they cannot enter a second time into their mother's womb to be born!'

Jesus answered, 'Very truly I tell you, no one can enter the kingdom of God unless they are born of water and the Spirit. Flesh gives birth to flesh, but the Spirit gives birth to spirit. You should not be surprised at my saying, "You must be born again." The wind blows wherever it pleases. You hear its sound, but you cannot tell where it comes from or where it is going. So it is with everyone born of the Spirit' (John 3:2-8).

Nicodemus had either seen or heard the reports of Jesus doing some pretty amazing things (John 2:23), but Jesus wants Nicodemus to know that if he is to really experience the new thing that God is doing in the world something revolutionary is needed.[1] Jesus says to Nicodemus that 'seeing' the kingdom of heaven requires being 'born again'. In Jesus' language, the kingdom of heaven is the new realm or new world where God reigns in Jesus and where God is obeyed by His loving and obedient people. In other words, it is the new cleaned-up, perfected world where people live as they were created to live: for God, free from the corruptions of sin.

When Jesus says that no one can 'see' the kingdom, He isn't talking about understanding or grasping what it is or having the eyes of faith to know about it; rather Jesus uses the word 'see' to mean 'experience'. For example, when someone says, 'I would love to *see* Europe', they don't mean they would love to understand or know about Europe, but rather that they would love to go there and actually experience it. In the same way, no one can 'see' God's kingdom unless they are born again. A few verses later, that becomes absolutely clear when Jesus expresses the same idea in a different way, saying that those who are not born again cannot '*enter* the kingdom of God.'

Nicodemus is completely bewildered by Jesus' suggestion that we need to be 'born again' to experience God's cleaned-up world. He says, 'How can someone be born when they are old?' It seems unlikely that Nicodemus is a complete idiot and has failed to grasp that Jesus is being metaphorical. It is much more likely that Nicodemus is simply extending the metaphor.[2] So Jesus says,

---

1. D. A. Carson, *The God Who Is There: Finding Your Place in God's Story* (Grand Rapids: Baker, 2010), 127. In much of what I say in this section I am indebted to Carson and his interpretation of John 3 found in that book, his commentary on John (D. A. Carson, *The Gospel According to John*, Pillar New Testament Commentary (Grand Rapids: Eerdmans, 1991)) and various online sermons.

2. Carson, *The God Who Is There*, 128.

effectively, that in order to enter God's new cleaned-up, perfected world, people need to start over from scratch – they need to be born again. And Nicodemus replies, 'But how can anyone start from scratch again? How can any of us undo the past? And how can any of us change the people that we are?'[3]

Jesus' answer to that question draws on Ezekiel chapter 36, which we looked at in the last chapter. Jesus says that a person must be born of 'water and the Spirit'. Remember God's promise in Ezekiel:

> I will sprinkle clean *water* on you, and you will be clean; I will cleanse you from all your impurities and from all your idols. I will give you a new heart and put a new *spirit* in you; I will remove from you your heart of stone and give you a heart of flesh. And I will put my *Spirit* in you and move you to follow my decrees and be careful to keep my laws (Ezek. 36:25-27) [emphasis added].

The combination of water and Spirit ties Jesus' words here with God's words through Ezekiel. Jesus is essentially saying, 'To enter the kingdom of God you need to experience what God promised through Ezekiel.'

But according to Jesus, the cleansing God promised in Ezekiel that every single person needs is not merely a small mopping-up operation; it is nothing less than the reconstruction of a person into a wholly other creation – we need to become new people.[4] Jesus says in verse 6:

---

3. As Leon Morris so wonderfully puts it, 'It is perhaps more likely that he is wistful rather than obtuse. A man, Nicodemus might have said, is the sum of all his yesterdays. He is the man he is today because of all the things that have happened to him through the years. He is a bundle of doubts, uncertainties, wishes, hopes, fears, and habits, good and bad, built up through the years. It would be wonderful to break the entail of the past and make a completely fresh beginning. But how can this possibly be done? Can physical birth be repeated? Since this lesser miracle is quite impossible, how can we envisage a much greater miracle, the remaking of a person's essential being? Regeneration is sheer impossibility!' (Leon Morris, *The Gospel According to John*, rev. ed., New International Commentary on the New Testament (Grand Rapids: Eerdmans, 1995), 190).

4. There is a strand of interpretation which has taken Jesus' comments to mean that a person needs to experience two baptisms to enter the kingdom of God – water baptism and Spirit baptism (e.g. Everett Ferguson, *Baptism in the Early Church: History, Theology, and Liturgy in the First Five Centuries* (Grand Rapids: Eerdmans, 2009), 142-45). But the fact that any reference to water falls away as Jesus goes on to focus entirely on the Spirit suggests that water is indeed a metaphor for a spiritual reality (as it is in Ezekiel and the whole OT!). See Carson, *John*, 191-92. Moreover,

Flesh gives birth to flesh, but the Spirit gives birth to spirit (John 3:6).

The contrast here is not between something concrete, like a human body, versus something which is spiritual, in the sense of unearthly. Rather, the contrast is between that which is mortal versus something which is immortal; something which belongs to this creation and is marred by sin versus something which belongs to God's new creation (cf. John 1:13).

The problem is that as people who are of this world, we cannot transform ourselves into something entirely new and different. It is utterly beyond us. As one writer says, 'There is no evolution from flesh to Spirit.'[5] Or as Don Carson explains:

> Pigs give birth to pigs; cockroaches give birth to cockroaches; bats generate bats; kind produces kind; flesh produces flesh. So how on earth do you take lost, self-centered, human beings, and actually connect them with the life of God? You are not going to produce such transformation by natural selection. You are not going to generate moral revolution by merely trying harder or by selective breeding. What you really must have is what Ezekiel said: an act of God himself, from his Spirit, so that we are changed, transformed. You must have that, or you cannot possibly be connected with the life of God.[6]

In short, for us to be connected with the life of God, and enter God's new cleaned-up, perfected world, we need to be cleaned up and remade through the work of the Holy Spirit.

In fact, when Jesus says we need to be born again, the term is ambiguous. It could also mean born 'from above'. That is, although we need to start over, it's not as though if we were just given that chance we would get everything right the second time around. We would still be people marred by sin. No matter how many chances we were given to live life over, we would never reach perfection. In other words, it's not simply that we need to be born *again*, we need

---

that interpretation pushes Jesus' metaphor to the limits and gives water baptism a significance it does not ever carry elsewhere in the New Testament. Water baptism is always a sign of an inner reality rather than an essential element in and of itself.

5. Edwyn Hoskyns, *The Fourth Gospel* (London, 1947), 204, as quoted in Morris, *John*, 194.

6. Carson, *The God Who Is There*, 130.

to be born 'from above' as a completely different kind of people – people who are free from sin.

What Jesus has in mind is not patching up one or two bits here and there but a completely new work. As John Calvin wrote:

> By the phrase *born again* is expressed not the correction of one part, but the renovation of the whole nature. Hence it follows, that there is nothing in us that is not sinful; for if reformation is necessary in the whole and in each part, corruption must have been spread throughout.[7]

The kind of cleansing that you and I need is not simply a mild bath or a quick spiritual shower that cleanses a mostly good person. We need nothing less than a total rebirth – a reconstruction that eliminates every evil and replaces it with a total commitment and love for the God who made us and loves us. And that is precisely what Jesus offers us. It is easy to look inside ourselves and despair over the tendrils of sin that seem to reach into every part of our lives. But Jesus offers to wash all that away.

How does a person experience that? Jesus answers that question a little later in verse 14:

> Just as Moses lifted up the snake in the wilderness, so the Son of Man must be lifted up, that everyone who believes may have eternal life in him (John 3:14-15).

The way that a person experiences the cleansing and remaking work of the Spirit is by looking to the Son of Man 'lifted up'. That is a reference to Jesus being 'lifted up' on the cross. The person who looks to Jesus in His death and resurrection, who 'believes in him', has eternal life. To quote Carson again:

> On his cross Jesus provided the means by which we have new birth. By his death we have life. By his crucifixion on a pole, we begin eternal life. The new birth is grounded in Jesus' death. That is what Jesus is saying. You and I receive the benefit of this not by trying harder or by being ultra-religious but by believing in Jesus.[8]

---

7. John Calvin, *Commentary on the Gospel According to John*, trans. William Pringle, 2 vols. (Bellingham: Logos Bible Software, 2010), 1:108.

8. Carson, *The God Who Is There*, 134. Some people might find that a slightly terrifying statement. That's because 'new birth' is often linked with the systematic theology category of regeneration which holds that a person cannot respond to God

According to Jesus, the cleansing by the Holy Spirit promised in Ezekiel comes through Him, and His death and resurrection.

There are so many things in life that I would love to have, but I know I probably never will. I will most likely never own a fancy house or a fast car. I'll probably never get to fly a helicopter or explore the bottom of the ocean in a submarine or travel into space and see the earth in a way that few people ever have. I'll never get to do those things because I don't have the time or the money or the opportunity. My only real hope is that some generous person gives them to me as a gift.

Of course, there's always a small chance that I might manage to get those things for myself. But what Jesus offers to give us as a gift is something we could never get for ourselves and that no other person could ever give to us. He offers to give us a fresh start as completely new people in God's new creation – in the new world that God is building in Jesus. And all we need to do to receive that incredible gift is look to Jesus and place ourselves in His hands.

Streams of Water Flowing from Within

Those ideas of cleansing through the Spirit that Jesus spelled out to Nicodemus find expression elsewhere in John too. Later in chapter 7, Jesus explains Himself even more clearly and shows the link between His death and the work of the Spirit.

---

without the prior work of the Spirit opening their eyes to the gospel and enabling them to turn to Jesus in faith and repentance. I am absolutely committed to that idea (as is Carson for that matter), and the idea is clearly found throughout the Gospel of John, not least when Jesus says that 'no one can come to me unless the Father who sent me draws them' (John 6:44). But it seems to me that there is a distinction between the New Testament idea of 'new birth' and the systematic theology concept of regeneration. New birth appears to be a broader idea that involves participation in the age to come which is inaugurated by the death and resurrection of Jesus (e.g. Andreas J. Köstenberger and Scott R. Swain, *Father, Son, and Spirit: The Trinity and John's Gospel*, New Studies in Biblical Theology 24 (Nottingham: Apollos, 2008), 130-31). To quote Carson again, 'Jesus is not presented as demanding that Nicodemus experience the new birth in the instant; rather, he is forcefully articulating what must be experienced if one is to enter the kingdom of God. ... The coming-to-faith of the first followers of Jesus was in certain respects unique: they could not instantly become "Christians" in the full-orbed sense, and experience the full sweep of the new birth, until after the resurrection and glorification of Jesus. If we take the Gospel records seriously, we must conclude that Jesus sometimes proclaimed truth the full significance and application of which could be fully appreciated and experienced only after he had risen from the dead. John 3 falls under this category' (Carson, *John*, 195-96). See also note 22.

The events take place during a seven-day celebration called the 'Feast of Tabernacles' or really, the 'Feast of Tents'. The feast was instituted by God to remember the years that the Israelites wandered around in the desert (see Lev. 23:33-44 and Deut. 16:13-15). They had been in the desert after leaving Egypt but instead of going straight to the Promised Land, their lack of trust in God led to them being condemned to wander the desert, living in tents for another forty years while that whole generation died out without ever seeing the Promised Land (see Num. 14). Nevertheless, during that time God provided for them in miraculous ways. One way was by providing water which came gushing from a rock (Exod. 17:1-7; Num. 20).

To remember that miraculous provision, by the time of Jesus, the Jews had inserted a creative addition into their celebration of the Feast of Tabernacles.[9] The High Priest would take a golden jug to the pool of Siloam in Jerusalem, scoop up some water and carry it in procession to the temple. The water would then be poured out before the Lord. The act was a recollection of God's miraculous provision in the time of Moses, but it was also an anticipation of God's promise that one day water would come flooding out from the temple to refresh and renew the world.

Ezekiel's Vision: A Trickle that Waters the World

Although the water pouring ceremony was a Jewish invention, the imagery of God flooding the world with life-giving water is a legitimate part of the Old Testament expectation of how God would fix the world. One of the key passages is Zechariah 14:

> On that day living water will flow out from Jerusalem, half of it east to the Dead Sea and half of it west to the Mediterranean Sea, in summer and in winter (Zech. 14:8).

Like in Jesus' words, the streams flowing from Jerusalem are 'living waters'. But Zechariah 14 is also significant because it links this event with the Feast of Tabernacles (Zech. 14:16).

However, a more expansive version of Zechariah's vision is also found in Ezekiel.[10] In the last chapters of Ezekiel, the prophet sees a vision of a temple:

---

9.   The details for this are found in Jewish Rabbinic literature dating from the early part of the third century A.D. (Mishnah Sukkah 4:9 and Tosefta Sukkah 3:3-13). See Carson, *John*, 322.

10.   Both Zechariah 14 and Ezekiel 47 are linked with the water-pouring ceremony by early Jewish sources (Tosefta Sukkah 3). See Craig S. Keener, *The Gospel*

The man brought me back to the entrance to the temple, and I saw water coming out from under the threshold of the temple toward the east (for the temple faced east). The water was coming down from under the south side of the temple, south of the altar. He then brought me out through the north gate and led me around the outside to the outer gate facing east, and the water was trickling from the south side.

As the man went eastward with a measuring line in his hand, he measured off a thousand cubits and then led me through water that was ankle-deep. He measured off another thousand cubits and led me through water that was knee-deep. He measured off another thousand and led me through water that was up to the waist. He measured off another thousand, but now it was a river that I could not cross, because the water had risen and was deep enough to swim in – a river that no one could cross. He asked me, 'Son of man, do you see this?'

Then he led me back to the bank of the river. When I arrived there, I saw a great number of trees on each side of the river. He said to me, 'This water flows toward the eastern region and goes down into the Arabah, where it enters the Dead Sea. When it empties into the sea, the salty water there becomes fresh. Swarms of living creatures will live wherever the river flows. There will be large numbers of fish, because this water flows there and makes the salt water fresh; so where the river flows everything will live. Fishermen will stand along the shore; from En Gedi to En Eglaim there will be places for spreading nets. The fish will be of many kinds – like the fish of the Mediterranean Sea. But the swamps and marshes will not become fresh; they will be left for salt. Fruit trees of all kinds will grow on both banks of the river. Their leaves will not wither, nor will their fruit fail. Every month they will bear fruit, because the water from the sanctuary flows to them. Their fruit will serve for food and their leaves for healing' (Ezek. 47:1-12).

It's clear from the details that what Ezekiel is seeing is symbolic – a trickle of water slowly gathers pace and becomes a virtual torrent. The trickle of water is coming from the temple, that is, from the

---

of John: A Commentary, 2 vols. (Grand Rapids: Baker Academic, 2012), 725-28. Even though the water-pouring ceremony was a Jewish invention, the point is that Jesus' words would have been understood against the background of what they believed the ceremony symbolised.

presence of God among His people. As they move further and further away from the temple, the water gets deeper and deeper. First it is ankle deep, then it is knee deep, waist deep, and finally too deep to pass. And this water is so powerful that it brings life and refreshment wherever it goes. When this fresh water hits the sea, it is powerful enough to turn salt water fresh. And all along the banks of the river and in the river itself, life thrives.

In the middle of Australia is a place called Lake Eyre, the lowest natural point in all of Australia. Most of the time, Lake Eyre is not a lake at all, it's mostly an empty salt pan surrounded by barren desert. But every now and again, enough rain falls in the north of Australia that some of it slowly makes its way down to Lake Eyre and it springs to life. What was barren, red desert becomes green plains. Fish appear almost from nowhere and birds and other wildlife somehow make their way there too. Just for a moment, lifeless desert comes to life.[11]

But Ezekiel's vision is not of a temporary Lake Eyre-type transformation. The picture of a river passing through a fruitful land, teeming with life, is reminiscent of the Garden of Eden, back in Genesis 1. That is not accidental. Ezekiel's vision is of a refreshing stream that goes out from God into the world and that remakes the world into how it was intended to be. So powerful is this cleansing work of God, that even what starts out as a small trickle is enough to engulf the world in restoration.[12]

And yet, soberingly, not everything is cleansed. Some places will remain wastelands. There is a hell in God's plan for the future, not just a new creation (e.g. Dan. 12:2; Matt. 13:41; John 5:29; Rev. 20:15).

A Better Water Source

So the golden jug filled with water was a well-meant effort both to remember what God had done (life-giving water from the rock in the desert) and to remember what God had promised (life-giving water stretching out to renew the world). But it would have been abundantly clear to anyone who paused to reflect that this small jug of water processing through the streets was not the end game. This jug of water was not going to flood the world and make all things

---

11. See, for example, https://www.abc.net.au/news/2019-05-09/lake-eyre-is-a-wild-river-system-left-to-run-its-course/11035506.

12. In that way, the vision of Ezekiel 47 is reminiscent of the flood too, in which God remakes the world through water (cf. Fesko, *Word, Water, and Spirit*, 256).

new. It would barely make it out the door of the temple before dissipating and drying up. Pretty underwhelming![13]

And so, at the end of seven days of golden jug processions, Jesus stands up and says something astonishing:

> Let anyone who is thirsty come to me and drink. Whoever believes in me, as Scripture has said, rivers of living water will flow from within them (John 7:37-38).

Jesus' claim is to be able to provide the fresh water for life like God had done for Israel in the time of Moses, but more importantly, as God had promised to do in the vision of Ezekiel. In fact, Jesus says something very similar to the Samaritan woman at the well:

> Everyone who drinks this water will be thirsty again, but whoever drinks the water I give them will never thirst. Indeed, the water I give them will become in them a spring of water welling up to eternal life (John 4:13-14).

But Jesus' claim is not simply about the renewal and refreshment of the world, but about the renewal and refreshment of individuals. In both John chapters 4 and 7, the water 'wells up' or 'flows' *within* the person. Again, Jesus chooses to use the image of water. He clearly isn't being literal but metaphorical. The image is of fresh, life-giving water flowing from within people's hearts, rather than the putrid stream of filth that issues from our hearts from the time of our conception onwards. In fact, John explains what Jesus means:

> By this he meant the Spirit, whom those who believed in him were later to receive. Up to that time the Spirit had not been given, since Jesus had not yet been glorified (John 7:39).

The rivers of living water are the Spirit, given to those who entrust themselves to Jesus. Jesus is combining God's promise of renewing the whole world, foreshadowed in Ezekiel 47, with His promise in Ezekiel 36 of renewing individuals.

Set against that bleak description of the human condition painted by Leviticus, the various cleansing rituals, and the Old Testament in general, it's hard to imagine what it must have been like to hear these words that Jesus spoke to the crowds. It's hard to imagine what

---

13.   Sadly, however, some of the Jews did expect great things from this small jug: 'all the waters created at the Creation are destined to go forth from the mouth of this little flask.' (Tosefta Sukkah 3:10)

it must have been like to suddenly realise that what God had long promised, Jesus had finally come to deliver. Likewise, for those of us who know the corruption of our own hearts and the darkness of our own thoughts and desires, the offer of Jesus is almost overwhelming. Jesus says that, if you trust Him, instead of your heart being a toilet pumping out sewerage, He'll give you a heart which is like a spring of fresh water. It's almost like a dream a heart which is not just clean, but which, one day, is inexhaustibly and incorruptibly clean.

Notably, in both John chapters 4 and 7, Jesus says that He is the source of this living water. But John 7 clarifies the exact mechanism by which that works. John tells us that in referring to the streams of living water, Jesus was referring to the Holy Spirit. But he also tells us that the Spirit would come in his cleansing role to those who believed in Jesus only after Jesus' glorification. In John's Gospel, Jesus' glorification refers to His death and resurrection. In other words, this new and long-promised work of the Spirit couldn't simply be dispensed haphazardly. It awaited Jesus' death for sins and powerful resurrection to life. It was His death and resurrection which ushered in this work of the Spirit and made it accessible to people whose lives were marred by sin. After all, how could the Spirit come and make His home in people unless there had been decisive and definitive atonement for sin; unless God's wrath against people had been put away? But Jesus, having buried our sins in the depths of the sea, pours out the Spirit on all who believe in Him.[14]

It is remarkable that Jesus offers to clean up our hearts even though, by nature, we are His greatest enemies. The gift of God's own renewing and revitalising Spirit is not a gift that God has reserved for His friends only. Unbelievably, it is a gift that He offers

---

14.   This is not to say that the Spirit was not at work in the lives of Old Testament believers. Clearly the Spirit was at work in them. For instance, David could say, 'Do not ... take your Holy Spirit from me' (Ps. 51:11), and others received the assistance of the Spirit too, such as Bezalel who was empowered by the Spirit to construct the temple (Exod. 31:2-5). But there seems to be a certain distance to the Spirit's work in the Old Testament which is removed in the New Testament. On the basis of John 14:17, James Hamilton describes the shift as from the Spirit being 'with' people to the Spirit being 'in' them (see James M. Hamilton Jr., *God's Indwelling Presence: The Holy Spirit in the Old and New Testaments*, NAC Studies in Bible & Theology (Nashville: B&H Academic, 2006)). This new intimacy is grounded in the definitive atoning work of Jesus. Moreover, the Spirit in the New Testament era is sent by the crucified, risen and ascended Jesus to unite us with Himself, hence bringing us all the benefits of the gospel. These benefits were foreshadowed in the Old Testament but only became a reality in Jesus' death and resurrection. See note 8.

to us who have hated and reviled Him and were set against Him. At the cost of His own life, Jesus has made reconciliation with God, so that whoever receives Him can also receive the life-giving gift of His Holy Spirit.

What's the Link to Baptism?

These are breathtaking truths. But it is worth asking whether any of these really have any connection with baptism. Sure, there are references to water, but is that enough? It's worth digging a little deeper to see the link.

Heading back to John 3, it helps to look at the wider context of Jesus' discussion with Nicodemus. Only a chapter earlier, Jesus was at a wedding in Cana where the hosts had run out of wine. Sitting in the corner were six stone jars that were used for holding the water needed to conduct the regular Jewish cleansing rites.[15] Jesus commands the servants to fill the jars to the brim with water and then draw out what is in them and take it to the master of the house. When the master of the house tastes what is given to him, it has become wine. At first sight, the miracle is merely about Jesus' provision of wine for an ill-prepared host. But on closer inspection it is clear that Jesus is setting up for the point He later makes much more explicitly to Nicodemus: the Old Testament Jewish cleansing rituals are coming to an end because Jesus is bringing the reality to which they pointed.[16] To put it another way, the jars for cleansing can now be filled with wine for celebrating because their original purpose is now obsolete.

Then in the section after Jesus' discussion with Nicodemus, we find Jesus baptising people through His disciples:[17]

> After this, Jesus and his disciples went out into the Judean countryside, where he spent some time with them, and baptized. Now John also was baptizing at Aenon near Salim, because there was plenty of water, and people were coming and being baptized (This was before John was put in prison.).

---

15. The kinds we looked at in the Old Testament, though like the golden jug for the Feast of Tabernacles, there were also some cleansing rites that were inventions of the Jews (e.g. Mark 7:1-5).

16. E.g. Andreas J. Köstenberger, 'John,' in *Commentary on the New Testament Use of the Old Testament*, ed. D. A. Carson and G. K. Beale (Grand Rapids: Baker Academic, 2007), 431.

17. That Jesus was baptising through the disciples is clear from John 4:1-2.

An argument developed between some of John's disciples and a certain Jew over the matter of ceremonial washing. They came to John and said to him, 'Rabbi, that man who was with you on the other side of the Jordan—the one you testified about—look, he is baptizing, and everyone is going to him.'

To this John replied, 'A person can receive only what is given them from heaven. You yourselves can testify that I said, "I am not the Messiah but am sent ahead of him." The bride belongs to the bridegroom. The friend who attends the bridegroom waits and listens for him, and is full of joy when he hears the bridegroom's voice. That joy is mine, and it is now complete. He must become greater; I must become less' (John 3:22-30).

Again, there is a link to Jewish purification – that had started the debate. But the dispute leads John's disciples to be concerned that people are leaving John's baptism in preference for Jesus' baptism. It's impossible to know, but I imagine the debate that led them to ask their question, went something like this:

John's disciples: You should be baptised by our teacher.

Jewish man: Why, when we already have our Jewish purifications?

John's disciples: Because our teacher is saying that God is about to fulfil all those purification rituals.

Jewish man: So why are people abandoning your master's baptism in favour of this fellow Jesus' baptism?

That is, the issue seems to centre on the relationship between John's baptism and Jewish purifications. But the existence of Jesus' baptism creates awkward questions for John's disciples that they can't yet answer.

Whatever the exact nature of the debate, it is clear that, while John's disciples (and others) have grasped that John's baptism is related to other ceremonial washing, they haven't quite grasped how John's baptism is related to Jesus and His baptism. The idea seems to be that although John's disciples have seen that John's baptism is somehow a fulfilment of the Old Testament cleansing rituals, they have failed to see that it is not *the* fulfilment. John points out that he is only the messenger announcing something greater. John is only from earth but Jesus comes from heaven (3:31) and gives the Spirit without measure (3:34). John's answer to his disciples is simple: go with Jesus and His baptism because, in Jesus, what those ceremonies and rituals were foreshadowing has now come about – the giving of the Holy Spirit.

We will return to these ideas again in chapter 5. But the key point for the moment is that across John chapters 2 and 3 we have this pattern that Jesus supersedes the Old Testament purification system (the wedding at Cana) because He brings the promised cleansing through the Spirit (Nicodemus), and Jesus' baptism somehow acknowledges and identifies that (the baptism controversy).

The Washing of Regeneration and Renewal

We saw in the introduction to this chapter that Paul uses the language of cleansing in numerous places to show that in Jesus the Old Testament hopes have been fulfilled. But one of the most significant places where he speaks about cleansing is Titus 3. There he draws together several important ideas in only a few sentences.

Paul writes to Titus and says he should encourage his church to live transformed lives that honour God. They ought to submit to the authorities, be obedient, be ready to do good, refrain from speaking evil of others, and so on (Titus 3:1-2). But that transformed life is grounded in what God has done in the lives of these Christians. Paul writes:

> At one time we too were foolish, disobedient, deceived and enslaved by all kinds of passions and pleasures. We lived in malice and envy, being hated and hating one another. But when the kindness and love of God our Savior appeared, he saved us, not because of righteous things we had done, but because of his mercy. He saved us through the *washing of rebirth and renewal* by the Holy Spirit, whom he poured out on us generously through Jesus Christ our Savior, so that, having been justified by his grace, we might become heirs having the hope of eternal life (Titus 3:3-7) [emphasis added].

Paul takes up the language of washing to describe God's work in the gospel.

Notice, first of all, that this 'washing' is a response to our corrupt natures – we were foolish, disobedient, led astray, malicious and hateful. Just as in the Old Testament, the hope for washing and cleansing is that it would change what lies deep within us.

But Paul also says that the washing is a work of 'rebirth and renewal of the Holy Spirit'.[18] The word 'rebirth', or 'regeneration', is only used twice in the whole of the New Testament, here and in Matthew 19:28. The Greek word, *palingenesia*, is a sandwich of two other words 'beginning' (*genesis*) and 'again' (*palin*), and it means something like 'new beginning' or even 'new birth'.[19] The word 'renewal' has a very similar meaning. It does not refer here to a gradual *process* of renewal but refers to a decisive restart – going back to 'new'. In other words, both are very similar to what Jesus says in John 3 about being 'born again'.[20]

The way Jesus uses 'regeneration' in Matthew 19:28 also gives us some insight into what Paul means in Titus 3.[21] Jesus says:

> Truly I tell you, at the renewal of all things [i.e. the *regeneration*], when the Son of Man sits on his glorious throne, you who have followed me will also sit on twelve thrones, judging the twelve tribes of Israel (Matt. 19:28).

18. The relationship between washing, rebirth, renewal and the Holy Spirit is grammatically tricky. It could be 'through the washing-of-rebirth and (through) the renewal-of-the-Holy Spirit' or 'through the washing of rebirth-and-renewal of the Holy Spirit.' But the fact that rebirth and renewal mean almost the same thing and that washing is generally a function of the Holy Spirit, suggest that whatever the precise grammatical relationship, thematically, washing, rebirth, renewal and the Holy Spirit's activity all constitute one singular work of God (cf. Phillip H. Towner, *The Letters to Timothy and Titus*, New International Commentary on the New Testament (Grand Rapids: Eerdmans, 2006), 782-84 and George W. Knight, *The Pastoral Epistles: A Commentary on the Greek Text*, New International Greek Testament Commentary (Grand Rapids: Eerdmans, 1992), 342-44).

19. E.g. Peter Trummer, 'Palingenesia,' ed. Horst Balz and Gerhard Schneider, *Exegetical Dictionary of the New Testament*, 3:8.

20. The language that Jesus uses is not exactly the same as the language Paul uses here. In John 3 Jesus says, *gennēthē anōthen*, which also means 'born again'. But we shouldn't get too caught up on the exact form of the words. It's possible to say the same thing in lots of different ways, and the two ideas are clearly the same.

21. The early church father, Clement of Rome, connected 'regeneration' (*palingenesia*) to the flood and Noah's preaching at that time: 'Noah, being found faithful, preached regeneration to the world through his ministry' (1 Clem. 9 [*Ante-Nicene Fathers* 1:7]; see Fesko, *Word, Water, and Spirit*, 226).

Jesus uses the term 'regeneration' to refer to the new world or new creation that He will establish in which He will rule together with His disciples. That hope is anchored in the Old Testament hope of a world put right. For example, God says through Isaiah:

> See, I will create new heavens and a new earth. The former things will not be remembered, nor will they come to mind (Isa. 65:17).

That new world will be a world of unparalleled goodness such that no one will remember the sadness of this contorted world. So too, the lives of people in that world will be full of joy and peace:

> 'They will build houses and dwell in them; they will plant vineyards and eat their fruit. No longer will they build houses and others live in them, or plant and others eat. For as the days of a tree, so will be the days of my people; my chosen ones will long enjoy the work of their hands. They will not labor in vain, nor will they bear children doomed to misfortune; for they will be a people blessed by the LORD, they and their descendants with them. Before they call I will answer; while they are still speaking I will hear. The wolf and the lamb will feed together, and the lion will eat straw like the ox, and dust will be the serpent's food. They will neither harm nor destroy on all my holy mountain,' says the LORD (Isa. 65:21-25).

God's plan to put the world right involves a new beginning for the whole world and the whole creation.

But the catch is that, in order for you and me to be part of that new creation, we need to become new creations too. The reason for that is pretty obvious. It would be totally inadequate for God to simply pick us up and transplant us into a new world because we would remain the corrupt and distorted people that we are and we would simply corrupt and distort that new world as well. If you take a filthy dog and let him loose on your pristine house, very soon the house will be filthy along with everyone else who lives in it. In order to inhabit God's new world, we need to be cleaned up, or in other language, we need to be made new. That's why Jesus says to Nicodemus, you can't enter the kingdom of God unless you're born again and made new.

What we find in the New Testament, then, is that Christians are not simply *part* of a new creation but new creations themselves:

> Therefore, if anyone is in Christ, he is a new creation.
> The old has passed away; behold, the new has come
> (2 Cor. 5:17 ESV).

God is not just making the world new; He is making *people* new as well. That is what Titus means when he says that through the Spirit believers have received the 'washing of rebirth and renewal'. He means that if we belong to Christ, we have been cleansed by the Spirit in such a way that we have begun again (renewal) and are now part of the new creation established in Jesus (rebirth/regeneration).[22] We are 'heirs having the hope of eternal life' (Titus 3:7).

A New Creation in Christ Jesus and through the Spirit

That is frankly amazing! Through the ministry of Jesus and the Spirit we become new creations. But how exactly does that work? And why, then, are we all still affected by sin? At this point, it is worth pausing to think a little more deeply about what exactly the problem with us is and how Jesus and the Spirit together work to remedy that.

According to the Bible, the problem with us, the reason that we are so thoroughly corrupted, is because we share in the effects of the sin of Adam who was the first to turn against God. When Adam and Eve sinned, they brought the corruption of sin flooding into our world and we bear the consequences of that. Paul explains in Romans 5:

---

22. Confusingly, the term 'regeneration' is used quite differently in the Bible from the way it is used in the discipline of systematic theology. Even within systematic theology the term is used in quite different ways. For instance, the sixteenth century theological statement, the Belgic Confession, sees regeneration as following faith, while another document from a similar time, the Canons of Dort, sees regeneration as the thing that engenders faith. In contrast, Calvin saw regeneration as synonymous with the theological category of sanctification – the progressive change of a person into the image of Christ. While it's okay to use words in different ways, it can be confusing, and we need to be aware of the distinction. The theologian Herman Bavinck writes, 'when dogmatics [i.e. theology] restricts the term to the implantation of the spiritual life, it is giving it a more restricted sense than that in which Scripture usually speaks of 'regeneration' (or 'birth from above' or 'birth from God') and must therefore be on its guard' (Herman Bavinck, *Reformed Dogmatics*, ed. John Bolt, trans. John Vriend, 4 vols. (Grand Rapids: Baker Academic, 2003-2008), 4:76-77). In this book, when I use the term 'regeneration', I mean it in the sense that the New Testament does. On which see note 8. To understand the big picture of regeneration in the Bible's storyline see, Graeme Goldsworthy, *According to Plan* (Nottingham: Inter-Varsity Press, 1991), esp. chapter 24.

> Therefore, just as sin entered the world through one man, and death through sin, and in this way death came to all people, because all sinned … (Rom. 5:12).

Paul is referring to Adam. He is saying that through Adam, sin entered the world. It was Adam (and Eve) who first sinned and so caused the plague of sin and hence death to be unleashed on the world.[23] Paul paints a picture of what that looks like in Ephesians 2:

> As for you, you were dead in your transgressions and sins, in which you used to live when you followed the ways of this world and of the ruler of the kingdom of the air, the spirit who is now at work in those who are disobedient. All of us also lived among them at one time, gratifying the cravings of our flesh and following its desires and thoughts. Like the rest, we were by nature deserving of wrath (Eph. 2:1-3).

To be born into this world, even simply to be conceived, is to be conceived and born a sinner, twisted and corrupted by sin, and so *by nature* an object of God's wrath. The sin that makes God opposed to us is wedded deeply into who we are and it thoroughly distorts us. As Martin Luther wrote:

> We are not sinners because we commit sin—now this one, now that one—but we commit these acts because we are sinners before we do so; that is, bad tree and bad seed produce bad fruit, and from an evil root nothing but an evil tree can grow.[24]

We have seen that idea repeatedly in the Old Testament. But the good news of the gospel is that Jesus has come in order that we might no longer be like Adam, but holy, righteous, perfect and good like Jesus. Paul explains in 1 Corinthians 15:

---

23.   In theology that idea is called 'original sin'. As ever, the Reformer John Calvin is both clear and sane. His comments on this text and on original sin are worth reading. See John Calvin, *Commentary on the Epistle of Paul the Apostle to the Romans*, trans. John Owen (Bellingham: Logos Bible Software, 2010), 200-201 and John Calvin, *Institutes of the Christian Religion*, ed. John T. McNeill, trans. Ford Lewis Battles, 2 vols., Library of Christian Classics (Louisville: Westminster John Knox, 2006), 2.1.5-11.

24.   Martin Luther, *What Luther Says*, ed. Ewald M. Plass (St. Louis: Concordia, 1959), 3:1299, as quoted in Gregg R. Allison, *Historical Theology: An Introduction to Christian Doctrine* (Grand Rapids: Zondervan, 2011), 354.

> For since death came through a man, the resurrection of the
> dead comes also through a man. For as in Adam all die, so
> in Christ all will be made alive. But each in turn: Christ,
> the firstfruits; then, when he comes, those who belong to
> him (1 Cor. 15:20-23).

The 'resurrection' that Paul has in mind is not simply moving from being physically dead to being physically alive. It includes that obviously. But it also includes moving from what he describes in Ephesians 2 as being 'dead in your transgressions and sins' to being 'created in Christ Jesus to do good works'. It is a move from being like Adam to being like Christ:

> just as we have borne the image of the earthly man, so shall
> we bear the image of the heavenly man (1 Cor. 15:49).

In order to enter God's new creation—God's kingdom—we need to cease to be like Adam and we need to be made like Jesus. That will take place finally, as Paul says, when Jesus returns. And yet, amazingly, that reality has already begun to work back into our present experience. Through the Spirit we are joined with Jesus so that just as when we were born the first time we were in the 'image' of Adam and we shared his sin and corruption, so now if we are born again by the Spirit we are remade in the image of Jesus and we share His holiness and righteousness. That is not to say that we become instantaneously perfect. Rather, instead, we end up straddling two realities – we remain partly old and yet have become new.

There is a helpful diagram by a man named Geerhardus Vos that shows what is meant:[25]

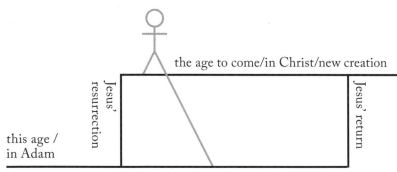

the age to come/in Christ/new creation

Jesus' resurrection

Jesus' return

this age / in Adam

---

25. See Geerhardus Vos, *The Pauline Eschatology* (Princeton: Geerhardus Vos, 1930), 38. (The man with the one ridiculously long leg is my addition!)

The point of this diagram is that Jesus' death and resurrection have ushered in a new age of the new redeemed and restored creation. But Jesus' launch of this new creation is not something He simply does 'out there', but something that He does in Himself. He has begun this new creation by becoming *himself*, through His death and resurrection, the first part of the new creation – the first new, redeemed and restored human being. He is the 'firstfruits of those who have fallen asleep' (1 Cor. 15:20). Jesus has put to death the old order and established the new perfected order *in Himself.*

So What About Us?

But how does that affect us? You and I begin our lives in 'this age' – in Adam. But when we are united to Jesus through faith, we are united to Jesus by the Holy Spirit. The result is that, what Jesus has done in history and what Jesus continues to be now, becomes ours. Through the Spirit we share in Jesus' death and His resurrection. In His death our old nature dies and we are 'born again' by sharing through the Spirit in Jesus' powerful resurrection life and new humanity. Thus, through the Spirit, we come to share in Jesus' new humanity and in the age to come.

That is an 'existential' reality. That is, it changes us at the very level of our existence. We are not simply declared to be new but we are born again into a new creation/humanity in the image of Jesus. It is a completely new start. It is not a gradual change, so that we somehow get closer and closer to heaven as life goes on. Rather, it is a decisive new reality – we are already seated with Christ in the presence of God (Eph. 2:6).

Nevertheless, until the return of Jesus to judge the living and the dead and to put away all sin and opposition to God, Christians remain as people who straddle two ages or two creations – the old age and the new age (see the man in the diagram). We have the firstfruits of the Spirit but we still live in an old body with its old corruptions. Through the Spirit we will increasingly be able to put to death in us the misdeeds of the body but, until we die or Jesus returns, we will always remain with a foot in this age. That is what Paul complains about in Romans 7 when he bemoans the fact that:[26]

---

26. It is worth saying that the meaning of Romans 7 is one of the most highly contested in the New Testament. Unnecessarily so, in my view. A proper understanding of the phased unfolding of God's new creation in Christ, together with an understanding of how Romans 7 functions as a stage in the argument being

> in my inner being I delight in God's law; but I see another law at work in me, waging war against the law of my mind and making me a prisoner of the law of sin at work within me. What a wretched man I am! Who will rescue me from this body that is subject to death? Thanks be to God, who delivers me through Jesus Christ our Lord! So then, I myself in my mind am a slave to God's law, but in my sinful nature a slave to the law of sin (Rom. 7:22-25).

That is, inwardly Paul delights in the things of God – he has the firstfruits of the new life in Christ. Yet he continues to be weighed down by this 'body that is subject to death' – his existence in a corrupted body in a corrupted world. The answer to that predicament is not to lose the body and to become a spirit floating around on a cloud, but for his body to be renewed. That hope finds expression in the very next chapter of Romans:

> And if the Spirit of him who raised Jesus from the dead is living in you, he who raised Christ from the dead will also give life to your mortal bodies because of his Spirit who lives in you (Rom. 8:11).

In Christ, through the Spirit, we have received spiritual renewal – the Spirit of the risen Christ dwells in us. But our mortal bodies need to be made immortal, imperishable and incorruptible (1 Cor. 15:50-54). So, Paul says later in Romans 8:

> We know that the whole creation has been groaning as in the pains of childbirth right up to the present time. Not only so, but we ourselves, who have the firstfruits of the Spirit, groan inwardly as we wait eagerly for our adoption to sonship, the redemption of our bodies (Rom. 8:22-23).

Creation has been groaning for cleansing and renewal, in the 'pains of childbirth'. That is, the present creation is waiting expectantly for a new creation to be 'born'. So too, believers who have the firstfruits of the Spirit, whose minds and spirits have been set free to know and love God, groan as they await the redemption and renewal of their bodies in the resurrection of their bodies from the dead.

---

developed over three chapters (Rom. 6–8), removes the perceived complexity. For the super keen, see my 'Who Is the 'I' in Romans 7:14-25?,' *Reformed Theological Review* 69 (2010): 119-30, and even better is David Peterson, *Possessed by God: A New Testament Theology of Sanctification and Holiness*, New Studies in Biblical Theology 1 (Leicester: Apollos, 1995), chap. 5.

If we know and belong to Jesus there is a sense in which we increasingly want to love and serve Jesus, a sense in which we increasingly delight in the things of God. But that desire and delight are frustrated by the fact that we continually seem to fall into sin. We keep stumbling. Like Paul, we keep doing the very things we don't want to do, or we fail to do the things we do want to do. Although we have been awakened in our inner being to the things of God, we long for another day—the return of Jesus—when our bodies will be renewed and the corruption of sin will be put away once and for all.[27]

Returning then to Titus, Paul is saying that the 'washing' that matters is the washing which makes people new creatures and enables them to share in the new creation/new humanity established in Jesus and in the image of Jesus. In His death and resurrection, Jesus has brought an end to the old humanity and has established in Himself a new humanity which is perfect, holy and righteous. By faith in Jesus, we share in that new humanity in Jesus. We share in that regeneration and renewal through the Holy Spirit who unites us to Jesus.

Jesus has come not simply to patch us up and to set us on the road to gradual improvement, but He has offered us a new beginning through being united with Him, by the Spirit, in His death and resurrection.

Cleansing through Justification

As in John's Gospel, Paul anchors this work of the Spirit uniting us with Jesus in Jesus' historical death and resurrection. He says that the 'washing of rebirth and renewal' has come 'having been justified by his grace'. God has saved us through the Spirit's washing of regeneration in which we are united to Christ. However, the Spirit is only poured out on us through Jesus' justifying work in His death and resurrection.

It is crucial to understand that the problem that the gospel remedies is twofold. There is the just wrath and condemnation of God against our sin that needs to be put away. But there is also the need for sin to be eradicated from within us. What good does it do to forgive people only to leave them mired in their sin? Conversely,

---

27. As Wesley Hill put it so eloquently in the title of his book, we are 'washed and waiting' (Wesley Hill, *Washed and Waiting: Reflections on Christian Faithfulness and Homosexuality* (Grand Rapids: Zondervan, 2010)).

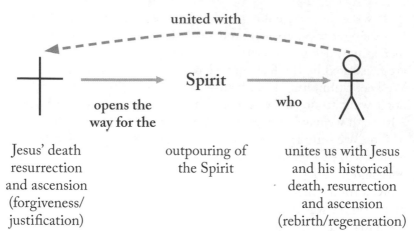

what good does it do to give people a new start if their history of rebellion and evil remain freshly planted in God's mind? But in Jesus, God has decisively dealt with both. And it is through the former—forgiveness and justification—that the latter comes— regeneration and renewal.

It is important to note that we are speaking here of the order of events in redemptive history rather than the experience of the individual Christian. That is, Jesus had to die and rise again in history so that the age could come in which the Spirit dwells in believers. For the Christian, however, forgiveness, the Spirit and union with Christ come together as a package deal. We do not receive one first and then the others sometime later.

Although the reason that cleansing through the Spirit follows forgiveness and justification is not spelled out in the passages we looked at above (e.g. John 7; Titus 3:3-7), the logic is clear. The reason is that God cannot come and dwell in people who are still the objects of His wrath. People first need to be reconciled to God through the atoning death of Jesus before they can become the temple of the living God. That idea becomes even clearer in the next passage we'll consider.

A Better Hope than Water and Goats

The final place we'll look to see the New Testament significance of washing is in Hebrews. In the examples so far in this chapter, the connection to Old Testament cleansing and washing have not been explicit but only been floating around in the background. But in Hebrews chapters 8 to 10, the writer is deliberately trying to explain the failure of the ceremonies in the Old Testament and how Jesus provides the ultimate solution. He begins by outlining the basic nature of the problem:

> For if there had been nothing wrong with that first covenant, no place would have been sought for another. But God found fault with the people and said:
> 'The days are coming, declares the Lord, when I will make a new covenant with the people of Israel and with the people of Judah. It will not be like the covenant I made with their ancestors when I took them by the hand to lead them out of Egypt, because they did not remain faithful to my covenant, and I turned away from them, declares the Lord. This is the covenant I will establish with the people of Israel after that time, declares the Lord. I will put my laws in their minds and write them on their hearts. I will be their God, and they will be my people. No longer will they teach their neighbor, or say to one another, "Know the Lord," because they will all know me, from the least of them to the greatest. For I will forgive their wickedness and will remember their sins no more.'
> By calling this covenant 'new,' he has made the first one obsolete; and what is obsolete and outdated will soon disappear (Heb. 8:7-13).

At its most basic, a covenant is an agreement bound by an oath.[28] The 'first covenant' is not the whole Old Testament, but the covenant that God made with the people through Moses – the covenant that enshrined all the rituals and sacrifices. God says that that covenant on its own was inadequate. It is not that the failure of that covenant caught God off-guard. Rather, the issue is that the covenant through Moses only *outlined* the promises but it did not actually *deliver* them, nor was it meant to. In fact, that old covenant is now passing away because the realities to which it pointed have come to fruition in the person and work of Jesus.

---

28. Paul R. Williamson, *Sealed with an Oath: Covenant in God's Unfolding Purpose*, New Studies in Biblical Theology 23 (Downers Grove: InterVarsity, 2007), 43. See, for example, Hebrews 6:17, 'Because God wanted to make the unchanging nature of his purpose very clear to the heirs of what was promised, he confirmed it with an oath.' Although the word 'covenant' is not used here, God's reaffirmation of His covenant with Abraham is clearly in view.

The problem that the writer identifies with that first covenant was that the people did not continue in the covenant. The problem was not with God but with the people. They turned away from God and, as a result, God turned away from them. Hence, God promises to do something new. He promises to actually change people – to put His laws in their minds and write them on their hearts.[29] Those are the same kinds of promises that we have seen communicated in the cleansing rituals of the Old Testament and in places like Ezekiel chapter 36. And once again, those things are anchored in atonement and forgiveness. God says, 'I will put my laws in their minds ... *For* I will forgive their wickedness and will remember their sins no more.' (Heb 8:10-12) The foundation of the cleaning up work that God will do in people is His decisive and final work of forgiving their sins, remembering them no more, and reconciling people to Himself.

The writer of Hebrews goes on to illustrate the limitations of the first covenant by using the construction of the tabernacle as a model of the differences between the two covenants. He says that the first covenant had the tabernacle (and later the temple), and the construction of the tabernacle had something to say about the two covenants. Just like there is a first and second covenant, the tabernacle had a first and second section:

> A tabernacle was set up. In its *first* room were the lampstand and the table with its consecrated bread; this was called the Holy Place. Behind the *second* curtain was a room called the Most Holy Place, which had the golden altar of incense and the gold-covered ark of the covenant. This ark contained the gold jar of manna, Aaron's staff that had budded, and the stone tablets of the covenant. Above the ark were the cherubim of the Glory, overshadowing the atonement cover. But we cannot discuss these things in detail now (Heb. 9:2-5) [emphasis added].

The first section was the Holy Place. All the priests in Israel could go into that first section. But there was also a second section, the Most Holy Place, and into that section only one person could go – the high priest. And even then, the high priest could only enter once a year, on the Day of Atonement, when he needed to offer sacrifices, not only for the people, but even for himself (Heb. 9:6-7). The writer says that this was supposed to indicate something very important:

---

29.   The words that the writer of Hebrews quotes are from Jeremiah 31:31-34.

> By this the Holy Spirit indicates that the way into the holy places is not yet opened as long as the *first* section is still standing … (Heb. 9:8 ESV) [emphasis added].

The writer says that the first and second sections were a 'parable' of the first and second covenants (i.e. old covenant and new covenant). The Holy Spirit was indicating that the way into the 'holy places', or the Most Holy place (the second section), was blocked so long as the first section/covenant was still standing. It was like this:

Most Holy Place
(represents)
'Second' or 'New' Covenant
(represents)
Access to God

Holy Place
(represents)
'First' or 'Old' Covenant
(represents)
Limited Access to God

This first section/covenant was blocking the way. It must be removed so that there can be free access to God.

In fact, there is some deliberate ambiguity here. It is not clear whether what blocked the way was the first section (the holy place) or the whole first tent (i.e. the tabernacle itself).[30] But the equation of the first and second sections with the first and second covenants renders that distinction irrelevant. It is not just the first section that kept people from God; the whole religious system of the first covenant kept people at a distance from God. Or rather, while it brought them closer into a kind of first section relationship with God, it couldn't bring them into the very presence of the living God.[31]

---

30. For instance, the NIV and CSB opt for the former, while the ESV opts for the latter.

31. In fact, there was kind of a catch-22. Cleansing and holiness were only possible in the presence of God, since God himself is the very source of holiness. We

In Tasmania, where I live, it seems to be quite common for people to want you to take your shoes off at the door. The reason is they don't want you to walk mud into their homes. You need to be clean before you can enter. In the same way, we need to be clean to be able to enter the very presence of God, but we need something far more than just taking off our shoes.

The problem with the first covenant was that it couldn't bring the thorough cleansing that was needed. The writer goes on to explain why:

> This is an illustration for the present time, indicating that
> the gifts and sacrifices being offered were not able to clear
> the conscience of the worshiper. They are only a matter of
> food and drink and various ceremonial washings [literally,
> 'baptisms'] – external regulations applying until the time of
> the new order (Heb. 9:9-10).

The problem was that the whole ritual system of washings and sacrifices did not make people fit for entering the very presence of God. More particularly, the issue was that the gifts and sacrifices could not 'clear' or rather 'perfect' the conscience of the worshipper. When we think of the conscience, we often think of it as the part of us that makes us feel bad for wrong stuff we've done in the past. But there are good reasons for thinking that the writer of Hebrews understands the conscience in a more comprehensive way. It seems that in chapters 9 and 10 he uses 'conscience' as a stand-in for the 'heart' referred to in the new covenant promise.[32] That is, the conscience represents the centre of a person's being in the same way that the heart is often used to refer to the centre of a person's being.[33] The conscience, like the heart, not only evaluates our past misdeeds but, more crucially, it shapes our whole lives including our present and future actions. In other words, the writer of Hebrews is not saying that the sacrifices and cleansing rituals could not make people feel better about the sins they had committed in the past (e.g.

---

can't be holy without being near to God. But our uncleanness means that we can't get near to God.

32. Perhaps the most obvious evidence for that is that the word 'heart' is completely missing in the section bracketed by the two quotations of Jeremiah's promise that God will write the law on His people's hearts (Heb. 8:10-12; 10:16-17). It is in the explanation of that very promise that the word 'heart' mysteriously disappears and the word 'conscience' seems to take its place.

33. E.g. Gareth Lee Cockerill, *The Epistle to the Hebrews*, New International Commentary on the New Testament (Grand Rapids: Eerdmans, 2012), 385, 401.

'clear the conscience'). Rather, he is saying that the sacrifices and cleansing rituals could not effect what God had promised to do in the new covenant – write the law on people's hearts.

The reason those ceremonies could not do that is obvious – they were merely external. In contrast, Jesus ushers in what the old covenant rituals could not:

> But when Christ came as high priest of the good things that are now already here, he went through the greater and more perfect tabernacle that is not made with human hands, that is to say, is not a part of this creation. He did not enter by means of the blood of goats and calves; but he entered the Most Holy Place once for all by his own blood, thus obtaining eternal redemption. The blood of goats and bulls and the ashes of a heifer sprinkled on those who are ceremonially unclean sanctify them so that they are outwardly clean. How much more, then, will the blood of Christ, who through the eternal Spirit offered himself unblemished to God, cleanse our consciences from acts that lead to death, so that we may serve the living God! (Heb. 9:11-14).

The old covenant rituals were just signs and symbols. Sure, they provided a kind of 'first section' access to God which was a great privilege, but they couldn't bring people into the very presence of God. That's because the blood of goats and calves offered in a tent somewhere in the Middle East and ashes mixed with water sprinkled on people's skin would never penetrate to the heart. In contrast, Jesus entered the presence of His Father, by means of His own blood poured out for our sins, and His sacrifice effected a cleansing that no Old Testament ritual ever did: it can 'cleanse our consciences [i.e. heart] from acts that lead to death, so that we may serve the living God'.[34]

It is Jesus' death that has ushered in the era of the new covenant. The reason is that the old covenant and the sins committed under it have been decisively put away:

> For this reason Christ is the mediator of a new covenant, that those who are called may receive the promised eternal

---

34. Notice again, that the purpose of purifying the conscience is not primarily to take away our feelings of guilt, but to enable us to serve God rather than keep giving ourselves to 'acts that lead to death'.

inheritance – now that he has died as a ransom to set them free from the sins committed under the first covenant (Heb. 9:15).

Jesus' death has ransomed or bought people out from under the first covenant and its rituals and its curse for disobedience. And now that it has been demolished, He has become the mediator of a covenant that brings direct access to God. Once again, it is Jesus who brings the cleansing foreshadowed in the Old Testament but not delivered. He brings it by His atoning death for sins which opens the way for the work of the Spirit to write the law on our hearts.

As a result, we can approach God with absolute confidence:

> Therefore, brothers, since we have confidence to enter the holy places by the blood of Jesus, by the new and living way that he opened for us through the curtain, that is, through his flesh, and since we have a great priest over the house of God, let us draw near with a true heart in full assurance of faith, with our hearts sprinkled clean from an evil conscience and our bodies washed with pure water (Heb. 10:19-22 ESV).

Our awareness of our own past sin and ongoing sinfulness often means we hang back from God, afraid of what He might do, and ashamed of letting Him see what we're really like. But if we know Jesus, we have no reason to avoid God. In fact, not only do we not need to avoid Him, but we can draw near to Him, know Him, love Him, be known and be loved by Him. We can draw near knowing that He accepts us and that we've been forgiven. We can draw near knowing that our hearts have been sprinkled clean and that inside He's made us new people. And we can draw near knowing that even our bodies have been washed and set apart for a new creation, and that although they groan, one day they'll be put right.

Finally, it is important to note that the writer calls the ineffectual Old Testament cleansing rituals 'baptisms' (Heb. 9:10). Clearly he sees that baptism itself somehow stands in line with those Old Testament cleansing rituals. But it is apparent that it is not baptism *itself* that the writer is interested in highlighting. After all, New Testament baptism is like the Old Testament baptisms in that it is merely an external washing. It is not New Testament baptism that fulfils the Old Testament cleansing rituals, rather it is the work of the Spirit that comes through the atoning death of Jesus that fulfils the Old Testament cleansing rituals. But as will become clear in the chapters ahead, just as the Old Testament cleansing rituals pointed forward to the promise of what God would do, baptism points back to what God has done in Jesus.

The Meaning of Cleansing in the New Testament

We saw in the Old Testament that our problem as human beings is that we are polluted by sin. Nevertheless, God promised a day would come when He would cleanse people with more than just water. With the coming of Jesus, that promise has begun to unfold in a new and spectacular way. The coming of Jesus heralded a new age where, having dealt on the cross with God's anger against sin, Jesus pours out the Holy Spirit on His people. Through the Spirit, people are born again into the new life that Jesus has begun in himself through His resurrection from the dead. And that cleansing has opened the way for us to have access to God – access that was blocked by sin and the inadequate provisions of the old covenant.

4. The Promise of a Saviour
Circumcision as a Sign of the Gospel Expected

I was at church recently when one of our service leaders began the service by reading these words from Paul:

> In him you were also circumcised with a circumcision not performed by human hands. Your whole self ruled by the flesh was put off when you were circumcised by Christ ... (Col. 2:11).

Wow, I thought, what must the non-Christian visitors be thinking!

There's no denying it, talking about circumcision is strange. I remember when I was doing my PhD on circumcision, I would often meet with my supervisor in a restaurant to talk about how my research was going. I always found myself speaking in hushed tones, desperately hoping no one would overhear. Yet strangely, circumcision is somehow a picture of the gospel.

But what's circumcision got to do with baptism? If you're new to Christianity or haven't ever read or heard much about baptism, you might wonder. But it helps to know that throughout the history of the church the connection between baptism and circumcision has been a key point of contention between those holding differing views on what baptism means and who it's for. Often the debate falls along party lines: those holding to believer's baptism don't see any meaningful connection,[1] while those holding to infant baptism think there is.[2] But even those who hold to believer's baptism are often still willing to recognise *some* connection between the two.[3]

At first glance, the idea that circumcision and baptism could be connected seems downright bizarre – one involves water, the other a knife; one leaves a person intact, the other doesn't; one is for men and women, the other is for men only. But there are also similarities – circumcision was the sign (in some way) of God's Old Testament people, while baptism is (in some way) the sign of God's New Testament people.

But the idea that circumcision and baptism are related is not just a theological invention, Paul discusses it in Colossians chapter 2. There he says that we were 'circumcised' with the 'circumcision of Christ, having been buried with him in baptism' (Col. 2:11-12 ESV). What Paul means by that is hotly debated, and we'll look at it more in the next chapter. But at least one thing is clear: Paul plainly sees that circumcision and baptism are related *somehow*. The only question is: how? In other words, the question is not *whether* a connection exists between baptism and circumcision, the question is *what* the nature of the connection is. Only having answered that can we then establish what implications, if any, that has for our understanding of baptism and who should receive it.

What's even more interesting is how often circumcision is floating around in other places where baptism crops up. We'll look more at

---

1. For example, Everett Ferguson notes, 'The most that can be said is that baptism is associated with the time or occasion of a person's participation in the circumcision of Christ' (Everett Ferguson, *The Church of Christ: A Biblical Ecclesiology for Today* (Grand Rapids: Eerdmans, 1996), 197).

2. For example, John Calvin writes, 'baptism is today for Christians what circumcision was for the ancients' (Calvin, *Institutes*, 4.14.24).

3. For instance, John Piper writes, 'even though there is an overlap in meaning between baptism and circumcision ..., circumcision and baptism don't have the same role to play in the covenant people of God because the way God constituted his people in the Old Testament and the way he is constituting the Church today are fundamentally different' (John Piper, 'How Do Circumcision and Baptism Correspond?,' *Desiring God*, August 29, 1999, https://www.desiringgod.org/messages/how-do-circumcision-and-baptism-correspond). Salter sees 'spiritual circumcision' as part of baptism, but argues that baptism is not a replacement for circumcision (Martin Salter, 'Does Baptism Replace Circumcision? An Examination of the Relationship between Circumcision and Baptism in Colossians 2:11-12,' *Themelios* 35 (2010): 15-29). Another notable exception is Paul K. Jewett, *Infant Baptism and the Covenant of Grace: An Appraisal of the Argument That as Infants Were Once Circumcised, so They Should Now Be Baptized* (Grand Rapids: Eerdmans, 1978).

the nature of the connection between baptism and circumcision in coming chapters. What I want to do in this chapter is come to terms with circumcision itself, and to see how, like cleansing, it was about God's promise of what He would do in Jesus.

The Start of a Strange Practice

The first place circumcision turns up in the Bible is in Genesis chapter 17 and it appears almost out of the blue.[4] God says to Abraham:

> I am God Almighty; walk before me and be blameless, that I may give you what I promised in my covenant between me and you, and may multiply you greatly (Gen. 17:1-2, my trans.).[5]

It is then that God commands Abraham to begin the practice of circumcision:

> Then God said to Abraham, 'As for you, you must keep my covenant, you and your descendants after you for the generations to come. This is my covenant with you and your descendants after you, the covenant you are to keep: Every male among you shall be circumcised' (Gen. 17:9-10).

Perhaps the strangest thing about Genesis 17 is that God promises to 'make' or, rather, 'give' His covenant to Abraham. That's strange because God already seems to have done that back in Genesis chapter 15. There, in response to Abraham's faith in God's promise, God established a covenant with Abraham. When

---

4.   What follows in this chapter is a very short summary of a very long book. Not everything can be said that I have tried to say there. So if you're not convinced by what I say here, check out that book: Karl Deenick, *Righteous by Promise: A Biblical Theology of Circumcision*, New Studies in Biblical Theology 45 (London: Apollos, 2018). I have included references to that book in what follows. It's also worth saying that not everything I am saying here has been said in that book either.

5.   Lots of translations have God saying that He will 'make' a covenant with Abraham, but the word is 'give'. Numerous times God promises to 'give' things to Abraham. God promises to give Abraham the land (Gen. 12:7; 13:15, 17; 15:18). Once Abraham asks why God hasn't yet 'given' him a son (Gen. 15:2). And in Genesis 17 itself, God promises to 'give' to Abraham the privilege of being the father of many nations (17:6), to 'give' to him the land (17:8), and to 'give' to him a son (17:20). In other words, what God means when He says that He will 'give' Abraham His covenant is not that He will make a new covenant with Abraham, but that He will begin to enact what was promised. See Deenick, *Righteous by Promise*, 16-19.

Abraham believed God, we're told that God 'counted it to him as righteousness' (Gen. 15:6). What follows is an elaborate exercise which would have meant more to Abraham than it does to us. God tells Abraham to gather a range of animals, cut them in half and lay the pieces side by side. Normally, what would follow is both parties walking down between the pieces as a symbolic act of their commitment to their promise.[6] In the language of Abraham's day, this was the way of making an iron-clad agreement. What is unusual in this instance is that instead of Abraham and God walking down together, Abraham remains fast asleep on the ground while God, represented by a mysterious smoking fire pot and flaming torch, passes between the pieces of animals alone. In other words, this commitment is God's commitment alone. It doesn't depend on Abraham.

So why in Genesis 17, then, does God say that He will give Abraham what He has promised *if* he walks before Him and is blameless? What does that mean?[7] It is sometimes suggested that 'blamelessness' is nothing more than a kind of genuineness – Abraham doesn't need to be perfect but sincere. The problem with that is that 'blamelessness' is often used to describe something far more comprehensive. It is used of God: God's work (Deut. 32:4), way (2 Sam. 22:31), law (Ps. 19:7) and knowledge (Job 37:16) are 'blameless', or we might say, 'perfect'. So too, in a peculiar passage in Ezekiel 28, an ancient king is pictured as being in the position that Adam and Eve were in before the fall into sin:

> You were blameless in your ways from the day you were
> created till wickedness was found in you (Ezek. 28:15).

But maybe one of the most significant is Psalm 15, where the writer asks, 'Lord, who may dwell in your sacred tent? Who may live on your holy mountain?' (Ps. 15:1). The answer is: 'The one whose walk is blameless, who does what is righteous, who speaks the truth from their heart...' (Ps. 15:2). In other words, the one who can dwell with God is the one who is perfect as He is perfect.

---

6. It was probably a way of saying, 'I'm going to do what I say, and if I don't this is what's going to happen to me.' For example, in Jeremiah, God says, 'Those who have violated my covenant and have not fulfilled the terms of the covenant they made before me, I will treat like the calf they cut in two and then walked between its pieces' (Jer. 34:18).

7. See Deenick, *Righteous by Promise*, 21-26.

That idea is confirmed by the way that similar terms are used in the New Testament.[8] So, for instance, Paul says that we were chosen in Christ 'to be holy and blameless before him' (Eph. 1:4 ESV). Jesus' purpose for the church is to 'present her to himself as a radiant church, without stain or wrinkle or any other blemish, but holy and blameless.' (Eph. 5:27). The aim of Jesus reconciling us to God by His death is so that He might 'present you holy and blameless and above reproach before him' (Col. 1:22 ESV). While God is the one who is able to 'present you blameless before the presence of his glory with great joy' (Jude 24 ESV). Notice that in each case what is in view is Jesus presenting His people on the last day with the spotless perfection that is necessary for them to live for eternity in the presence of God.

For you and me to meet God and to live with God in peace and joy we need to be utterly and completely blameless. God is not interested, in the long-term, in genuine but deeply flawed people. He does not simply want people who mean well or have good intentions but who still reject Him, hurt others or destroy His world from time to time, regardless of whether that's on purpose or by mistake. God's great gospel plan for the world is not for it to be populated by people who are forgiven but who are still constantly sliding back into sin and so constantly in need of forgiveness. He wants a people who are holy and blameless, just like He is.

Sometimes we can fall into a kind of acceptance and contentment with the presence of sin in our lives and in the lives of others. But we should never be content with sin. Sure, God is willing to forgive us, and if we're His children through faith in Jesus, our sin doesn't expel us from His family or cast us under the cloud of eternal judgment. But we shouldn't allow ourselves to make peace with sin or to simply accept as inevitable what God means to eradicate.

The Demand and the Provision

What God was calling Abraham to was not simply genuineness but perfection. He was calling him to the perfections of God Himself. The full realisation of what was promised depended on walking blamelessly before God. But we've also seen that in Genesis 15, God had reckoned Abraham to be righteous already. That is, God

---

8. See Deenick, *Righteous by Promise*, 97-104.

somehow considered Abraham to already have the righteousness and blamelessness that he needed but didn't yet fully possess. We also saw that the fulfilment of what God promised in Genesis 15 was dependent exclusively on God, and not on Abraham at all. So how can God now call Abraham to the impossible goal of being blameless? The solution to that riddle lies in understanding the most common way that 'blamelessness' language was used in the Old Testament.[9]

Out of the ninety-one times that 'blamelessness'[10] is used in the Old Testament, it is used fifty-one times in the context of the sacrificial system to refer to animals that are 'without blemish' or 'without defect'. So, for instance:

> If the offering is a burnt offering from the herd, you are to offer a male *without defect*. You must present it at the entrance to the tent of meeting so that it will be acceptable to the LORD. You are to lay your hand on the head of the burnt offering, and it will be accepted on your behalf to make atonement for you (Lev. 1:3-4) [emphasis added].

This passage makes clear that the animal acts as a substitute. The person bringing the offering was to lay their hands on the head of the animal to symbolise that this animal was to die in their place. The sacrificed animal would then be accepted to 'make atonement for you'. But the condition is that the animal must be 'without defect'. The reason for this exercise, however, is the lack of blamelessness of the person bringing the offering.

The sacrificial system gives us a big clue for how we are to understand God's call for Abraham to be 'blameless'. Although the sacrificial system was only established well after Abraham lived, for those who practiced the rituals of the sacrificial system, that practice would have shaped their understanding of what God had said to Abraham in Genesis 17:1. The sacrificial system showed that the ideal of 'blamelessness' was still real and that something needed to be done when they didn't live blamelessly. But it also showed that there was a path to some kind of perfection and blamelessness for those who were obviously not perfect or blameless. In other words, the sacrificial system held out the hope of grace and mercy without watering down God's demand for absolute perfection.

---

9. See Deenick, *Righteous by Promise*, 26-29.
10. The Hebrew word is *tamim*.

That relationship between moral blamelessness and the sacrificial system might seem like a long bow to draw, but several facts support drawing that connection. First and foremost is the way the New Testament picks up the language of 'blamelessness'.[11] We have already seen how the New Testament uses the language of 'blamelessness' to refer to Jesus' presentation of His people before the Father at the last day in absolute perfection. But the New Testament also uses the same language to refer to Jesus' own sacrifice of Himself. So, Peter describes Jesus as the 'lamb without blemish or defect' through whom we have been 'redeemed from the empty way of life handed down to you from your ancestors' (1 Pet. 1:18-19).

Perhaps most significant, from our perspective, is what the writer of Hebrews says. In comparing the failure of the Old Testament sacrifices and cleansing rituals, he says:

> The blood of goats and bulls and the ashes of a heifer sprinkled on those who are ceremonially unclean sanctify them so that they are outwardly clean. How much more, then, will the blood of Christ, who through the eternal Spirit offered himself *unblemished* to God, cleanse our consciences from acts that lead to death, so that we may serve the living God! (Heb. 9:13-14) [emphasis added].

As we have seen, the Old Testament rituals just cleaned up people's outsides to make them outwardly spotless; whereas the sacrifice of Jesus, who offered Himself without blemish, will 'cleanse our consciences/hearts'. In other words, it is through Jesus' blameless sacrifice of Himself that He will present His people as blameless before the Father at the last day.

The sacrificial system, therefore, presented the demand that people needed to be truly blameless and it foreshadowed the hope that one day God would make people truly blameless through a blameless substitute. But it also presented the hope that God would consider people blameless in the meantime even though they weren't.

The same truth was embodied in circumcision. God required Abraham to be blameless and holy and had promised that *He* would get Abraham there. But circumcision also ratified the fact that God considered Abraham righteous already, simply on the basis of

---

11. See Deenick, *Righteous by Promise*, 98-100.

Abraham's faith in God's promise, even though Abraham was not actually completely righteous and blameless in practice. That is what the Bible calls 'justification'.

The greatest problem that you and I face, together with Abraham, is that we are not what we should be. We are supposed to be blameless, but we are not. Sin permeates our lives. And despite our best efforts to keep it at bay we keep doing the very things that God hates. The story of Abraham's life is filled with indiscretions. So too, is the life of his descendants. But, coupled with the sacrificial system, circumcision presented a hope. It presented a hope that even though presently we are not blameless and righteous, there can be forgiveness for that through the sacrifice of a blameless substitute in our place. But circumcision also presented the hope that what we are not now, one day we will be. The gospel presents the same hope. As the theologian Herman Bavinck wrote:

> A person is ungodly in an ethical sense, but on account of the righteousness of Christ that person becomes righteous in a [legal] sense. ... [They are like] a child who, having been graciously adopted by a wealthy man, can as a future heir be called rich even though at the moment he or she does not yet own a penny. God declares sinners righteous, adopts them as children, promises them Christ and all his benefits; for that reason they are called righteous and will one day gain possession of all the treasures of grace.[12]

Strange as it might seem to us, God chose circumcision to be the sign that people could be heirs of God's promises in Jesus simply through receiving those promises by faith. And He chose it to be a confirmation of the truth that whoever believed could already be called rich even though they did not yet possess all the treasures of God's grace.

Why Circumcision? Why Not Just a Tattoo?

God's covenant with Abraham confirmed that God alone would bring about what He had promised. So although God called Abraham to walk before Him and be blameless, the fulfilment of

---

12. Bavinck, *Reformed Dogmatics*, 4:213.

that still lay in God's hands. And the sacrificial system gave people the resources to understand how to live in the gap between the future promise—perfection—and the present reality—imperfection. But what does all that have to do with circumcision?

The key to that lies in recognising that in Genesis 17 God says that He will 'establish' His covenant with the yet to be born Isaac.[13] When Genesis 17 begins, Abraham already has a son, Ishmael. But Ishmael is a son that Abraham had with his wife's servant, Hagar (see Gen. 16). God promises that Abraham will have another son, the one God promised, and this son will be through his wife, Sarah. But Abraham asks God to just accept Ishmael instead:

> If only Ishmael might live under your blessing! (Gen. 17:18).

To which God replies:

> Yes, but your wife Sarah will bear you a son, and you will call him Isaac. I will *establish* my covenant with him as an everlasting covenant for his descendants after him (Gen. 17:19) [emphasis added].

God tells Abraham that Ishmael will indeed be blessed, but the covenant will not be established with him. Instead, the covenant will be established with Isaac.

Although lots of people share in the blessings of God's covenant with Abraham, and although all the males in Abraham's household are circumcised (whether they are his children or not), the covenant itself is only established with two people in Genesis 17 – Abraham and Isaac. The covenant will be perpetuated not through all Abraham's children, or through all his household, but through one child, and through his child after him.[14]

---

13. See Deenick, *Righteous by Promise*, 39-44.

14. The Bible scholar, T. Desmond Alexander, writes, 'Although the male members of Abraham's household are circumcised, including Ishmael, the Lord emphasizes that the covenant will be established with Isaac, and him alone (Gen. 17:19, 21). The uniqueness of Isaac's position regarding the covenant is underlined by the exclusion of Ishmael even though he is also circumcised. This introduces an important distinction between those who may enjoy the benefits of this covenant and the one through whom the covenant will be established. Whereas the former includes all who are circumcised [and those who are not!], the latter appears to be restricted to a single line of descendants' (T. Desmond Alexander, *From Paradise to the Promised Land: An Introduction to the Pentateuch*, 3rd ed. (Grand Rapids: Baker, 2012), 102).

That idea is borne out by later references in the Bible to the same covenant. For example, God says in Exodus:

> And I will bring you to the land I swore with uplifted hand to give *to Abraham, to Isaac and to Jacob*. I will give it to you as a possession. I am the LORD (Exod. 6:8) [emphasis added].

The covenant passes down through a line of promise – Abraham, Isaac, Jacob.

That is even clearer once we zoom out and see the overall structure of the book of Genesis, both in its use of genealogies and its reference to a 'seed' or descendant of Abraham.[15] In Genesis 3:15, right after Adam and Eve plunged the world into sin, God made a promise:

> And I will put enmity between you and the woman, and between your offspring ('seed') and hers; he will crush your head, and you will strike his heel (Gen. 3:15).

What God is talking about here is not simply an ongoing battle between the Serpent (Satan) and the descendants of Eve (human beings). Rather, God has in mind a single descendant of Eve ('he') whom Satan will set out to destroy, but who, though bruised by the encounter, will ultimately destroy Satan.

The rest of Genesis is, in effect, a search for that single descendant. That can be seen in the way the book is structured around genealogies. Several times throughout Genesis we find the repeated phrase: 'these are the generations of ....'[16] Some of those genealogies are broad and simply record the spreading out of humanity. But others link in with the main storyline of Genesis and show how these key characters follow on through the line of promise, from Eve to Noah, from Noah to Abraham, from Abraham to Isaac, and from Isaac to Jacob.[17] What the genealogies and the narratives as a whole do is to shine the light on particular figures or descendants, and often particular descendants to the exclusion of others: Isaac *not* Ishmael, Jacob *not* Esau, Joseph *not* his eleven brothers.

Those two ideas together—the focus on a particular descendant and the restriction of the covenant to Isaac—suggest that what God

---

15. See Deenick, *Righteous by Promise*, 44-48.

16. You can find them in Gen 2:4; 5:1; 6:9; 10:1; 11:10, 27; 25:12, 19; 36:1, 9; 37:2.

17. E.g. Hamilton, *Genesis*, 1:9-10; 248-249.

is doing in Genesis 17 is narrowing down the field to show who it is through whom He will bring about this promised descendant of Eve. It will be a descendant of Abraham and, in turn, of Isaac.[18]

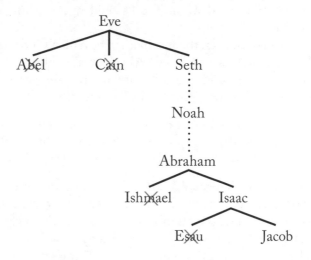

Interestingly, this focus on a single individual also connects back with the flood. What God was calling Abraham and his descendant to be is exactly what Noah was supposed to be – righteous and blameless. As we saw, in the flood, God was beginning again with the one man, Noah, and his family. But Noah's failure to be completely righteous and blameless meant that something more was needed. Now with Abraham, God is saying that He's looking to begin again. One day, from Abraham, would come a descendant through whom God would start again – He would make a new humanity and a new creation.

That focus on a particular descendant also suggests why *circumcision* is the sign,[19] rather than, say, a tattoo. After all, that would have been both less painful and more visible! But the most obvious explanation for why the sign was circumcision is because it was about God's promise to provide a *descendant* of Abraham through whom He will save a people for Himself. One cannot avoid the obvious (and possibly awkward) truth that circumcision

---

18. Frequently, too, it will be the unexpected descendant: Jacob not Esau (Gen. 25:23-26), Judah not Rueben (Gen. 49:3-4, 8-12), and Ephraim not Manasseh (Gen. 48:13-20).

19. See Deenick, *Righteous by Promise*, 48-50.

is performed on the very body part responsible for procreation. That is because it is bound up with the promise of a descendant. Circumcision was the emblem of the promise of a descendant of Abraham around whom God would re-form humanity and all of creation.

Moreover, even the mechanism by which God would do that was hinted at in Genesis. When Abraham and Sarah finally bore a child they were 'as good as dead', but from the almost death of Abraham came life. The writer of Hebrews notes:

> And so from this one man, and he as good as dead, came descendants as numerous as the stars in the sky and as countless as the sand on the seashore (Heb. 11:12).[20]

So too, in Genesis 22, after Isaac was finally born, God called Abraham to sacrifice Isaac. Although God stopped Abraham at the last minute, the almost sacrifice of Abraham's 'one and only son' (Heb. 11:17) became a hint of exactly how God intended to fulfil His promises to Abraham through Abraham's descendant.

Although we may not think of it like this, circumcision was a great gift from God. It was a sign to remind people of God's great gospel promise that one day, through one of Abraham's descendants, God would save a people for Himself who would be holy and blameless in His sight. It was a great gift because people like Abraham, and you and me, are prone to forget that God has a good plan. We too easily become overwhelmed by what's going on in the world around us, or in our own lives, or in our churches, or in our own hearts. We look at the world and we despair because it looks and feels sometimes like Satan is winning – the world is turning away from God, the church is languishing in apathy or has abandoned the gospel, and we aren't growing in holiness as much as we would hope. We become fixated on the present problems and forget that God has made promises He intends to keep. God has worked and is working in Jesus to put the world right, to end sin and death, to restore creation, to begin again with a new man, to redeem a people for Himself, to redeem those who trust Him. And

---

20. Similarly, Paul writes, 'Against all hope, Abraham in hope believed and so became the father of many nations, just as it had been said to him, "So shall your offspring be." Without weakening in his faith, he faced the fact that his body was *as good as dead*—since he was about a hundred years old—and that Sarah's womb was also dead.' (Rom. 4:18-19).

circumcision, strange as it was, was a reminder of that promise. It didn't make people righteous. It didn't save them. But it reminded people of what God had promised to do. And although we don't need to practice circumcision anymore because the one who was promised has finally come, we can still look back at circumcision as a great gift that pointed to the good news that we can be caught up in.

Circumcision and Those Who Did and Didn't Receive It

But perhaps one of the most important questions we might ask is: what was the connection between the sign and the individual who received it?[21] Was it a guarantee of salvation? Was it a contract between that person and God that the person had to keep – a promise that, if they were faithful, God would be faithful? And what about the fact that only men received the sign? What do we make of that?

When God commands Abraham to begin the practice of circumcision in Genesis 17, He commands him to circumcise every single male who is part of his household community. God says:

> For the generations to come every male among you who is eight days old must be circumcised, including those born in your household or bought with money from a foreigner – those who are not your offspring. Whether born in your household or bought with your money, they must be circumcised. My covenant in your flesh is to be an everlasting covenant. Any uncircumcised male, who has not been circumcised in the flesh, will be cut off from his people; he has broken my covenant (Gen 17:12-14).

Clearly, then, circumcision is important. But already in Genesis 17 there are strong indications that the sign was less about the individual and more about the promise itself and the community as a whole. What happens with Ishmael and Sarah provides two useful examples.

In the case of Ishmael, although the covenant is not established with him, he still receives the sign of circumcision and is somehow

---

21. See Deenick, *Righteous by Promise*, 49-50.

caught up in its blessings. When Abraham asks God to establish the covenant with Ishmael, although God refuses, He still blesses Ishmael:

> And as for Ishmael, I have heard you: I will surely bless him; I will make him fruitful and will greatly increase his numbers. He will be the father of twelve rulers, and I will make him into a great nation (Gen. 17:20).

Conversely, Sarah, Abraham's wife, is not circumcised at all and yet she also shares in some of the blessings:

> As for Sarai your wife, you are no longer to call her Sarai; her name will be Sarah. I will bless her and will surely give you a son by her. I will bless her so that she will be the mother of nations; kings of peoples will come from her (Gen. 17:15-16).

Neither Ishmael nor Sarah are direct recipients of God's covenant with Abraham – the covenant is with Abraham and Isaac and with the line of promised descendants after him. Nevertheless, Ishmael and Sarah are caught up in what God is doing on account of their connection with Abraham. They are blessed because of their relationship with him. But still, only Ishmael receives the sign of circumcision.

The same is true of the other men and women in Abraham's household. Although they are not singled out for blessing, they are obviously caught up in God's blessings to Abraham simply by being caught up with Abraham and Isaac. They will benefit from God blessing Abraham simply by living under Abraham's roof – if God gives Abraham land and possessions, they'll benefit indirectly.[22] For instance, if a friend was to invite you to live as part of his family and then someone gives him a million dollar harbourside mansion, you would also get to enjoy it and live in it, even though it doesn't belong to you. You would enjoy it because of your relationship with your friend. The same was true of those in Abraham's household. They were part of a community gathered around the promise of what

---

22. In that way, God's covenant with Abraham is like the later covenant that God makes with King David. God makes a covenant with David and with the line of individual kings who descend from David. That covenant too is only with individuals, nevertheless, the whole community of God's people shares in the blessings of God's commitment to David because David and his descendants are the rulers through whom God blesses His people.

God was doing through Abraham and his descendant. Nevertheless, still only half of Abraham's household was circumcised – the men and not the women. The implication is that what mattered was not circumcision itself but being gathered around and caught up in God's promise to Abraham.

That is not to say that all those people were 'saved', but the principle that was on display at the material level was an invitation to participate in what was true at a spiritual level. Sharing in the physical blessings of land and children through physical/relational proximity is ultimately a picture of sharing in the spiritual blessings through spiritual/relational proximity with the promised seed. God's promise to Abraham was not simply about land, but about making for Himself a people who were holy and blameless. Participation in that blessing required not just living in the same house as Abraham but sharing Abraham's faith, or what the Old Testament calls 'circumcision of the heart' (we'll come to that later).

But notice something crucially important: circumcision did not mark out who were the recipients of the physical promises to Abraham, and it certainly did not mark out who were the recipients of the spiritual promises to Abraham. So what did it do?

We saw above that circumcision communicated the content of God's promise – it was the sign reminding the people that through one of Abraham's descendants God would bring blessing to the world and make a people for Himself who are holy and blameless. Because the promise was of a *male* descendant from the *man* Abraham, only the men were circumcised. Nevertheless, broadly speaking, circumcision served to delineate the community in which that promise was taught and guarded and, in general, believed.

Moreover, circumcision did not simply identify parents and their children as belonging to that community. It included slaves and anyone else who lived in the household where the promise of God was recognised. And later, anyone could join themselves to the community through the males in that household community being circumcised (Exod. 12:48). Circumcision did not guarantee that everyone in that community believed. It did not guarantee that every male who had received it had really believed God's promise to Abraham. Just as it did not imply that the women did not believe because they had not and could not receive circumcision. All it did was signify and mark out the community where that promise was believed and passed on from generation to generation. Circumcision marked out a community of people and the promise of a Messiah around whom the community was gathered. It invited those in that community, and those outside of it (as we'll see), to share in the spiritual blessing that God had promised Abraham by embracing the promised descendant signified in circumcision.

That is not to say that circumcision was a matter of indifference. God had told Abraham that any male who was not circumcised would be cut off (Gen. 17:14). In fact, Moses almost lost his life because he was uncircumcised (Exod. 4:24-26).[23] To say that circumcision functioned at a community level is not to say that it could be thrown aside. That is for two reasons. In the first place, to reject circumcision was implicitly a rejection of the underlying promise of God. There was no hope for the person who rejected what God had promised to do through Abraham and his descendant. This was just as true for men, who could be circumcised, as much as it was for women, who could not. The cutting off of *men* who were not circumcised was a sign of God's rejection of both men *and women* who rejected His promise of salvation through a descendant of Abraham. Second, God had commanded circumcision to be done because it conveyed the truth of the gospel. Therefore, to abandon circumcision was to risk losing sight of the promise itself.

The key point is this: circumcision was not the sign of who shares in the blessings and who doesn't, but a sign of what the promise was – a descendant of Abraham who would save a people to be holy and blameless in God's sight. It wasn't about being born into a family where your parents were believers, but about whether you were connected by faith with what God was doing through Abraham and his promised descendant.

Uncircumcision as a Sign of Judgment on the Circumcised

That distance between who received the sign and the actual receipt of the promise is demonstrated in a profound way by the events recorded in Joshua 5.[24] What happens there shows that circumcision functioned more at the community level than at the individual level.

Having just crossed the Jordan into the Promised Land in fulfilment of God's promise to Abraham (Gen. 15), God instructs

---

23.   For more on this mysterious episode see Deenick, *Righteous by Promise*, 76-82.

24.   See Deenick, *Righteous by Promise*, 66-76.

Joshua that all the Israelite men must be circumcised. What follows is a long explanation of why that was necessary. It turns out that none of the men among the Israelites were circumcised. God had commanded Abraham never to stop the practice of circumcision, but for forty years it had been on hold. Joshua 5 tells us:

> At that time the Lord said to Joshua, 'Make for yourself flint knives and start circumcising the sons of Israel again.' And Joshua made flint knives for himself and he circumcised the sons of Israel at the 'Hill of Foreskins'.
>
> And this is the reason Joshua circumcised all the people: those who came out of Egypt—all the men of fighting age—died in the wilderness on the way after coming out from Egypt. For all the people who came out were circumcised, but all the people born in the wilderness on the way after coming out from Egypt were not circumcised. [They were not circumcised] because for forty years the sons of Israel walked in the wilderness until the whole nation was finished off – the men of war who had come out from Egypt who did not listen to the voice of the Lord, to whom the Lord swore they would not see the land which he swore to their fathers to give to us, a land flowing with milk and honey (Josh. 5:2-6, my trans.).

The logic of this circumcision event is this: although the men who came out of Egypt were circumcised, those who were born in the wilderness were not circumcised. They were not circumcised because Israel had to wander in the desert for forty years until all the circumcised men who came out of Egypt had died.

Just as God had *sworn* to Abraham that He would give him the land (Gen. 15), God had also *sworn* to those who came out of Egypt that they would not see the land because of their unbelief. When Moses had sent spies to the Promised Land, the people had panicked and failed to trust God and so refused to go up (Num. 13-14). Therefore God had said:

> not one of those who saw my glory and the signs I performed in Egypt and in the wilderness but who disobeyed me and tested me ten times – not one of them will ever see the land I promised on oath to their ancestors. No one who has treated me with contempt will ever see it (Num. 14:22-23).

According to Joshua, the interruption in the practice of circumcision during the wilderness years was a sign of God's judgment: what God had promised to Abraham, the wilderness generation would never receive.

But notice how the sign works: it is those who *are* circumcised that die in the wilderness and do not enter the land, while it is those who had remained uncircumcised for forty years that do enter the land. The uncircumcision of the children was a sign of judgment on the parents. In that way, we see again that the sign function of circumcision works at a community level, not at the level of the individual. Joshua 5 shows us that circumcision was not making a statement about whether any particular individual was saved or not saved. It was a sign to the community of what God was doing and it was an invitation to those within the community to respond to that with faith and repentance. Just as the practice of circumcision within the community of God's people was a sign of His promise to Abraham and a call to believe in that promise, so also the interruption in the practice of circumcision for forty years was a sign of God's judgment on the community and so a call for repentance also.

Circumcision as a Sign of Hope for the Uncircumcised

But the most significant statement about the distance between circumcision itself and the receipt of the promise comes from the pen of the apostle Paul, in what can only be described as possibly the greatest act of theological reversal ever accomplished. Paul completely turns the common Jewish understanding of circumcision on its head.[25]

In Romans 4, Paul is explaining how a person receives the blessing of forgiveness. Quoting Psalm 32, he writes:

> Blessed are those whose transgressions are forgiven, whose sins are covered. Blessed is the one whose sin the Lord will never count against them (Rom. 4:7-8).

Paul says that those who are forgiven are blessed. But then he asks the important question: who is that blessing of forgiveness for?

---

25. See Deenick, *Righteous by Promise*, 180-84.

> Is this blessedness only for the circumcised, or also for the uncircumcised? We have been saying that Abraham's faith was credited to him as righteousness. Under what circumstances was it credited? Was it after he was circumcised, or before? It was not after, but before! And he received circumcision as a sign, a seal of the righteousness that he had by faith while he was still uncircumcised (Rom. 4:9-11a).

Some people in Paul's day thought you couldn't be forgiven and couldn't be right with God without circumcision. After all, hadn't God commanded that it be done, and hadn't He commanded that anyone who wasn't circumcised should be cut off? But Paul here makes a startling observation: circumcision didn't make Abraham righteous; instead it was given to him as a 'seal' of the righteousness he already had when he was uncircumcised. In other words, circumcision can't be the thing that made Abraham right with God.

A seal in Paul's day, much like in our day, was used to show either ownership (perhaps of a slave or an animal) or authenticity (perhaps of a document).[26] When Paul uses the same language in other places, he means the latter. So he says in Ephesians 1 that believers have been 'sealed' with the Holy Spirit who is 'the guarantee of our inheritance until we acquire possession of it' (Eph. 1:13-14 ESV). In the same way, Abraham's circumcision ratified and 'sealed' what God had already declared to be true back in Genesis 15: that Abraham was righteous on the basis of faith (Gen. 15:6).

We need to be careful to see that what Paul is saying circumcision meant for Abraham, it did not mean for others later on (at least not in exactly the same way). Paul is not making a claim here about what circumcision signified about every Israelite man who received it. He is making a claim about what it signified about Abraham. The sign of circumcision was a seal of *Abraham's* righteousness by faith. Abraham's circumcision was a unique event. It was Abraham alone with whom God made a covenant in Genesis 15. It was Abraham alone who was reckoned as righteous in Genesis 15. And it was with Abraham alone that circumcision was first instituted. Paul says that, when God gave the sign of circumcision to Abraham in Genesis 17, it was a confirmation, seal or ratification of what God had already declared to be true: that Abraham was righteous by faith.

26. Tim Schramm, 'Sphragis,' in *Exegetical Dictionary of the New Testament*, ed. Horst Balz and Gerhard Schneider, 3 vols. (Grand Rapids: Eerdmans, 1990-1993), 3:316-17.

That Paul is focussed on the unique role of Abraham and his circumcision is clear from what he goes on to say:

> So then, he is the father of all who believe but have not been circumcised, in order that righteousness might be credited to them. And he is then also the father of the circumcised who not only are circumcised but who also follow in the footsteps of the faith that our father Abraham had before he was circumcised (Rom. 4:11b-12).

He says that Abraham's circumcision made him the 'father' of two important groups. Abraham's circumcision puts him in a kind of one-off position. Nevertheless, he is their father in the sense that they are like him in some way.

In the second group, Paul identifies those who are like Abraham in that: (1) they are circumcised, but (2) they are not *only* circumcised, they also share Abraham's trust in God. The key move Paul is making here is to show that not everyone who was circumcised was right with God. Circumcision was not an automatic free pass to salvation. Rather, circumcision was a reminder of how righteousness had come to Abraham – through faith.

The first group are those who are: (1) *un*circumcised but (2) also share Abraham's faith. They are like Abraham in that they are righteous by faith apart from circumcision, just like Abraham was. In fact, Paul says that part of the very purpose of Abraham's circumcision was to communicate something to these people who, though uncircumcised, trusted God like Abraham did. It is important to notice that Abraham's circumcision did not merely seal his righteousness by faith, but it sealed the 'righteousness that he had by faith *while he was still uncircumcised.*' That is, circumcision signified its own apparent unimportance – righteousness is by faith *apart from circumcision.* The Jews of Paul's day thought that circumcision was a sign of their special privilege: that they were 'in' with God. But Paul says that what they took to be a sign of their special privilege was actually God's sign of His love for the whole world. Abraham's circumcision (as well as all later acts of circumcision) were a sign that God's grace extended to the uncircumcised![27]

---

27. As Leon Morris writes, 'Even that ordinance which was most typically Jewish was for the purpose of embracing the Gentiles!' (Leon Morris, *The Epistle to the Romans*, Pillar New Testament Commentary (Grand Rapids: Eerdmans, 1988), 203).

Once we understand the unique function of Abraham's own circumcision it becomes much easier to see what the circumcision of others later on was intended to communicate. According to Paul, circumcision functioned uniquely in Abraham's life: it sealed the righteousness by faith he had apart from circumcision. Every later act of circumcision was a remembrance of what was true of Abraham. It was not a statement about the individual being circumcised. It was *not* a seal that they too were righteous by virtue of their circumcision. It was a reminder that others, not just the one being circumcised, could be righteous too if they exercised the same faith as Abraham.

Circumcision preached the gospel in advance. It testified that salvation was by faith in the God of Abraham regarding His future promises – promises that would come through Abraham's descendant. It testified that salvation was for all people, whether Jew or Gentile, simply on the basis of faith. And every act of circumcision proclaimed that. Paul says the circumcision of an Israelite boy was actually a sign of God's love for people who were not circumcised or brought up hearing the gospel. It was a sign that they too could be saved by receiving God's promise of righteousness through the blameless descendant of Abraham.

Getting Circumcision into the Heart

It is clear, then, that physical circumcision was just a sign. It was a sign of God's promise to save a people for Himself through a descendant of Abraham, and it was a sign that anyone could receive that by taking hold of the promise by faith. But how did a person take hold of the promise by faith? What did that mean? What did that look like in day to day experience?

The answer to that can be found by understanding one of the ways that circumcision is used as a metaphor. Strange as it might seem, the Old Testament uses circumcision as a metaphor in several ways: ears can be circumcised or uncircumcised (Jer. 6:10), as can lips (Exod. 6:12) and even fruit trees (Lev. 19:23). But maybe the most important circumcision metaphor in the Old Testament is a circumcised heart.

A Humble Heart

The best passage in which to get our head around what that means is Leviticus 26.[28] There God calls His people to live obedient lives before Him. The chapter begins:

> If you follow my decrees and are careful to obey my commands, I will send you rain in its season, and the ground will yield its crops and the trees their fruit (Lev. 26:3-4).

The people are to obey God, and if they do, the result will be blessing. The blessing that God has in mind is specifically the blessings promised to Abraham:

> I will look on you with favor and make you fruitful and increase your numbers, and I will keep my covenant with you. ... I will put my dwelling place among you, and I will not abhor you. I will walk among you and be your God, and you will be my people (Lev. 26:9-12).

The language of 'make you fruitful and increase your numbers' is drawn from God's covenant with Abraham (Gen. 17:20). God's promise to 'walk' among them and to be their God is also language reminiscent of Genesis 17.

So if the people are obedient, God's covenant with Abraham will be rolled out. But if they don't obey God, things will go very badly indeed. The middle verses in Leviticus 26 are filled with warnings of increasing doom and destruction if the people fail to carry out God's commands. God will bring terror, disease, drought, famine and defeat upon them. At each step there will be a chance for them to listen and return to God (Lev. 26:14, 18, 21, 23, 27), but if they don't, they will simply spiral further and further down into God's judgment and rejection, with the ultimate step being exile from the Promised Land (Lev. 26:31-35).

However, in verse 40 a note of hope is sounded:

> But if they will confess their sins and the sins of their ancestors—their unfaithfulness and their hostility toward me, which made me hostile toward them so that I sent them into the land of their enemies—then *when their uncircumcised hearts are humbled* and they pay for their sin, I will remember

---

28. See Deenick, *Righteous by Promise*, 53-60.

my covenant with Jacob and my covenant with Isaac and
my covenant with Abraham, and I will remember the land
(Lev. 26:40-42) [emphasis added].

In other words, despite their disobedience, there is hope. But
the hope lies in God remembering His promise to Abraham. If
the people humble their 'uncircumcised hearts' then God will
remember His covenant with Abraham and He will bring about
all that He has promised.

The kind of humbling that God has in mind is the same as that
which He later speaks about to Solomon:

> if my people, who are called by my name, will humble
> themselves and pray and seek my face and turn from their
> wicked ways, then I will hear from heaven, and I will forgive
> their sin and will heal their land (2 Chron. 7:14).

By speaking of 'humbling' their uncircumcised heart, Leviticus 26
gives us a window into what it means to 'circumcise' their heart.
Circumcising their heart has to do with humbling themselves
before God, confessing their sins and putting their hope in God's
commitment to do what He promised Abraham – to raise up a
descendant who will put things right.

No Longer Stiff-necked

The same idea is found in Deuteronomy 10.[29] Once again, the
demand is for absolute holiness:

> And now, Israel, what does the LORD your God ask of you
> but to fear the LORD your God, to walk in obedience to him,
> to love him, to serve the LORD your God with all your heart
> and with all your soul, and to observe the LORD's commands
> and decrees that I am giving you today for your own good?
> (Deut. 10:12-13).

But in the context of such a high demand God tells the people:

> *Circumcise your hearts*, therefore, and do not be stiff-necked
> any longer (Deut. 10:16) [emphasis added].

What is clear is that a circumcised heart is the opposite of being
stiff-necked, or literally, having a hard or stubborn heart. The gap

---

29. See Deenick, *Righteous by Promise*, 60-63.

between the demand to love God with their whole heart and the reality of not loving God like that is bridged by their humble trust in the promise of God symbolised in circumcision.

That becomes even clearer when we look at the chapter before. In the preceding chapter, Moses has recounted the episode with the golden calf. The people of God had made an idol to worship, and just as God was about to destroy them Moses interceded on their behalf (Exod. 32). What is striking is the basis on which Moses intercedes. Moses says:

> Remember your servants Abraham, Isaac and Jacob. Over-look the stubbornness of this people, their wickedness and their sin (Deut. 9:27).

So too, Moses says to the people earlier in chapter 9:

> It is not because of your righteousness or your integrity that you are going in to take possession of their land; but on account of the wickedness of these nations, the LORD your God will drive them out before you, to accomplish what he swore to your fathers, to Abraham, Isaac and Jacob. Understand, then, that it is not because of your righteousness that the LORD your God is giving you this good land to possess, for you are a stiff-necked people (Deut. 9:5-6).

The solution to their lack of holiness is God's commitment to what He has promised Abraham. The people can get on board with that by humbling themselves and trusting in God's promise. In the absence of absolute holiness, a tender, circumcised heart takes hold of God's promise to Abraham.

God's Promise in Your Heart and in Your Mouth

What happens, then, in Deuteronomy 30 is that God makes it clear that even that simple act of humbling themselves and taking hold of God's promise is too much for the people.[30] Even that must be a work of God. Moses says:

> The LORD your *God will circumcise your hearts* and the hearts of your descendants, so that you may love him with all your heart and with all your soul, and live (Deut. 30:6) [emphasis added].

---

30. See Deenick, *Righteous by Promise*, 64-66.

Nevertheless, God says that holiness is not beyond them because His words are in their hearts and mouths:

> Now what I am commanding you today is not too difficult for you or beyond your reach. It is not up in heaven, so that you have to ask, 'Who will ascend into heaven to get it and proclaim it to us so we may obey it?' Nor is it beyond the sea, so that you have to ask, 'Who will cross the sea to get it and proclaim it to us so we may obey it?' No, the word is very near you; it is in your mouth and in your heart so you may obey it (Deut. 30:11-14).

The words that were in the hearts and mouths of the people of Israel, the words that were within reach, were the words of God's promise to Abraham:

> This day I call the heavens and the earth as witnesses against you that I have set before you life and death, blessings and curses. Now choose life, so that you and your children may live and that you may love the LORD your God, listen to his voice, and hold fast to him. For the LORD is your life, and he will give you many years in the land he swore to give to your fathers, Abraham, Isaac and Jacob (Deut. 30:19-20).

Deuteronomy 30 shows that God's demand for complete obedience and perfect love for Him is not relinquished. Yet as impossible as that goal is, it is not impossible, because the demand is met by God through His promise to Abraham received by faith in their hearts and mouths (see Deut. 30:6 above).

Perhaps most striking of all, however, is that these words of Moses were uttered to God's people near the end of the forty-year period when circumcision had been on hold. The absence of circumcision was a daily reminder to them of God's judgment because of their unbelief. But in that context, Moses does not tell them to begin physical circumcision again (not yet). He urges them to embrace in their hearts the very thing that circumcision symbolised: the hope of salvation through humble repentance and trust in God's promise to Abraham. In other words, what really mattered was not the sign, but believing and trusting in what the sign pointed to.

In the New Testament, Paul takes these words from Deuteronomy 30 and says that they are fulfilled in the gospel:

But the righteousness that is by faith says: 'Do not say in your heart, "Who will ascend into heaven?"' (that is, to bring Christ down) 'or "Who will descend into the deep?"' (that is, to bring Christ up from the dead). But what does it say? 'The word is near you; it is in your mouth and in your heart,' that is, the message concerning faith that we proclaim: If you declare with your mouth, "Jesus is Lord," and believe in your heart that God raised him from the dead, you will be saved' (Rom. 10:6-9).

Although it's utterly impossible for you and me to make ourselves completely perfect and holy and to make ourselves love God with our whole heart and every fibre of our being; it's also not impossible. It's not impossible because God promises to do that very thing for us and in us. Through Jesus He has promised to make us holy and blameless, and all we need to do to receive that precious gift is turn from our sin, humble ourselves before Him and entrust ourselves to Jesus as Lord and resurrected Saviour.

Like the people of Israel, we cannot be stiff-necked and resistant to the authority of Jesus. We need to humble ourselves before Him, confess our sin and trust in Him. God's word of promise, that Jesus is Lord and Saviour, must be in our mouths and in our hearts. And if it is, if we believe that promise and call on God through Jesus, then God forgives us and will transform us to be like Jesus. Circumcision embodied that hope. And to humbly believe that promise was to have a circumcised heart – it was to believe the gospel proclaimed in advance.

It is important to note, that while circumcision of the heart was fundamentally an act of God, it was still a real possibility for people living in Old Testament times. Often theologians have equated circumcision of the heart with Jeremiah's new covenant promise to write the law on people's hearts or with the New Testament's concept of regeneration.[31] However, the two are distinct. Circumcision of the

---

31. E.g. Michael F. Bird, *Evangelical Theology: A Biblical and Systematic Introduction* (Grand Rapids: Zondervan, 2013), 534. Interestingly, Hamilton argues that circumcision of the heart and regeneration are the same but that they are distinct from the law being written on the heart (Hamilton Jr., *God's Indwelling Presence*, 47). In my view, circumcision of the heart is distinct from regeneration and the law written on the heart. The law written on the heart refers to complete obedience and love for God. Regeneration is the *means* by which the law is written on the heart. And circumcision of the heart is the faith and trust that God will do those things in the person of Jesus Christ. In the Old Testament, believers only possessed the circumcision of the heart.

heart is trust in God's promise – it is humble repentance and faith. It is turning away from sin and trusting God for all that He promised in His covenant with Abraham. But circumcision of the heart does not itself refer to the content of all that the covenant promised. The promise of the new covenant is the fundamental reconstitution of a person through their union with the crucified and risen Lord Jesus Christ – a reality that awaited the crucifixion and resurrection of Jesus. Those in the Old Testament whose hearts God had circumcised awaited that promise with expectant hope and trust.

The Fulfilment of Circumcision

Before moving on from looking at circumcision, it will help to look at one New Testament passage that draws together many of these ideas. In Philippians 3, Paul makes a determined effort to show that the fulfilment of circumcision is found ultimately in Jesus.[32]

Paul begins by warning his readers to look out for the fake circumcision people:

> Watch out for those dogs, those evildoers, those mutilators of the flesh. For it is we who are the circumcision, we who serve God by his Spirit, who boast in Christ Jesus, and who put no confidence in the flesh ... (Phil. 3:2-3).

Paul says that circumcision, properly understood, is about more than a flesh wound. Real circumcision receives the Spirit through Jesus Christ.

To prove his point, Paul lists all his earthly accomplishments that might give him a reason to be confident before God:

> circumcised on the eighth day, of the people of Israel, of the tribe of Benjamin, a Hebrew of Hebrews; in regard to the law, a Pharisee; as for zeal, persecuting the church; as for righteousness based on the law, faultless (Phil. 3:5-6).

The last is possibly the most significant: Paul says that he was 'faultless' or 'blameless' with respect to righteousness under the law. That is, he had (or he thought he had) fulfilled the very thing that God had called Abraham to in Genesis 17. But when Jesus revealed

In the New Testament the three are part of one indivisible package. You cannot have one without the other.

32. See Deenick, *Righteous by Promise*, 111-30.

Himself to Paul, Paul realised that everything he thought he had achieved was worthless:

> But whatever were gains to me I now consider loss for the sake of Christ. What is more, I consider everything a loss because of the surpassing worth of knowing Christ Jesus my Lord, for whose sake I have lost all things … (Phil. 3:7-8).

What matters is not circumcision, but Jesus to whom circumcision pointed. Without Jesus, circumcision is just mutilation. It is through Jesus that the real righteousness and blamelessness come. Paul says:

> I consider them garbage, that I may gain Christ and be found in him, not having a righteousness of my own that comes from the law, but that which is through faith in Christ – the righteousness that comes from God on the basis of faith. I want to know Christ – yes, to know the power of his resurrection and participation in his sufferings, becoming like him in his death, and so, somehow, attaining to the resurrection from the dead (Phil. 3:8-11).

So what was the problem with Paul's blamelessness? It was blamelessness according to the law but without realising that the aim of circumcision and the law was to point to Jesus. The aim was to take hold of Jesus.

It's a bit like seeing a road sign that says, 'Sydney: 200kms'. No one stops by the side of the road sign and says, 'Wow. We've finally made it,' because the destination is still 200 kilometres away. The road sign is not the destination. In the same way, Paul and others had mistaken circumcision (and the law in general) for the destination rather than merely the road sign that pointed the way to the destination.[33] But circumcision is not the destination, Jesus is. Those who got caught up with the signpost of circumcision missed Jesus, and so missed the true destination. But Paul had finally come to see that circumcision was only the signpost. He'd come to see that the *truly* circumcised are not those who are circumcised in the flesh, but those who 'boast in Christ Jesus', and who give up everything, circumcision included, to know Christ and be found in Him. To put it in Old Testament language: those are really 'circumcised' (that is, recipients of God's promise to Abraham) are those whose hearts are circumcised – they have taken hold, by humble repentance and faith, of God's promise

---

33. Or as Paul says in Galatians 3:24, 'the law was our guardian until Christ came that we might be justified by faith.'

to make a righteous and blameless people for Himself through a righteous and blameless descendant of Abraham, Jesus Christ.

That also helps to explain why once Jesus had come, circumcision became simultaneously irrelevant and potentially dangerous.[34] It was because the aim of circumcision was to point to the coming of Jesus and Jesus had now come.[35]

What you and I need is not circumcision, nor is it baptism for that matter. What we need is Jesus. We need to be connected with Him by faith – by entrusting ourselves to Him. We need to share not only in what He's done in history, in His life, death and resurrection; we also need to share in who He is now. Every day we need *Him*. We need to share in His life that He's living right now. We need to be conformed more and more every day to His death. We need to share more and more in His resurrection power. We need His life and power to be at work in us.

Everything else we might think we need, whatever it is, is rubbish. It's worthless. It won't help us to grow. It won't help us to become more like Jesus. It won't help us take hold of the eternal life to which we've been called. What we need is Jesus Himself – to know Him, to gain Him, to be found in Him, to know the power of His resurrection, sharing in His sufferings, and becoming like Him in His death.

---

34.   So Paul can on the one hand say, 'Circumcision is nothing and uncircumcision is nothing.' (1 Cor. 7:19). But he can also say, 'Mark my words! I, Paul, tell you that if you let yourselves be circumcised, Christ will be of no value to you at all.' (Gal. 5:2).

35.   The twelfth century theologian Rupert Tuitiensis wrote: 'Now see how great a sacrilege it would be, after the arrival of [Abraham's] seed, to still impose on one's flesh a sign of his circumcision. No, in fact according to the truth written beforehand, undertaking circumcision is the profession that his seed is being expected. Whoever is circumcised professes that he is expecting that the seed that was promised to Abraham would come, even if not by knowledge, but nevertheless by that sign. But he, namely Christ, has already come, has already been born, and since he has been given as a blessing to all nations the truth of God has been fulfilled. Therefore whoever is still circumcised denies that he has come, the one he pronounces by such a sign that he is expecting to come, and for this reason he denies that the one who has already come is the Christ. Rightly and truly therefore the Apostle says: if you are circumcised, Christ will be of no benefit to you.' (Rupert Tuitiensis, *De Trinitate* 5.31 [my trans.], see J-P Migne (ed.) Patrologia Latina. 217 vols. Paris, 1844-1864, 167:395).

The Meaning of Circumcision

What, then, was the meaning of circumcision? It was a sign, given by God, to communicate the gospel.[36] It was a sign that pointed to the blameless seed of Abraham through whom God would save a people for Himself and make a community of righteous and blameless people. God had counted Abraham righteous on the basis of his faith alone and God confirmed that in the sign of circumcision. Every subsequent act of circumcision was a reminder to *everyone*, not primarily even to the person being circumcised, that righteousness was available to all, both circumcised and uncircumcised, on the basis of faith alone. What is more, it was a sign that one day God would make that righteous declaration a reality in the lives of His people through a 'seed' or descendant of Abraham who would give His life as a ransom for many. God's plan was never simply to declare people not guilty. His plan has always been to transform them to be holy and righteous like His Son, Jesus.

It is important to point out that circumcision of the heart is not the fulfilment of circumcision.[37] Rather, Jesus was the fulfilment of circumcision. Circumcision of the heart was a metaphor for receiving and trusting God's promise to send a Messiah or, this side of the coming of Jesus, a metaphor for accepting that God's promise has been fulfilled in Jesus. In fact, circumcision of the heart was both a reality and necessity in the Old Testament – people needed to trust God's promise then as much as now.

But the call to have circumcised hearts also demonstrates the fact that the sign itself did not indicate who was swept up in God's covenant plan and who wasn't, who was 'in the covenant' and who was 'out', who was saved and who wasn't. Rather, it was a call to all who heard of it or saw it to receive God's promise by faith. There were many men who were circumcised who needed to heed that call. There were many women, who were not circumcised, who needed

---

36. Circumcision is described as a sign at its institution in Genesis 17:11 and also by Paul in Romans 4:11.

37. That is a common misunderstanding (e.g. John D. Meade, 'Circumcision of Flesh to Circumcision of Heart: The Typology of the Sign of the Abrahamic Covenant,' in *Progressive Covenantalism: Charting a Course between Dispensational and Covenant Theologies*, ed. Stephen J. Wellum and Brent E. Parker (Nashville: B&H Academic, 2016), 152-157; Fred Malone, *The Baptism of Disciples Alone: A Covenantal Argument for Credobaptism versus Paedobaptism*, 2nd ed. (Cape Coral: Founders Press, 2007), 116; and Fesko, *Word, Water, and Spirit*, 294).

to hear that call. And there were many outside Israel who needed to hear that call also.

To be sure, circumcision was an entrance requirement for men who wanted to join the community of God's promise. And if a person rejected circumcision, it would lead to them being cut off from that community. But in both cases, the issue was the underlying promise that circumcision symbolised. To join the community required identification with the promise of what God would do in Abraham's descendant, while rejection of circumcision implicitly meant rejection of that promise. In other words, while circumcision was a kind of rough marker for the community gathered around the promise, what really mattered was circumcision of the heart; that is, the acceptance, by humble repentance and faith, that ones only hope lay in God's promise of a blameless descendant of Abraham who would make His people blameless. But that also explains why circumcision is no longer practised by Christians – because we're no longer waiting. The promised descendant of Abraham has arrived; His name is Jesus. In the next chapter, we'll begin to see how that relates to baptism.

5. The Saviour is Announced

John's Baptism as a Sign of the Gospel about to be Fulfilled

It may come as a surprise to you that there is really very little extended theological reflection in the New Testament on baptism. Apart from John the Baptist's ministry, most of what is said about baptism is little more than reports of people being baptised (mostly in the Gospels and Acts) or passing comments about baptism. That suggests, again, that a lot of the heavy lifting in laying the foundations for baptism was done by the Old Testament. That's good news because if you've made it this far in the book, you have those foundations in your head – the same kind of foundations that Jesus' early Jewish disciples would have had.

Nevertheless, there are several important places where baptism is mentioned in the New Testament. The aim of this chapter and the next is to look at those and to see how they connect with that Old Testament foundation. In this chapter we'll focus on the ministry of John the Baptist, while in the next chapter we'll look at some of the key passages from the rest of the New Testament.

The Messenger Comes: John the Washerman

It is quite striking to think that if you pick up any of the four Gospels one of the first topics you will encounter is baptism.[1] It

---

1. In Matthew's Gospel you have to wait until chapter 3. In Luke you have to wait until chapter 3 as well, but his first three chapters tell the intertwining story of

doesn't take long before baptism comes flooding onto the scene, and it comes in the person of John the Baptist. That suggests that whatever John the Baptist was trying to communicate through his baptism ministry, it was important and even foundational for the whole of the New Testament.

Interestingly, people suggest all kinds of backgrounds to the baptism ministry of John.[2] Some people suggest that the background for what John was doing lies in a first-century Jewish practice of baptising new converts.[3] Others suggest that the background can be found in another Jewish community from a place called Qumran.[4] But it seems odd to look to those places to find the background to John's baptism when both he and the Gospel writers go to great lengths to anchor his ministry in the expectations of the Old Testament.[5] John was showing that all God promised in the Old Testament regarding cleansing His people was about to be fulfilled in Jesus.[6]

In chapter 2, we saw that through Malachi, in the final pages of the Old Testament, God promised that He would come in

---

Jesus and John the Baptist. In John's Gospel, he has only just finished telling us about how Jesus was with God and was God from before all eternity when he suddenly skips to John the Baptist in verse 19. But in Mark he doesn't even wait that long; John the Baptist arrives in verse 2!

2. For a thorough survey of suggested backgrounds to baptism more broadly, see Ferguson, *Baptism*, chaps. 2 and 4.

3. E.g. Joachim Jeremias, 'Der Ursprung Der Johannestaufe,' *Zeitschrift für die neutestamentliche Wissenschaft und die Kunde der älteren Kirche* 28 (1929): 312-20.

4. E.g. Beasley-Murray thinks, 'John was indebted to the sectaries for raw material hard to come by elsewhere.' Nevertheless, Beasley-Murray thinks that John's expectations were anchored in the Old Testament as well. See George R. Beasley-Murray, *Baptism in the New Testament* (1962; reprint, Milton Keynes: Paternoster, 2005), 39-44.

5. It is not that first-century washing rituals undergirded John's ministry but that the Old Testament hope and expectation undergirded both. But John was showing that the fulfilment lay in Jesus, not in the rituals of the first-century Jews.

6. Fesko suggests that the background of John's baptism lies chiefly in its geographical connection with Israel passing through the Jordan in Joshua 4, and by extension, then, its connection with the Red Sea and the flood (see Fesko, *Word, Water, and Spirit*, 213-14 and chap. 2, note 26). Although, undoubtedly a connection exists, it could hardly be primary, since the Gospel writers and John himself anchor John's ministry in other parts of the Old Testament, such as Malachi 3.

person to clean up His people in a way they had never been able to do themselves. But God also promised through Malachi that before He came in person, He would send a messenger who would prepare the way:

> I will send my messenger, who will prepare the way before me (Mal. 3:1).

The messenger himself wouldn't do the cleaning up work. It would be God, who came after, who would do the cleaning up work.

It is telling, then, that as Mark begins his Gospel, he quotes from Malachi 3:

> The beginning of the good news about Jesus the Messiah, the Son of God, as it is written in Isaiah the prophet: **'I will send my messenger ahead of you, who will prepare your way'** – 'a voice of one calling in the wilderness, "Prepare the way for the Lord, make straight paths for him."' And so John the Baptist appeared in the wilderness, preaching a baptism of repentance for the forgiveness of sins (Mark 1:1-4) [emphasis added].

But Mark also combines the reference to Malachi with a quotation from Isaiah:

> **A voice of one calling: 'In the wilderness prepare the way for the LORD; make straight in the desert a highway for our God.** Every valley shall be raised up, every mountain and hill made low; the rough ground shall become level, the rugged places a plain. And the glory of the LORD will be revealed, and all people will see it together. For the mouth of the LORD has spoken' (Isa. 40:3-5) [emphasis added].

Again, the point is that God is coming to His people and they will see His glory. But before He comes, someone else is coming to prepare the way before Him.

Mark follows these two quotes immediately and quite dramatically with the simple but profound statement: 'And so John the Baptist appeared ....' Mark wants us to understand that John the Baptist is the direct fulfilment of both these Old Testament promises.[7] John

---

7. Later in chapter 4, Malachi also identifies this messenger as another 'Elijah': 'See, I will send the prophet Elijah to you before that great and dreadful day of the Lord

is the one sent by God to prepare the way for God Himself to visit His people.[8]

That much is also clear from some of what John himself says. John is desperate to make plain that he is only the messenger. He insists:

> After me comes the one more powerful than I, the straps of whose sandals I am not worthy to stoop down and untie (Mark 1:7).

John is placing himself in the pattern of the messenger of Malachi 3. He is not worthy to stoop down and untie the sandals of the one who is to come because the one who is to come, the one for whom he is preparing the way, is none other than God Himself, come into our world in the person of Jesus Christ.[9]

The God whom we meet in the Bible and for whom John prepares the way is not a 'standoff-ish' sort of God who yells at us from heaven and demands what we can never do. He is a God who stoops down and humbles Himself to become one of us and do for us what we could never achieve. He comes to us in grace and mercy to offer us not just arbitrary gifts but Himself. And in offering Himself to us, He offers to do all that is needed so that we can know Him.

Cleansing with the Holy Spirit

Clearly John himself as well as the Gospel writers see his ministry as anchored in God's Old Testament promises to come to His people and clean them up. That's deeply significant because the way John

---

comes.' (Mal. 4:5). God's promise here is not that the actual Elijah who had already lived and died would return as His messenger, but an Elijah-like figure would appear. When John the Baptist came, he came in the dress and style of Elijah. For instance, Mark tells us, 'John wore clothing made of camel's hair, with a leather belt around his waist, and he ate locusts and wild honey.' (Mark 1:6). Elijah is described in similar language in the Old Testament (see 2 Kings 1:8). If that wasn't a clear enough link, then Jesus Himself tells us what we are to think of John the Baptist: 'he is the Elijah who was to come.' (Matt. 11:14). Moreover, the fact that John's ministry occurs 'in the wilderness' suggests that Mark saw John as fulfilling that part of Isaiah's prophecy that the messenger would prepare the way 'in the wilderness'.

8. In fact, Jesus Himself later confirms that John fulfils Malachi 3 when He says, 'This is the one about whom it is written: "I will send my messenger ahead of you, who will prepare your way before you."' (Matt. 11:10).

9. That is even more clear in John 1:15: 'John testified concerning him. He cried out, saying, "This is the one I spoke about when I said, 'He who comes after me has surpassed me because he was before me.'"'

prepares for God to come and clean up His people is through baptism. Not only did John appear, he appeared 'preaching a baptism of repentance for the forgiveness of sins' (Mark 1:4). He was preparing people for God's great cleaning work by washing them with water.

John is at pains to point out that what he is doing is not the main event. His baptism is merely a symbol of something better. He says:

> I baptize you with water, but he will baptize you with the
> Holy Spirit (Mark 1:8).

Once again, John is picking up on God's promise in Ezekiel 36 that one day He would 'sprinkle clean water' on His people. That imagery would find its fulfilment in the people receiving a 'new heart' and a 'new spirit'. God Himself would 'put my Spirit in you and move you to follow my decrees and be careful to keep my laws' (Ezek. 36:26-27). John says he can't be the Messiah because all he is doing is washing people with water. The bath that people were taking under John's ministry didn't make them the new people that God had promised to make them in the Old Testament. They came out of the River Jordan with the same polluted hearts with which they had entered. John is simply preparing the way for someone else. The one who comes after him will wash people with the Spirit. Only the Spirit can provide the deep cleansing that we need in order to be people who love and serve God with our whole being.

And what was true of John's baptism is also true of the baptism that we practice. Christian baptism, though different from John's baptism (as we'll see), is the same in the sense that no one who is baptised goes into water and comes out a different person. No one goes into the water without the Spirit and comes out with Him. I know people who have been taught wrongly that the way to deal with sin in them is by being rebaptised. But that's like going back to relying on the shadows in the Old Testament. As John points out, water is completely unable to penetrate to the heart. What we need is not water, but the work of God by the Spirit that comes through Jesus. The water is only a symbol of a deeper reality – Jesus' promise of the Spirit to those who believe in Him.[10]

---

10. I take this to be the meaning of 'baptism with the Spirit'. It does not refer to something that happens *after* we become a Christian, but is that great promise of God that is fulfilled *when* we become a Christian.

Cleansing with Fire

But in Matthew and Luke's Gospels, John the Baptist adds another important word. While in Mark and John he refers only to Jesus baptising with the Holy Spirit, in Matthew and Luke he says that Jesus will baptise both with the Holy Spirit and *with fire*. He declares:

> I baptize you with water for repentance. But after me comes one who is more powerful than I, whose sandals I am not worthy to carry. He will baptize you with the Holy Spirit *and fire*. His winnowing fork is in his hand, and he will clear his threshing floor, gathering his wheat into the barn and burning up the chaff with unquenchable fire (Matt. 3:11-12) [emphasis added].

The reference to fire is again strongly reminiscent of Malachi where God promises that He will come as a 'refiner's fire' and will refine His people like gold and silver. Yet here the reference to fire seems like bad news not good news. 'Fire' here is an act of judgment, not salvation. It is 'unquenchable fire'.[11] What's going on?

To understand we need to go back to Malachi 3. There God said that He is not only coming to purify His people, He is also coming to judge those who remain committed to doing evil. God says:

> So I will come to put you on trial. I will be quick to testify against sorcerers, adulterers and perjurers, against those who defraud laborers of their wages, who oppress the widows and the fatherless, and deprive the foreigners among you of justice, but do not fear me ... (Mal. 3:5).

The ferocity of that judgment becomes clear at the very end of Malachi:

> 'Surely the day is coming; it will burn like a furnace. All the arrogant and every evildoer will be stubble, and the day that is coming will set them on fire,' says the LORD Almighty. 'Not a root or a branch will be left to them' (Mal. 4:1).

What becomes clear is that God's intention to come into His world in person has one indivisible purpose, but is achieved in two radically contrasting ways.[12] God is coming to clean up the world

---

11. The other time that fire is used in Matthew 3 it is also an act of judgment: 'The ax is already at the root of the trees, and every tree that does not produce good fruit will be cut down and thrown into the fire' (Matt. 3:10).

12. It also becomes clear in the New Testament that God is so long-suffering and compassionate that His coming to His world in person in both salvation and

and to burn away the filth of sin, but that cleaning up process can take place either through God cleaning up people by His Spirit or by God removing from His world and judging with unquenchable fire those who persist in rebellion against Him.[13]

That might sound harsh but it's a reminder both of God's hatred of sin and of the fact that the world can't be fixed without sin being comprehensively destroyed. It is impossible to rescue and redeem us without sin being eradicated, one way or the other. That's why the ultimate salvation of those who believe in Jesus, the ultimate and final rescue from sin, is inseparable from the final judgment. There can be no end to sin in anybody's life without the destruction of sin in the world. Look what God says about the new heavens and the new earth in Revelation:

> Nothing impure will ever enter it, nor will anyone who does what is shameful or deceitful, but only those whose names are written in the Lamb's book of life (Rev. 21:27).

There are two ways to clean up God's world and to remove evil from it: either by removing the evil from within people or by removing

---

judgment is stretched out across the two comings of Christ. God has come to us first in mercy, in the person of Jesus 2000 years ago, and He will come again in judgment when Jesus returns to judge the living and the dead.

13.   I suspect that James Dunn is correct to see a twofold use of fire here: for refinement as well as judgment (James D. G. Dunn, *Baptism in the Holy Spirit: A Re-Examination of the New Testament Teaching on the Gift of the Spirit in Relation to Pentecostalism Today*, 2nd ed. (SCM Press, 2010), 10-14; also Beasley-Murray, *Baptism*, 37-38), much in the same way that the waters of the flood are both an instrument of cleansing and judgment. Notably, too, when the Holy Spirit descends at Pentecost he comes as tongues of fire (Acts 2:3). In Mark 10:38, Jesus describes his baptism as undergoing the wrath of God: 'You don't know what you are asking .... Can you drink the cup I drink or be baptized with the baptism I am baptized with?' Although the disciples seem to understand Jesus in terms of sharing in the privileges of His kingdom (eating at Jesus' table and being cleansed and made fit for God's kingdom [cf. 10:37]), Jesus is referring to His death. The cup is the cup of God's wrath (cf. Isa. 51:17) and the baptism is His death. In other words, the disciples' participation in Jesus' kingdom comes at a huge cost. Just as Jesus will cleanse the world with fire, He Himself will undergo the cleansing judgment of God as a ransom on behalf of His people. But it is not that baptism represents judgment, but rather baptism represents cleansing and that cleansing in turn is achieved *through* judgment – either our own or Jesus' judgment in our place. The disciples will indeed share in the blessings of Jesus' kingdom (Mark 10:39) through His atoning death and resurrection. But they must also follow Him from suffering to glory as they take up their cross and follow Him (Mark 8:34-9:1; also 1 Pet. 4:12-14).

evil people from the world. And John says that Jesus has come to do precisely that. Jesus has come to sort out the world.

John says that Jesus' 'winnowing fork is in his hand'. A winnowing fork was used by farmers to sort the wheat from the chaff. After picking their wheat, farmers would beat and crush it on a hard surface called a threshing floor. But in order to separate the bit you want (the grain) from the rubbish (the chaff) they would scoop up forkloads of wheat and throw it in the air into a light breeze. The heavier grain would then fall back down onto the threshing floor while the lightweight chaff would be blown away by the wind. Later, the chaff would be gathered up and burned. John says that Jesus will do precisely that, but with people.[14] He will cleanse evil from the world by separating the good from the bad.

Although the destruction of evil might seem like a deeply distressing idea, it's important to understand that it is also part of the good news of the gospel. For those of us who have not suffered terribly much, it may not seem like such great news. But for those who have experienced terrible evil, it really is. For those who have been raped, abused, beaten, or seen their families and friends murdered, the notion of God's justice and the end of evil is not abhorrent but tremendously comforting. Rebecca Pippert writes:

> Think how we feel when we see someone we love ravaged by un-
> wise actions or relationships. Do we respond with benign intol-
> erance as we might toward strangers? Far from it .... Anger isn't
> the opposite of love. ... God's wrath is not cranky explosion,
> but his settled opposition to the cancer ... which is eating out
> the insides of the human race he loves with his whole being.[15]

A Cleansing Received through Humble Repentance

But notice that Jesus is not separating people who are fundamentally good from people who are fundamentally evil. As Alexander
Solzhenitsyn wrote:

---

14. The word that John uses to describe Jesus gathering up and burning the chaff is a cleansing word – He will 'clean out' (*diakatharizō*) the threshing floor. See R. T. France, *The Gospel of Matthew*, New International Commentary on the New Testament (Grand Rapids: Eerdmans, 2007), 115.

15. Rebecca Pippert, *Hope Has Its Reasons* (Harper, 1990), chap. 4, as quoted in Timothy Keller, *The Reason for God: Belief in an Age of Scepticism* (London: Hodder & Stoughton, 2008), 73.

If only it were all so simple! If only there were evil people somewhere insidiously committing evil deeds, and it were necessary only to separate them from the rest of us and destroy them. But the line dividing good and evil cuts through the heart of every human being. And who is willing to destroy a piece of his own heart?[16]

Rather, Jesus is cleansing the world by giving His Spirit to some people and then casting others out. Everyone is evil, and the world will be cleansed of our evil *either* through washing with the Spirit *or* with the fire of judgment.

But who receives what? According to John, the answer lies in repentance but also somehow in baptism. John begins his ministry with these words:

> Repent, for the kingdom of heaven has come near (Matt. 3:2).

Similarly, the Gospel writers describe John's baptism as a 'baptism of repentance for the forgiveness of sins' (Mark 1:4; also Luke 3:3; cf. Matt. 3:11).[17] And we are told that people from Judea and Jerusalem were going out to John in the wilderness and were being baptised by him and 'confessing their sins' (Mark 1:5; also Matt. 3:5).

But John's message was not simply about confessing sins but also about abandoning sin and living a changed life:

> 'What should we do then?' the crowd asked.
>
> John answered, 'Anyone who has two shirts should share with the one who has none, and anyone who has food should do the same.'
>
> Even tax collectors came to be baptized. 'Teacher,' they asked, 'what should we do?'
>
> 'Don't collect any more than you are required to,'" he told them.
>
> Then some soldiers asked him, 'And what should we do?'
>
> He replied, 'Don't extort money and don't accuse people falsely – be content with your pay' (Luke 3:10-14).

---

16. Aleksandr Solzhenitsyn, *The Gulag Archipelago 1918-56: An Experiment in Literary Investigation*, ed. Edward E. Ericson, Jr, trans. Thomas P. Whitney and Harry Willetts (1985; reprint, London: Vintage, 2018), 75.

17. Again, John is standing in line with the message of Malachi. God had said that His messenger would conduct a ministry of encouraging people to repentance. He would 'turn the hearts of the parents to their children, and the hearts of the children to their parents' (Mal. 4:6).

What John was calling the people to was not perfection but to a life of genuinely seeking to live for God and honour God. He says:

> Produce fruit in keeping with repentance. And do not think you can say to yourselves, 'We have Abraham as our father.' I tell you that out of these stones God can raise up children for Abraham. The ax is already at the root of the trees, and every tree that does not produce good fruit will be cut down and thrown into the fire (Matt. 3:8-10).

John warns that if people do not repent then judgment is coming. God has His axe ready to strike the tree and cut it down. The only remedy is for people to genuinely repent and to bear the fruit of repentance.[18]

The danger that the people faced was the historic danger of the people of Israel: that they would claim to know God and be in a relationship with God, while in reality just continuing to live their own way, with total disregard for God. John warns the Jewish people not to think, 'We have Abraham as our father'. Although John doesn't mention circumcision, it is clearly in view. The risk was that the Jewish people might think they would be saved through their family connection with Abraham (a connection which was highlighted by circumcision) and so they didn't need to deal with sin. They could have their cake and eat it too – they could hang on to sin and be saved. But as we saw in the last chapter, circumcision was not a guarantee of salvation but a call to humble repentance and trust in God's promise through Abraham. John says God can raise up people like that – people like Abraham who trust and follow God. God can raise them up not only from outside Israel, but even from inanimate stones![19]

John's message to the people is exactly the same message God spoke to His people in the Old Testament through Jeremiah:

---

18. The same is true in Malachi's message: "'Ever since the time of your ancestors you have turned away from my decrees and have not kept them. Return to me, and I will return to you," says the Lord Almighty.' (Mal. 3:7). To 'return' is the language the Old Testament often uses for repentance. In the following verses, God explains what 'returning' would involve. It involved an end to robbing God (by paying their tithes) and no longer saying it's futile to serve God. In other words, it involved not only a return to God but a change in how they lived.

19. In that way, John's message is essentially the same as Paul's message in Romans 4 – God's salvation is not for the circumcised but for those who trust God like Abraham did, whether circumcised or uncircumcised. See the section 'Circumcision as a Sign of Hope for the Uncircumcised' on page 90 above.

'If you, Israel, will return, then return to me,' declares the LORD. 'If you put your detestable idols out of my sight and no longer go astray, and if in a truthful, just and righteous way you swear, "As surely as the LORD lives," then the nations will invoke blessings by him and in him they will boast.'

This is what the LORD says to the people of Judah and to Jerusalem: 'Break up your unplowed ground and do not sow among thorns. Circumcise yourselves to the LORD, *circumcise your hearts*, you people of Judah and inhabitants of Jerusalem, or my wrath will flare up and burn like fire because of the evil you have done – burn with no one to quench it' (Jer. 4:1-4) [emphasis added].

God calls the people to repentance; that is, to circumcise their hearts. These people were physically circumcised but that didn't make them children of God. They were claiming to know God but continuing to hang on to all their cherished sins. What really mattered was turning away from sin, humbly seeking God, and trusting in what God had promised He would do through the Saviour descended from Abraham.

Yet hanging onto sin remains a pressing problem still today. People don't necessarily believe that being born into the right family will save them, but the view is still prevalent that you can embrace sin and nurture it, and God will still be happy with you provided you claim God's promises for yourself. But that's not repentance.

We tend to think that the main way people deny the gospel is by becoming an atheist or by leaving Christianity altogether. But the problem is often far more subtle. The people of Israel in the Old Testament rarely completely abandoned God. What they did was accept the truth of God's promises, claim them for themselves, but then hang onto sin and rebellion against God. Moses warned the people in Deuteronomy:

Make sure there is no man or woman, clan or tribe among you today whose heart turns away from the LORD our God to go and worship the gods of those nations; make sure there is no root among you that produces such bitter poison.

When such a person hears the words of this oath and they invoke a blessing on themselves, thinking, 'I will be safe, even though I persist in going my own way,' they will bring disaster on the watered land as well as the dry. The LORD will never be willing to forgive them; his wrath and zeal will burn against them. All the curses written in this book will fall on them, and the LORD will blot out their names from under heaven (Deut. 29:18-20).

When John says, 'do not think you can say to yourselves, "We have Abraham as our father"', the problem is not simply that they trust in their family heritage. Rather, they trust and claim the promise God made to Abraham but fail to realise that receiving that promise means they must abandon their sin and humble themselves before God. You can't grab hold of Jesus while you're still grasping onto sin.

Yet it's easy enough for people to still fall into the same trap. Many people are more than willing to claim the forgiveness which God offers in Jesus but without accepting Jesus' authority and rule over their life. They want to keep their sin and be forgiven for it. They want to keep living life their own way, and they want God to accept them while they do that. They want to hang onto their bitterness and resentment, or love money, or overlook the poor, or steal from others, or sleep with their boyfriend or girlfriend, or embrace a gay identity. They want to do any or all those things or many others besides *and* claim God's forgiveness and acceptance. But you can't have the forgiveness of Jesus without turning from sin. The German theologian, Dietrich Bonhoeffer, described that kind of gospel as 'cheap grace'. It is 'the preaching of forgiveness without repentance and baptism without church discipline'. It is a kind of fake 'grace' that leads to the 'justification of sin' rather than to the 'justification of the repentant sinner, who leaves and turns back from his sin.[20]

A Cleansing in Expectation of the Promised Descendant

Yet it's important to realise that John was not simply calling people to turn from sin and not trust in their family heritage, but he was also calling them to explicitly put their hope in the promised Messiah who was about to arrive. Humble repentance is only one side of the coin of John's baptism. Repentance is about turning – turning from one thing to another. John was not only calling people to turn *from* sin. More importantly, he was calling them to turn *to* Jesus.

---

20.   Dietrich Bonhoeffer, *Nachfolge*, ed. Martin Kuske and Ilse Tödt, 3rd ed. (Gütersloh: Gütersloher Verlagshaus, 2008), 30 (my trans.).

John was announcing the imminent arrival of God's long-promised Messiah, and his baptism was a call to identify with that hope. John says that pointing to Jesus was the central purpose of his baptism ministry:

> 'I myself did not know him, but **the reason I came baptizing with water was that he might be revealed to Israel**' [emphasis added].
>
> Then John gave this testimony: 'I saw the Spirit come down from heaven as a dove and remain on him. And I myself did not know him, but the one who sent me to baptize with water told me, "The man on whom you see the Spirit come down and remain is the one who will baptize with the Holy Spirit." I have seen and I testify that this is God's Chosen One' (John 1:31-34).

People often wonder why it was that Jesus was baptised by John. After all, Jesus had no sins to confess and nothing of which to repent. But John tells us – it was to reveal Jesus. And in the context of God's promise to Abraham, it makes perfect sense. Israelite after Israelite was coming to John because they recognised that they needed to repent. They came to confess their sin, turn away from it, and put their hope in the promised Messiah. Then, one day, along comes Jesus. He looked like any other Israelite. He looked like He was repenting and confessing sin. But then, having been baptised, as He left the water the Holy Spirit descended on Him in the form of a dove, and God Himself spoke from heaven, saying: 'This is my Son, whom I love; with him I am well pleased' (Matt. 3:17).[21] What was the message? The message was that this man had no need of the same cleansing as every other child of Abraham or every other human being. This is the long-awaited blameless seed of Abraham who already possesses the promised Holy Spirit and by whom God will clean up His people.

John's baptism, at least in part, was designed to show that God was on the cusp of fulfilling His promise to cleanse the world. All

---

21. Notably, James Dunn highlights that it was not in the baptism itself that the Spirit descended but after Jesus was baptised and while He was praying (Luke 3:21). The implication being that the descent of the Spirit is not connected with baptism itself. That is further confirmed by the fact that John's Gospel does not mention Jesus' baptism at all. It was not John's baptism that brought in the new age of the Spirit, nor was it John's baptism of Jesus, per se, rather it was the person and character of Jesus Himself. Many had been baptised by John, but the Spirit only descended on Jesus. See Dunn, *Baptism*, 32-37.

through the Old Testament, God had promised that He would cleanse sin and evil from the world. John was showing that God was about to do precisely that, and his baptism was a call to identify with that hope. But not by identifying with John but by identifying with Jesus – John was only baptising with water but Jesus would baptise with the Spirit.

Somewhat ironically, perhaps, John's baptism was about people identifying with the core message of circumcision: repentance from sin and trust in God's promised Messiah descended from Abraham. John was not introducing a new idea but clarifying an old one: what matters is not what family you belong to, but whether you've turned away from sin and trusted in the rescue of God through His promised Messiah. In particular, what matters is trusting the Messiah, Jesus, *who has now appeared.*

If one problem is that people try to claim the salvation of God in Jesus without making any genuine effort to abandon sin, the other problem is that people try to kill and leave sin without actually connecting up with Jesus. They try to kill sin by their own cunning schemes and efforts. They beat themselves, put on camel's hair undies, try to make up for the sin in their past and attempt to work the sin out of their hearts. But it's completely ineffective and they're left either proud and deluded like the Pharisees, thinking that they've made themselves acceptable to God, or they're discouraged and mistaken like Martin Luther, realising that they can't make themselves right with God and despairing that they ever will be. What we need is not only to genuinely seek to leave sin, but to take hold of Jesus and all that God offers us in Him. And the promise offered in baptism is that if we do that, God will forgive us and make us clean.

John's Baptism and Christian Baptism

But thinking about John's baptism raises an important question: what was the difference between his baptism and the baptism that we practice today?

The answer lies in John's location in the history of God's great salvation program. We've already seen how John distinguishes between his plain old water baptism and Jesus' Spirit baptism. John's baptism only washed people on the outside, but Jesus was coming to fulfil God's Old Testament promise to wash people on the inside

– to wash their hearts by pouring out God's Spirit upon them. But how does that relate to the practice of water baptism itself? Is there a difference between the water baptism of John and the water baptism that Jesus commanded his disciples to practice (Matt. 28:19)?[22]

The answer can be found in one episode in Acts 19. There Paul finds a number of disciples in Ephesus who had received John's baptism but nothing more. Paul says to them:

> 'Did you receive the Holy Spirit when you believed?'
> They answered, 'No, we have not even heard that there is a Holy Spirit.'
> So Paul asked, 'Then what baptism did you receive?'
> 'John's baptism,' they replied.
> Paul said, 'John's baptism was a baptism of repentance. He told the people to believe in the one coming after him, that is, in Jesus.' On hearing this, they were baptized in the name of the Lord Jesus. When Paul placed his hands on them, the Holy Spirit came on them, and they spoke in tongues and prophesied. There were about twelve men in all (Acts 19:2-7).

Notice carefully what Paul says. He says that John's message was to 'believe in the one coming after him, that is, in Jesus.' These people had obviously heard John's message, committed themselves to God in humble repentance and faith, and they were awaiting God's promised Messiah, but they had not yet heard that the Messiah was Jesus. As a result, they had not received the Holy Spirit that

---

22. D. Broughton Knox argues that Jesus' disciples only water baptised as a kind of remnant of John's baptism but that Jesus never actually commanded it – Jesus only commanded a kind of metaphorical baptism, 'immers[ing] the nations into the revealed character of God'. Among the numerous problems with this view is: (1) the fact that not all the disciples appear to have had a background in John's ministry as Knox maintains (e.g. Levi [Luke 5:27]); (2) although Jesus Himself never baptised, the disciples clearly did so at His instruction rather than from their own initiative (John 3:22; cf. 4:2), (3) one would think that if water baptism was so unimportant, Jesus might have mentioned the move away from it more explicitly and chosen less confusing words when He commanded the disciples to baptise people from all nations (Matt. 28:19); and (4) if John's baptism was really part of the old dispensation and 'outside the kingdom of God' as Knox maintains, and if Jesus dropped water baptism after He 'took over the leadership' of John's ministry (as Knox also questionably maintains), it seems quite implausible that the disciples would 'revive' the practice and begin their ministry in the new dispensation with such a conscientious continuation of a practice their leader had so deliberately abandoned (e.g. Acts 2:38; 10:47). See D. B. Knox, *Church and Ministry*, ed. Kirsten Birkett, vol. 2 of *D. Broughton Knox Selected Works* (Kingsford: Matthias Media, 2000), 263-309, esp. 270, 273, 282.

John said would come through Jesus. However, once they hear about Jesus, they are baptised 'in the name of the Lord Jesus' and immediately they receive the promised Holy Spirit.

It's important to realise that John's baptism was anticipatory. People were being baptised *in expectation* of the coming of the Messiah. Until Jesus was revealed, John's baptism simply testified that *someone* was coming soon, and it called people to put their trust or renew their trust in God's promise, but it didn't identify *who* was coming. It wasn't until Jesus appeared at the River Jordan to be baptised by John that anyone knew who it was to whom they needed to entrust themselves. Once Jesus had come, however, people needed to specifically identify with Him. They needed to acknowledge that Jesus was the Messiah God had promised – they needed to be baptised 'into the name of Jesus Christ' (Acts 10:48). That's why these people who had received John's baptism later needed to be rebaptised. It wasn't because they needed to repent and turn to God. They'd already done that. It was because their faith had to be explicitly in God's work in the person of Jesus Christ.

The same was true, in a sense, on the day of Pentecost when 3,000 Jews and God-fearers were baptised. It would be a mistake to think that all the people gathered on that day to hear Peter and the other disciples were either godless hypocrites or were caught up in trying to please God by their own obedience. Undoubtedly, some of them were genuine believers who trusted in God as He had revealed Himself in the Old Testament and who, like Simeon, were awaiting the consolation of Israel (Luke 2:25). So, when Peter said to them, 'Repent and be baptized, every one of you, in the name of Jesus Christ for the forgiveness of your sins' (Acts 2:38), he didn't simply mean 'start following God from today'. For some of them, it would have meant that: a completely new beginning. But for others, like those Paul met in Ephesus, it meant moving from trusting in God and in the expectation of His *coming* Messiah, to trusting in God and His Messiah Jesus who had *finally arrived* and through whom came forgiveness and the indwelling of the Spirit.[23]

What is fundamentally at stake is a change of era – from the Old to the New; from the present age to the age to come. That new age

---

23. As Beasley-Murray notes, 'baptism was a fitting conclusion to the gospel proclamation; for baptism in the Name of the Lord Jesus connoted not alone a cleansing from sin but an expression of dissociation from the rejectors of the Messiah and a means of association with the Messiah and His people.' (Beasley-Murray, *Baptism*, 98).

has begun through the incarnation, death, resurrection and ascension of Jesus. We participate in that age through faith in Jesus.[24]

The people in the Old Testament were like people on a train platform waiting for the train to arrive. Some people, like Simeon, were on the right platform waiting for the right train. Others, like Paul before his conversion and the Pharisees, were not on the right platform and not even looking in the right direction. Still, even for those who were on the right platform and who had a relationship with God through that faith, they still had to hop on when the Jesus train finally arrived.[25]

The coming of Jesus changed the explicit object of faith from a promised person to an actual person. That change is what marks out the difference between John's baptism and Christian baptism. And that, in turn, marks out what lies at the very heart of baptism – identification with Jesus as the Messiah and Saviour of the world. And through identification with Jesus comes the Holy Spirit who unites us with Jesus and the powers of the coming age.

---

24. For a helpful discussion, see Dunn, *Baptism*, chap. 4.

25. My thanks here must go to one of my theology classes for helping me develop the Jesus train illustration. More mundanely, one Bible scholar, comparing Abraham's faith and ours, puts it like this: 'The only difference is that Abraham, according to Paul, was justified by believing (= trusting) that God would fulfil the divine promise in the future, while the one who believes in Christ trusts that God has already acted in the resurrection of Jesus Christ. So Christian faith is belief in God, but precisely belief that God has been faithful in and through the resurrection of Jesus from the dead. ... [T]hough Abraham may be a model of faith and essentially the faith that justifies is a trust in the faithfulness of God such as Abraham had, it is faith that God has acted in the resurrection of Jesus Christ and with the cooperation of Jesus Christ so decisively that henceforth faith in God cannot be expressed except as a faith in Christ which amounts to the confession *Jesus is Lord*' (Veronica Koperski, 'The Meaning of Pistis Christou in Philippians 3:9,' *Louvain Studies* 18 (1993): 211-13 [emphasis original]).

6. The Saviour Who is Here

Baptism as a Sign of the Gospel Fulfilled

John the Baptist's baptism ministry heralded the arrival of God's promised Saviour, Jesus. He announced that all that God had promised in the Old Testament, pictured in water, was now coming to fulfilment. To receive God's gift of the Spirit, people had to link up with Jesus. Those themes continue through the writings of the rest of the New Testament.

In this chapter we'll be looking at some of the key passages from the New Testament that speak about baptism. We'll see how they use lots of the imagery from the Old Testament to explain the meaning of baptism and to show that all that was promised has finally been realised in the person and work of Jesus.

Clothed in the Promised Descendant of Abraham

The arrival of Jesus has brought the long-awaited Holy Spirit and the hope of finally being forgiven and cleaned up. All people need to do to receive that gift is to receive Jesus and entrust themselves to Him. But it seems that some early Christians were turning back to the Old Testament rituals, especially circumcision, in an effort to clean themselves up. That's the issue Paul addresses in his letter to the Galatians.[1] And strikingly, in addressing that issue, he shows us how baptism connects with God's fulfilment in Jesus of the promise signified by circumcision.

At the beginning of chapter 3, Paul says:

> You foolish Galatians! Who has bewitched you? Before your very eyes Jesus Christ was clearly portrayed as crucified. I would like to learn just one thing from you: Did you receive the Spirit by the works of the law, or by believing what you heard? Are you so foolish? After beginning by means of the Spirit, are you now trying to finish by means of the flesh? (Gal. 3:1-3).

The problem is that the Galatians, who had begun well, were finishing the Christian life poorly. They had begun with faith but now were seeking to 'finish' or be 'perfected' by means of the flesh.[2] Hence Paul says:

> So again I ask, does God give you his Spirit and work miracles among you by the works of the law, or by your believing what you heard? So also Abraham 'believed God, and it was credited to him as righteousness' (Gal. 3:5-6).

Although Paul doesn't explicitly mention circumcision in these verses, it is certainly in view. Earlier in his letter he has spoken about a conflict over circumcision that had arisen between him and Peter in which Peter had withdrawn from eating with those who were not circumcised (Gal. 2:11-16). So also, the last two chapters are filled with references to circumcision.[3] There, Paul warns that their views on circumcision are putting them at risk of abandoning the gospel:

> Mark my words! I, Paul, tell you that if you let yourselves be circumcised, Christ will be of no value to you at all (Gal. 5:2).

---

1. See Deenick, *Righteous by Promise*, 185-208.

2. There is a kind of double reference going on here. The underlying Greek term (*epiteleō*) generally only means to complete something or reach a goal. But Paul's broader use of this and related terms often looks ahead to the final goal of believers being perfectly remade in the image of Christ. The related term 'perfection' (*teleios*) is one of a number of terms the Greek translators of the Old Testament used to render the Hebrew term 'blameless' (*tamim*) and its related verb. That term was bound up with God's promise to Abraham in circumcision. Paul also uses the expression in his discussion of the true goal of circumcision in Philippians 3. See Deenick, *Righteous by Promise*, 102-5.

3. See Gal. 5:2, 3, 6, 11; 6:12, 13, 15.

Ironically, the Galatians were trying to obtain what was promised in circumcision (righteousness and perfection) by zealously hanging on to their practice of circumcision and other Old Testament rituals like food laws rather than clinging to Jesus (cf. Gal. 2:11-16).

But according to Paul, the blessing of righteousness and perfection promised to Abraham doesn't come through circumcision, but through Jesus and the Spirit. He says in verse 13:

> Christ redeemed us from the curse of the law by becoming a curse for us, for it is written: "Cursed is everyone who is hung on a pole." He redeemed us in order that the blessing given to Abraham might come to the Gentiles through Christ Jesus, so that by faith we might receive the promise of the Spirit (Gal. 3:13-14).

The 'blessing given to Abraham'[4] that Paul has in mind is none other than 'the promise of the Spirit'. That promised Spirit does not come through rituals and procedures like circumcision but through faith in Jesus. It is only the Spirit that can bring the new creation to life in us and make us new creatures. No law or human effort can achieve that. But neither can any law or human effort earn us access to the Spirit. According to Paul, the purpose of Jesus' death was to free us from the law[5] so that what was promised to Abraham might finally be given. While the law stood, it blocked the coming of the promised Spirit and the new creation. That's because we were at enmity with God. The wrath of God needed to be put away before the promise of God's personal presence in His people could be fulfilled.

But having established that, Paul goes on to demolish the Galatians' view of circumcision. In fact, what he's really doing is showing what circumcision always meant. He starts by saying that

---

4. Or strictly speaking, 'the blessing of Abraham'. That is, the one promised to him in the gospel preached 'beforehand' (see Gal. 3:8-9). Abraham did not yet possess the Spirit in the New Testament sense. Since, as we have seen, the outpouring of the Spirit awaited the death and resurrection of Jesus.

5. The law pronounced a curse on anyone who did not continue to do everything written in it. Paul quotes that curse from Deuteronomy in Gal. 3:10: 'Cursed is everyone who does not continue to do everything written in the Book of the Law.' The problem was that the law was utterly incapable of bringing about the new creation that it so eagerly looked forward to. It highlighted the hope through its sacrifices and rituals, but it couldn't bring them about. The mistake that many Jewish people made was to think that the law was itself the good news. Instead, the law only preached the good news in advance. As Paul goes on to say, it locked people up until the coming of Jesus who fulfilled everything the law offered but could never achieve. (Gal. 3:22-23).

the purpose of Jesus' death was so that the 'blessing of Abraham' could come to the Gentiles, not just to Abraham's descendants and not just to those who were circumcised.

But Paul has only just made that expansive move when he throws in another massive curve ball: God's promise was only ever to one person! Paul shows that the promise given to Abraham was not actually a promise to Abraham and *all* his descendants but to Abraham and only *one* of his descendants – his 'seed'. Paul writes:

> The promises were spoken to Abraham and to his seed. Scripture does not say 'and to seeds,' meaning many people, but 'and to your seed,' meaning one person, who is Christ (Gal. 3:16).

All through the Old Testament everyone was waiting for this 'seed'. As we've seen, circumcision signified that promise. Circumcision was never about marking out who was saved and who wasn't. It was about proclaiming a promise that through one of Abraham's descendants God would save a people for Himself, and circumcision called on people to believe that promise in their heart. But now Jesus has come, and so the promise of a seed of Abraham, signified in circumcision, has been fulfilled.[6]

So the question becomes: if the promise was to Jesus and to Jesus alone, then how does someone share in that promise and inheritance? The simple but profound answer is that you link up with Jesus through faith so that what belongs to Him becomes yours as well. Paul says in verse 26:

> So in Christ Jesus you are all children of God through faith, for all of you who were baptized into Christ have clothed yourselves with Christ. There is neither Jew nor Gentile, neither slave nor free, nor is there male and female, for you are all one in Christ Jesus. If you belong to Christ, then you are Abraham's seed, and heirs according to the promise (Gal. 3:26-29).

To be a child of God, an heir according to the promise of God and 'Abraham's offspring', comes from 'belonging' to Christ. He is

---

6.   Again, that is why circumcision is no longer required, because the person to whom it pointed has arrived. The promise has been fulfilled. It also explains why continuing circumcision can be catastrophically dangerous, as Paul points out in Gal. 5:2 – because it risks denying that the fulfilment of all God's promises lies in Jesus.

Abraham's heir, *par excellence*. Those who are in Him, then, share in all that God promised Abraham through Him.

Another way of saying that, according to Paul, is that we are 'clothed with Christ'. That has two implications. First, it means we take on Jesus' identity and status so that everything that belongs to Him becomes ours and what is true of Him is considered to be true of us too. Hence, because He has an eternal inheritance from God, we have an eternal inheritance. Because He is a child of God, we are children of God, adopted into the family. Because He is righteous, we are righteous. What He has achieved for us in His humanity, He shares with us.

But second, clothing ourselves with Jesus changes us. It's not just that our status changes but *we* change. We become more like Him. We're not just adopted into God's family, we're reborn into God's family – our DNA changes (metaphorically speaking). The very fabric of who we are changes. That's why there's no more Jew or Gentile, slave or free, male or female, because those things no longer define us now that our identity is defined by Jesus' identity and now that we've been reborn into a new creation in the image of Jesus. You are no longer just your parent's child, or the son of Adam, or Abraham, or whoever (though you remain those things too). You're a child of God through faith in Christ Jesus.

Sometimes we like to think that when we put on new clothes we can become different people. The ads we see promise us that. They promise that if we have that new hat or new coat or new jeans we'll be cool, sexy, popular, confident and successful. And so often we believe it, even when we know it's stupid. But despite all the marketing hype, when we put on the new clothes and head to work or to a concert or to a friend's party, we still know that deep down we're the same people. Our clothes fail to change us and they fail to change our destiny.

But imagine if there was a set of clothes that you could put on that would really change you. Imagine a suit or a dress that could change your future and your destiny. Imagine a pair of clothes that you could put on so that life would never be the same again. Imagine a pair of clothes that you could put on that would not only change your life now but could give you an eternal inheritance that will never perish, spoil or fade. And imagine if those same clothes didn't just change your destiny, they changed you. Imagine that they were clothes whose own qualities infused themselves into you and mingled together with you in such a way as to wash away everything that was evil and corrupt, and replace it with everything that was noble, good, pure and holy. Those are the kind of clothes that, if most people found, they would go out, sell everything they had, and buy them (Matt. 13:44-46). They would drop everything they were doing to get them (cf. Matt. 22:1-14). The kind of cleansing we have in the gospel by being linked up with Jesus gives us an entirely new identity with a totally new inheritance. When God looks at us, He sees a descendant of Abraham, a child of the promise.

Baptised into the Promises of Circumcision

But Paul also links 'clothing yourself with Christ' with baptism. He says that the Galatians are sons of God through faith. Why? *Because* as many of them as have been baptised have also put on Jesus or believed in Jesus (Gal. 3:27). What does he mean? How is baptism related to faith and putting on Jesus?

What Paul is not saying is 'you are sons of God because you believed/put on Christ and that was then symbolised in baptism.' Paul is not thinking, then, of baptism as a testimony to faith. If that were the case, you would expect Paul to have put it the other way around: 'you are sons of God because, as many of you as have believed/clothed yourselves with Christ, have been baptised.' But he doesn't put it that way. Baptism comes before 'clothing yourself with Christ' by faith.

Nor is Paul simply referring to a spiritual baptism rather than an actual physical act.[7] So, 'you are sons of God because as many of you as have been washed/baptised by the Spirit have (in so doing) put on Christ.' That view wouldn't fit the logic of Galatians. Paul is very careful in Galatians to show that the Holy Spirit is the inheritance that comes through identification with Christ, rather than the other way around – they are heirs of the Spirit through Christ (Gal. 3:7, 9, 14, 22, 29; 4:7). A person receives the Spirit because of identification by faith with Christ and the deliverance from the law that comes through Him (esp. Gal. 3:2). Again, that being the case, if Holy Spirit baptism was meant it would have to come second: 'as many of you as have put on Christ, have been baptised (by the Spirit).'

---

7. See, for example, James D. G. Dunn, *The Epistle to the Galatians*, Black's New Testament Commentaries (London: Continuum, 1993), 203-4 and Dunn, *Baptism*, 109-13.

So what does it mean? The trick is that the phrase 'all of you' or 'as many of you' speaks only to extent. It simply says that the group who experienced one event (baptism) is as big as the group who experienced another event (clothing yourself with Christ), but it doesn't tell us the logical relationship between one event and the other.[8] So, for instance, in Matthew 14:36, 'as many as' touched Jesus robe were healed. In that case, it was *by* touching Jesus' robe that they were healed. On the other hand, in Acts 4:34, 'as many as' owned property, sold it and brought the money to the apostles. In that case, owning property was not the means by which they sold it! That clearly makes no sense. Rather, the point is that all those people in the first category— land owners—went on to take another subsequent action – they sold their property.[9]

In Galatians, then, Paul could mean one of two things. He could mean, 'as many of you who were baptised have clothed yourself with Christ *by* being baptised.' But given what Paul has been arguing about circumcision, it makes no sense to suppose that he now attributes to baptism what he was trying to prove was not true of circumcision. He is at pains to point out that circumcision did not incorporate a person into the gospel promise. Circumcision did not make them sons. Faith and belonging to Christ and clothing themselves with Christ made them sons. So it is unlikely that Paul is trying to convince the Galatians to move away from the physical act of circumcision by telling them that the real way they inherit Abraham's promise is through the physical act of baptism.

Rather, Paul means 'you are sons through faith because, having been baptised, you have (subsequently) actually clothed yourself with Christ'! His emphasis in this passage is on faith and it remains

---

8. E.g. Frederick W. Danker et al., *A Greek-English Lexicon of the New Testament and Other Early Christian Literature*, 3rd ed. (Chicago: University of Chicago Press, 2000), 729.

9. Indeed, it would have been possible for some people to own property and not sell it. And it's quite possible that some did. We probably shouldn't take Luke as being exhaustive – every single person without fail. Clearly, Mary retained a house (Acts 12:12; so I. Howard Marshall, *Acts: An Introduction and Commentary*, Tyndale New Testament Commentaries 5 (1980; reprint, Downers Grove: IVP Academic, 2008), 116). Rather, Luke is trying to emphasise how extensive this attitude was. See David G. Peterson, *The Acts of the Apostles*, Pillar New Testament Commentary (Grand Rapids: Eerdmans, 2009), 205-6.

on faith, rather than moving from faith to baptism.[10] Moreover, Paul switches from speaking about what has been done to the Galatians to what they have done to themselves. They were baptised (passive), but they have 'clothed *themselves*'. If it was baptism (even as an expression of faith) that achieved the clothing you would expect Paul to continue in the passive voice, and so say, 'as many of you as were baptised were clothed (passive) with Christ.'[11]

But perhaps more importantly, in the other places where Paul talks about 'clothing yourself with Christ' it is always without reference to baptism, and it is viewed as an ongoing part of the Christian life. For example:

> Rather, *clothe yourselves* with the Lord Jesus Christ, and do not think about how to gratify the desires of the flesh (Rom. 13:14) [emphasis added].
>
> ... and *put on* the new self, created to be like God in true righteousness and holiness (Eph. 4:24) [emphasis added].
>
> Do not lie to each other, since you have taken off your old self with its practices and have *put on* the new self, which is being renewed in knowledge in the image of its Creator.... Therefore, as God's chosen people, holy and dearly loved, *clothe yourselves* with compassion, kindness, humility, gentleness and patience (Col. 3:9-12) [emphasis added].

'Clothing yourself with Christ' represents both the beginning of the Christian life and also the ongoing action of the Christian life.[12]

---

10. Many think Paul does shift the focus to baptism. Douglas Moo notes, 'What is somewhat surprising is the shift from faith as a means of union with Christ in verse 26 to baptism in verse 27.' (Douglas J. Moo, *Galatians*, Baker Exegetical Commentary on the New Testament (Grand Rapids: Baker, 2013), 251). It would be surprising if Paul did make that shift, but he doesn't.

11. That is what he does in Romans 6 where he employs a very similar phrase: 'as many of us who were baptised (passive) into Christ Jesus, were baptised (passive) into his death' (Rom. 6:3; my trans.). Elsewhere too, where the second action is carried out by the first (i.e. the one linked with 'as many as'), the second action is a passive verb (e.g. Matt. 14:36; Mark 6:56). Where the second verb is active, the action represents a distinct action to the first and is often subsequent (e.g. Mark 3:10; Luke 4:40; John 1:12; Acts 10:45). Also, the fact that both verbs in Galatians 3 occur in the aorist tense does not imply that the actions are simultaneous (e.g. Mark 6:30; Luke 9:10; John 1:12; 4:29; Acts 10:45; Rev. 1:2; 13:15). Indeed, a change in voice and/or person suggests that the two are not simultaneous.

12. As Dunn notes, 'the middle voice and the parallel uses (especially Rom. 13:14; Col. 3:10; Eph. 4:24) indicate, it signifies an act of the will – a responding to Christ and a commitment to Christ whereby the life and character (that is, the Spirit) of Jesus is received (henceforth to be manifested in a new way of life), and whereby

To illustrate the point that Paul is making, imagine if he had said, 'You are all sons of God through faith, for as many of you who were circumcised, have clothed yourselves with Christ.' What would he most likely mean by that? Given that the whole argument of his letter is that it is faith that matters, he would most likely mean that they are sons of God, not because they were circumcised, but because having been circumcised they actually believed. Of course, Paul doesn't say that about circumcision in those words. Nevertheless, that is the whole point of his letter. And what is true of circumcision, he here says is true of baptism. In the same way that faith (i.e. circumcision of the heart) completed circumcision, so also faith completes baptism and continues to complete baptism as we continue to clothe ourselves with Christ every day.[13]

But as we saw above, clothing ourselves with Christ is not only about being a son of God, it is about being Abraham's seed and heir with Christ of the promised Holy Spirit. Surprisingly, however, that is signified in baptism. Baptism signifies putting on Christ. It is not that baptism is a fulfilment of circumcision. Jesus is the fulfilment of circumcision. But baptism is the means by which we identify with Jesus as the promised descendant of Abraham through whom all God's promises come. And that baptism is completed by *actually* clothing ourselves with the one to whom baptism points.

Sometimes people ask, if baptism just replaces circumcision, why didn't the apostles say that when people misunderstood circumcision? When circumcision rose up as a point of controversy, why didn't they say, 'Don't you know that we don't need to be circumcised anymore? That's been replaced by baptism.'[14]

The answer to that question is relatively straightforward. It's because that would have simply transferred the misunderstanding from circumcision to baptism. The problem was not circumcision, per se, but the fact that people misunderstood it to be a sign of who was in and who was out. The problem was that people had

---

participation in the καινὴ κτίσις ['new creation'] (6:15), in the new humanity of Christ is granted (3:29).' (Dunn, *Baptism*, 110).

13.   Moo argues that baptism is the 'capstone' of a person coming to Christ (Moo, *Galatians*, 251). But, in fact, Paul's point is exactly the opposite. Faith is the completion of baptism!

14.   Thomas Schreiner argues exactly that in his commentary on Galatians (Thomas R. Schreiner, *Galatians*, Zondervan Exegetical Commentary on the New Testament 9 (Grand Rapids: Zondervan, 2010), 257).

failed to realise that circumcision was about pointing people to the promised seed of Abraham, Jesus Christ, and the need for personal faith in Him. Replacing one misunderstood sign with another misunderstood sign doesn't solve the problem. You can be baptised instead of circumcised until the cows come home, but if you don't meet Jesus, it's all a waste of time.[15]

That doesn't mean that baptism is unimportant. Rather, baptism is the picture of the gospel that preaches the message that if you entrust yourself to Jesus, the promised seed of Abraham, it's like putting on new clothes, such that all that belongs to Jesus now belongs to you.

Saved Along with a Better Noah

But baptism is not just a symbol of being clothed with the promised descendant of Abraham. It is also about being connected up with one who is better than Noah.

During a section of his letter encouraging his readers to endure suffering, Peter briefly launches into an explanation of baptism and a comparison with Noah and the flood.[16] Speaking about Noah's ark, Peter writes:

> God's patience waited in the days of Noah, while the ark was being prepared, in which a few, that is, eight persons, were brought safely through water. Baptism, which corresponds to this, now saves you, not as a removal of dirt from the body but as an appeal to God for a good conscience, through the resurrection of Jesus Christ, who has gone into heaven and is at the right hand of God, with angels, authorities, and powers having been subjected to him (1 Pet. 3:20b-22 ESV).

---

15. Indeed, the fact that Paul doesn't mention that baptism is a sign of personal faith that has replaced circumcision seems to be a much greater problem for the typical Baptist position. In the Baptist position, whereas circumcision was a sign that people were included in the people of God because of their family, now God's people only includes those who have faith in Jesus and baptism is a declaration of that personal faith in Jesus. In that view, saying baptism replaced circumcision would have ended the discussion.

16. The connection with suffering is that just as Noah was saved from an evil generation by the flood, so also Peter's readers will ultimately be saved from their suffering at the hands of evil people through their participation in the cleansing and renewing work of Jesus.

Peter says that the flood somehow symbolised or prefigured baptism. Just as Noah was saved by the flood, so believers are somehow saved by baptism.[17]

Strikingly, Peter says that it is baptism that 'now saves you'. But immediately he clarifies what he means by that: it is not the external washing with water that saves a person, rather, it is the thing baptism represents that saves you. Peter describes it as an 'appeal to God for a good conscience'. The resonance between Peter's language here and the language of Hebrews is striking. Just as the various 'baptisms' of the Old Testament could not cleanse the conscience but only made people outwardly clean (Heb. 9:10-14), so also the external rite of baptism only removes dirt from the body. What really matters is a 'good conscience'.[18]

We saw when we looked at Hebrews that a cleansed conscience is not about no longer feeling guilty for the past, but it is a renewed heart and mind with which we can serve God. It is the fulfilment of God's Old Testament promises to write the law on His people's hearts. That cleansed conscience comes through the work of Jesus: He gives us a new heart that can rightly discern and choose what pleases God. Similarly, for Peter, the outcome of a good conscience is not living 'the rest of their earthly lives for evil human desires, but rather for the will of God' (1 Pet. 4:2). Moreover, a good conscience comes through 'the resurrection of Jesus Christ'. It comes through the resurrection of Jesus Christ because it is through the resurrection of Jesus that 'he has given us new birth into a living hope' (1 Pet. 1:3). According to Peter, that fulfils what God had foreshadowed in the worldwide flood in the days of Noah.

As we saw in chapter 2, in the flood, God destroyed everything in the world except Noah, seven of his family members and a collection of animals. God was cleaning up the world after it had become polluted by evil and He was beginning again with Noah

---

17.   It might seem strange to us to think that Noah was saved *by* the flood rather than *from* the flood, but Peter thinks differently. The flood was the means by which God cleaned up the world and destroyed evil and gave Noah and his family a new start (D. A. Carson et al., eds., *New Bible Commentary: 21st Century Edition*, 4th ed. (Leicester: Inter-Varsity Press, 1994), 1381).

18.   Some see 'putting off the dirt of the flesh' as a reference to circumcision (the key person being William Joseph Dalton, *Christ's Proclamation to the Spirits: A Study of 1 Peter 3:18-4:6*, 2nd ed., Analecta Biblica 23 (Rome: Editrice Pontificio Istituto Biblico, 1989), 199-206), but the absence of circumcision from the rest of Peter's letter would seem to make that quite unlikely.

and his family. The problem was that simply starting again with the same old people fixed nothing. Almost as soon as they had left the ark, the family fell into sin because they were the same sinful people they had been before they entered the ark and passed through the flood. God had chosen the 'blameless' and 'righteous' Noah but he was still a man riddled with sin.[19] In the generations that followed, God promised that where Noah had failed to be the righteous and blameless beginning of a new humanity, from Abraham would come a blameless seed through whom God would save a people for Himself and start again. And the world had been waiting ever since. But Peter says that what couldn't be achieved even with Noah and a worldwide flood, has now been achieved in Jesus.

In Jesus, God has launched the flood version 2.0. Just as in the flood God cleaned up the world and began again with one man and his family, so God has begun again with one man, Jesus. But unlike with Noah, where the people remained the same old sinful people on the other side, those who trust in Jesus are decisively changed.[20] Through Jesus we're given a new conscience/heart with which to serve God. God is going to clean up evil from the world once and for all. But if we link up with Jesus, we not only come through that 'flood' unscathed, we come through as new people cleaned up by Jesus and raised with Him to a new kind of life.

An Appeal to God

But how is that related to baptism? What does baptism itself do? The NIV describes baptism as a 'pledge of a clear conscience toward God.' In that view, baptism represents our pledge to God to maintain a clear conscience.[21] The problem with that

---

19. It needs to be said that God was not caught off guard by Noah's failure. He always knew that salvation could only come through His perfect Son Jesus and not through any of us.

20. Strikingly, Noah and his son, Ham, between them, engaged in debauchery, lust and drunkenness (Gen. 9:18-27). These are the very things that Peter says Christians have been rescued from (1 Pet. 4:3).

21. This view is often linked with baptism practices found in the early centuries after the New Testament where the person being baptised would be asked whether they believed in Jesus and they would answer by expressing their trust and commitment to Jesus. But there are theological and linguistic problems with this link. My own view is that those practices arose due to a misunderstanding of the term Peter uses, influenced by the later use of the same term in the secular world for making contracts. Though we reach the opposite conclusion, I have been much helped

view is that it sees us committing to give to God what he has promised to give to us – a good conscience or a new heart.[22] It is much more likely that, as with the ESV, Peter means 'appeal' or 'petition'.[23]

In the back of Peter's mind seems to be a strange document called the Book of Enoch which is not in the Bible but was floating around in Peter's day.[24] In that book, it describes God's judgment coming on the world through the flood. Those who are going to be judged

---

in this section by Martin Williams who provided me with an unpublished section from his dissertation on 1 Peter.

22. The parallels with the language used in Hebrews of 'baptism', water and conscience, suggest that Peter is (unsurprisingly) operating from the same theological thought world as the writer of Hebrews and is speaking about the same realities here (cf. also Ezek. 36:25-27). Maurer suggests that Ps. 51:10 may lie in the background: 'Create in me a pure heart, O God, and renew a steadfast spirit within me.' Christian Maurer, 'Sunoida, Syneidēsis,' ed. Gerhard Kittel and Gerhard Friedrich, trans. Geoffrey W. Bromiley, *Theological Dictionary of the New Testament*, 10 vols. (Grand Rapids: Eerdmans, 1964-1976), 7:918-19.

23. E.g. Thomas R. Schreiner, *1, 2 Peter, Jude*, New American Commentary 37 (Nashville: Broadman & Holman, 2003), 195-97. The reason for the confusion is that the word doesn't occur anywhere else in the New Testament. It occurs a few times in the Greek translations of the Old Testament to mean 'decree' or 'oracle' (Dan. 4:17 [Theodotion]; Sir 33:3). In classical Greek, the related terms simply mean 'question' but typically in the sense of asking *about* something rather than asking *for* something (Moisés Silva, ed., 'Erōtaō, Etc,' in *New International Dictionary of New Testament Theology and Exegesis*, 5 vols., 2nd ed. (Grand Rapids: Zondervan, 2014), 2:286-89). The same is true of the related terms in the New Testament, though there are still quite a few cases where those related terms seem to mean 'appeal' (about thirty times; e.g. Matt. 15:23; 16:1; Luke 4:38; 1 Thess. 5:12; 2 Thess. 2:1; 1 John 5:16; 2 John 5). The term itself also occurs in later centuries (outside the Bible) to describe contracts and agreements (e.g. Ceslas Spicq, *Theological Lexicon of the New Testament*, ed. James D. Ernest, 3 vols. (Peabody: Hendrickson, 1994), 2:32-33). But even there the term originally referred to the request or petition that formed the basis for the contract (see John H. Elliot, *1 Peter: A New Translation with Introduction and Commentary*, Anchor Bible 37B (New York: Doubleday, 2000), 680). More significant, however, is its use in the book of Enoch, which Peter is clearly relying on (see below).

24. The Book of Enoch, or 1 Enoch, was written somewhere between 200 B.C. and A.D. 50 (Craig A. Evans, *Ancient Texts for New Testament Studies: A Guide to the Background Literature* (Grand Rapids: Baker Academic, 2011)). It was not written by Enoch but supposedly recounts events and dreams from his life. It seems to have been a well-known writing around the time of Jesus. Peter refers to it again in 2 Pet. 2:4, and Jude even quotes from it (Jude 14-15). But although some New Testament authors make use of it, it was never considered to be part of the Bible. When Peter and Jude refer to 1 Enoch, they seem to do so in order to connect with the thought-world of their readers.

ask Enoch (a righteous man) to petition God on their behalf and on behalf of their children. The word that Enoch uses to describe that petition is closely related to the one that Peter uses.[25] Enoch says:

> And they asked that I write a memorandum of *petition* for them, that they might have forgiveness, and that I recite the memorandum of *petition* for them in the presence of the Lord of heaven. For they were no longer able to speak or to lift their eyes to heaven out of shame for the deeds through which they had sinned and for which they had been condemned. Then I wrote out the memorandum of their *petition*, and the requests concerning themselves, with regard to their deeds individually, and concerning <their sons> for whom they were making request, that they might have forgiveness and longevity (1 Enoch 13:4-6).[26]

But God's answer is final: He will not listen.

Peter is clearly not endorsing the account that book gives of those events. For instance, in contrast to the Book of Enoch, Peter sees humanity rather than angelic beings as the core problem. It is human beings who are unrighteous and need to be saved.[27] Nevertheless, Peter is riffing on those events. His point is that whereas in that story Enoch's supposed intercession failed, in the case of Jesus it works. Whereas in the days of Noah the unrighteous were condemned and only Noah and his family were saved, now Jesus has died, 'the righteous for the unrighteous, to bring you to God' (1 Pet. 3:18). What Enoch failed to achieve in that myth, God has really and truly done in Jesus. Where even 'righteous' Enoch and 'righteous' Noah failed, Jesus has succeeded, since He now stands at the Father's right hand to present our petitions to God. Unlike in the days of Noah where only a handful of people

---

25. The term Peter uses (*eperōtēma*) is a compound form based on the same stem as the term found in Enoch (*erōtēsis*). But both generally mean the same thing. See Silva, 'Erōtaō, Etc,' 2:287. Each occurrence of that term in the book of Enoch book means 'petition' or 'request' to God (1 Enoch 10:10; 13:2, 4, 6; 14:4, 7; 15:2; 16:2).

26. George W. E. Nickelsburg, *1 Enoch 1: A Commentary on the Book of 1 Enoch, Chapters 1-35, 81-108*, ed. Klaus Baltzer, Hermeneia (Minneapolis: Fortress, 2001), 237.

27. See also 2 Pet. 2:4-10, where Peter again uses the Book of Enoch to make a point about corrupt humanity.

were saved, now everyone who calls out to God through Jesus will be saved.

Baptism as a petition or appeal to God can be found in other places too.[28] For instance, in Acts 22:16, Paul recounts how a man named Ananias had said to him:

> And now what are you waiting for? Get up, be baptized and wash your sins away, calling on his name (Acts 22:16).

Significantly, Ananias links baptism with the metaphor of washing. Baptism is a picture of washing away sins. But he clearly also sees that it is not baptism itself that achieves the washing away of sins. It is 'calling on his name' that achieves that.

Baptism is a symbol of God cleaning up the world and beginning again with His blameless and righteous Son, the man, Jesus Christ. But baptism is more than just a sign, it is also the means by which we appeal to God to participate in all that God has achieved in Jesus.

Buried with the Messiah

Baptism offers us the hope of better clothes and coming through a flood into a new cleaned-up world as new people with a better Noah. But it also offers the hope of death, burial and resurrection. In Romans 6, Paul writes:

> What shall we say, then? Shall we go on sinning so that grace may increase? By no means! We are those who have died to sin; how can we live in it any longer? Or don't you know that all of us who were baptized into Christ Jesus were baptized into his death? We were therefore buried with him through baptism into death in order that, just as Christ was raised from the dead through the glory of the Father, we too may live a new life.

---

28. Regarding Peter's words in Acts 2:38, 'Repent and be baptized, every one of you, in the name of Jesus Christ for the forgiveness of your sins. And you will receive the gift of the Holy Spirit,' David Peterson writes: 'The expression "gift of the Spirit" recalls Jesus' promise to those who pray (Luke 11:13; cf. Acts 8:20; 10:45; 11:17). Christian baptism can be regarded as a means of prayer to God for the gift of the Spirit.' Nevertheless, 'the link cannot be pressed too strongly since the gift of the Spirit sometimes precedes and sometimes follows baptism in other contexts (cf. 8:12, 14-17; 9:17-18; 10:44-48; 19:5-6).' (David G. Peterson, *Transformed by God: New Covenant Life and Ministry* (Nottingham: Inter-Varsity, 2012), 63).

> For if we have been united with him in a death like his,
> we will certainly also be united with him in a resurrection
> like his. For we know that our old self was crucified with
> him so that the body ruled by sin might be done away with,
> that we should no longer be slaves to sin – because anyone
> who has died has been set free from sin (Rom. 6:1-7).

So far in Romans, Paul has been explaining the gospel: that salvation is not based on what we do but is by grace through faith in Christ Jesus. In chapter 5, he has explained how just as Adam's sin brought condemnation, Jesus' death has brought reconciliation and justification (Rom. 5:10) because the condemnation of our sin has been taken by Jesus.

But if Jesus has suffered the condemnation meant for us and we're no longer guilty in God's eyes, then what's to stop anyone just living how they want? Why not go on sinning, given we already have a blank cheque for God's forgiveness? That's the question Paul goes on to answer. And he answers it by talking about baptism.

Paul asks the Roman Christians whether they realise that baptism symbolises more than just linking up with the objective facts of what Jesus has done *for* us but also symbolises our participation *in* those things for ourselves. In particular, it symbolises participation in Jesus' death. Paul says:

> Or don't you know that all of us who were baptized into
> Christ Jesus were baptized into his death? (Rom. 6:3).

Paul does not mean that baptism itself unites us with Jesus. He only mentions baptism once in the whole of his letter to the Roman Christians (here in this passage). Everywhere else in his letters it is faith that unites us to Jesus. The gospel reveals a righteousness that is 'by faith' (Rom. 1:17).[29]

Moreover, his question is not about the simple fact of their baptism. He doesn't say, 'Don't you realise you were baptised?' He says, 'Don't you realise you were baptised *into his death*?' [emphasis added]. His question is driving at whether they recognise that baptism points to more than just linking up with Jesus but also points to linking up specifically with His death. Or in other words, 'Don't you realise the message of baptism includes baptism into

---

29. E.g. Douglas J. Moo, *The Epistle to the Romans*, New International Commentary on the New Testament (Grand Rapids: Eerdmans, 1996), 366.

Jesus' death?' Or even, 'Don't you realise that being washed in Jesus means being washed in His death?'

The fact that Paul is focussed on the meaning rather than the mere fact of their baptism is seen in how he goes on to apply the truth of baptism to their lives. Baptism does not change them automatically, but rather they need to live a life consistent with the meaning of baptism. They are to count themselves 'dead to sin but alive to God in Christ Jesus' (Rom. 6:11). The logic works like this: baptism signifies linking up with Jesus in His death, and so for that reason count yourself as dead to sin. Baptism also signifies linking up with Jesus in His resurrection, and so consider yourself alive to God. It is not the *fact* of baptism that will change their life, but a proper understanding of its *meaning*.[30]

The Shampoo of Death

Behind Paul's words here are all those Old Testament cleansing ceremonies that involved, not only sacrifice *on behalf of the people* to ransom them from the consequences of their sin, but the application of water to the person themselves; and not only water, but water mixed with death in the form of either blood or ashes.

Perhaps the most enigmatic example of that is the one found in Numbers 19. There, God gives the people a procedure to go through if they come into contact with human death, such as a dead body or a human bone. For starters, a spotless red heifer was to be sacrificed. Unusually, though, it was to be done 'outside the camp' (Num. 19:3). Its body was then to be burned and the ashes gathered up and stored outside the camp. When a person came into contact with human death, they would gather some of the ashes into a jar, mix them with water, then take some hyssop and sprinkle everything that had come into contact with death – the people, and in the case where someone had died in a tent, all the things that were in the tent.

Again, like with the other cleansing ceremonies, the idea is that death is a contagion. It is the ultimate contagion. But what makes this cleansing ceremony so puzzling is that the remedy to contact with death is more contact with death! They are sprinkled with the ashes of the heifer.

---

30. As in Galatians, it is not that their baptism encapsulates what they have already believed, but baptism represents that truth which they must believe and must continue to believe and live out.

The ceremony of Numbers 19 (and other cleansing ceremonies that mix blood/death with water) showed that the remedy to the contagion of sin that leads to death is actually death itself. The ashes and the blood were a kind of Old Testament shampoo that showed that death itself must cleanse us from what pollutes us. But how do you come into contact with death safely? The ceremony of Numbers 19 and other cleansing rituals foreshadowed the way. Somehow, through the death of a substitute, there could be not only forgiveness for what we've done, but we can come into contact with that death in such a way that we are also cleansed from what pollutes us.

Paul says that the fulfilment of all those ideas is found in Jesus' own death. In Romans 5, Paul has laid out how the contagion of sin has led to the spread of death. And now in Romans 6, he points out the remedy to that is not only atonement (e.g. Rom. 5:9), but also cleansing through sharing in Jesus' death. His death was not only on our behalf to ransom us from the guilt of our sin. His death is also something that we are joined up with experientially so that we are cleansed from the pollution of sin that leads to death.

It seems that some people in the Roman church had understood the basic idea that baptism symbolised identification with Jesus as God's Messiah, but they hadn't completely understood how comprehensive that was. But Paul says that being united with Jesus by faith means not only that His death atoned for our sins and we have been reconciled to God, it also means being 'buried with him', 'united with him in a death like his', 'crucified with him' and 'united with him in a resurrection like his'. His death and resurrection not only create a new legal reality – we are free from condemnation (Rom. 8:1); it also creates a new us – our 'old self' was 'crucified with him so that the body ruled by sin might be done away with, that we should no longer be slaves to sin' (Rom. 6:6). Believers are united with Jesus in everything that He has achieved for them. It is not just that Jesus died in our place, but that we died with Him. It is not only that He was buried, but that we were buried with Him. It is not simply that He was raised, but that we are raised with Him. His work is not only *for us*, it is *in us* and it fundamentally changes and reconstitutes us. And that work in us comes through the promised Holy Spirit.

The kind of cleansing that baptism symbolises involves nothing less than wholesale death and resurrection. This is not a minor mopping up operation but a complete destruction of the old and a recreation of the new, as in the flood. That recreation comes through the Holy Spirit uniting us with the person of Jesus, especially in His powerful death and resurrection.

Misunderstanding what baptism symbolises radically undermines the gospel. If baptism merely symbolises connecting up with Jesus and His atoning death in our place then the gospel simply becomes, 'Jesus died for my sins, and I can go on living however I like.' But baptism communicates more than that. It communicates that Jesus came not only so that we could be forgiven but so that we could be freed from the power and presence of sin. Day by day, through the Holy Spirit, Jesus' powerful death for sins is destroying the sin that remains in us and His powerful resurrection is bringing us to life.

That means we can't just go on living as we were before. We can't go on as before, not only because to go on giving ourselves to sin would deny all that Jesus had done for us, but, more to the point, because Jesus' death and life are at work in us, changing us. And if we're united to Him, we can't avoid that.

That doesn't mean we suddenly become perfect. As Paul goes on to explain in Romans 7 and 8, as long as our unrenewed bodies remain, we are caught in a battle with sin and we groan waiting for the children of God to be revealed (Rom. 8:19). But, in Jesus, we are not condemned by the existence of that battle. We are justified. We are right with God despite the ongoing battle with sin. And if the Spirit of God lives in us then we will keep fighting that battle and keep putting to death the misdeeds of the body until the day comes when our bodies too are renewed in the image of Jesus Christ. As Paul says in Romans 8:

> But if Christ is in you, then even though your body is subject to death because of sin, the Spirit gives life because of righteousness. And if the Spirit of him who raised Jesus from the dead is living in you, he who raised Christ from the dead will also give life to your mortal bodies because of his Spirit who lives in you (Rom. 8:10-11).

Circumcised with the Circumcision of Jesus

So baptism is about being cleaned up by Jesus through the promised Holy Spirit. It's about being clothed in Jesus, brought safely through the flood with Jesus, and being buried and raised with Jesus. But most weirdly of all, it's about being circumcised with the circumcision of Jesus. What's all that about? Washing makes sense. Being clothed makes sense. So does being buried. But circumcised with Jesus' circumcision! What's going on there?[31]

Throughout Colossians, Paul is encouraging the Colossian church to remain faithful to the gospel. It turns out that the Colossians, like the Galatians, were starting to look to other things to try to grow in the Christian life. In 2:16-23 Paul writes:

> Therefore do not let anyone judge you by what you eat or drink, or with regard to a religious festival, a New Moon celebration or a Sabbath day. These are a shadow of the things that were to come; the reality, however, is found in Christ. Do not let anyone who delights in false humility and the worship of angels disqualify you. Such a person also goes into great detail about what they have seen; they are puffed up with idle notions by their unspiritual mind. They have lost connection with the head, from whom the whole body, supported and held together by its ligaments and sinews, grows as God causes it to grow.
>
> Since you died with Christ to the elemental spiritual forces of this world, why, as though you still belonged to the world, do you submit to its rules: 'Do not handle! Do not taste! Do not touch!'? These rules, which have to do with things that are all destined to perish with use, are based on merely human commands and teachings. Such regulations indeed have an appearance of wisdom, with their self-imposed worship, their false humility and their harsh treatment of the body, but they lack any value in restraining sensual indulgence (Col. 2:16-23).

Paul wants the Colossians to know that these rituals and rules don't help them grow and continue in the Christian life. The way you continue is the way that you begin. Earlier he writes:

---

31. See Deenick, *Righteous by Promise*, 130-38.

> So then, just as you received Christ Jesus as Lord, continue to live your lives in him ... (Col. 2:6).

In other words, you don't simply begin the Christian life with Jesus and then move onto other things. You continue in the Christian life through Jesus too.

Strangely, however, Paul goes on to justify that by talking about circumcision. In verse 9, he says:

> For **in him** the whole fullness of deity dwells bodily,
>   And **in him** you have been filled, who is the head of all rule and authority.
>   **In whom** also you were circumcised with a circumcision made without hands, by putting off the body of the flesh, by the circumcision of Christ, having been buried with him in baptism.
>   **In whom** you were also raised with him through faith in the powerful working of God, who raised him from the dead (Col. 2:9-12).[32]

It may not be immediately obvious to us why Paul brings up circumcision, but what is clear is that Paul wants the Colossians to understand that everything they have, they have *in Christ*. In verses 9-12, he uses four phrases that all begin with 'in him' or in 'whom'.[33] He also uses a number of expressions that speak about sharing in something *with Christ* – they have been 'buried with him' (2:12), 'raised with him' (2:12), and 'made alive together with him' (2:13).

The Circumcision of Christ

But what have they received *in Christ*? In the first place, they have been filled. The fullness of God's deity dwells in God the Son and because believers have been joined with Christ (by the Holy Spirit)[34] they somehow share in that. It's not that we become divine, but the

---

32. I have modified the ESV here.

33. Mysteriously, many translations (and some scholars) ignore the parallelism between these phrases and translate the last 'in whom' as 'in which' – referring to baptism, rather than to Jesus. But given the clear parallelism that seems very strange. Moreover, throughout this whole section Paul is chiefly concerned with what the Colossians have *in Christ*. The section is filled with 'in him' and 'with him' expressions, as noted above. For more, see Deenick, *Righteous by Promise*, 130-31.

34. Although Paul does not make the Spirit's role explicit here.

fullness of who Christ is changes us – we live in Him and are rooted and built up in Him (Col. 2:6-7).[35]

In the second place, they have been circumcised and they have been raised from the dead. But what does it mean that they have been 'circumcised with a circumcision made without hands'? Paul explains with the two following phrases: they have been 'circumcised ... *by* putting off the body of the flesh' and '*by* the circumcision of Christ.'

When Paul speaks about 'putting off the body of the flesh' he is not merely referring to our physical bodies, but to our physical bodies as symptomatic of our existence in a fallen world that is distorted and marred by sin.[36] In verse 13, he links being 'dead in your sins' with the 'uncircumcision of your flesh':

> When you were dead in your sins and in the uncircumcision of your flesh, God made you alive with Christ (Col. 2:13).

By the 'uncircumcision of your flesh', Paul does not so much mean that because the Colossians were Gentiles they were physically uncircumcised (though that is certainly part of what he means). Rather, to be 'uncircumcised in your flesh' is roughly equivalent to being 'dead in your sins'. Apart from Christ and apart from the promise of Christ, the Colossians were dead in sin – corrupted in their very being and unable to rescue themselves. Similarly, a few verses later Pauls speaks about 'the indulgence of the flesh' (2:23 ESV). He clearly has in view the flesh as a source of corruption and sin.

In the next chapter, Paul also picks up on the same language of 'putting off'. He says:

> Do not lie to each other, since you have *taken off* your old self with its practices and have *put on* the new self, which is being renewed in knowledge in the image of its Creator (Col. 3:9-10) [emphasis added].

---

35. David W. Pao, *Colossians and Philemon*, Zondervan Exegetical Commentary on the New Testament 12 (Grand Rapids: Zondervan, 2012), 163.

36. In fact, our physical bodies and our existence in this sinful world are obviously inseparable. When Paul explains the resurrection in 1 Corinthians 15, he points out that this corruptible and mortal body which we inhabit must be transformed in order for us to participate in the new creation.

Paul wants the Colossians to realise that in Christ they have 'put off' the body of death, or the old self, and have 'put on the new self' – the new life in the image of Christ.

What is required is nothing less than a complete transformation. It is not just a part of us that needs to be destroyed and remade but all of us. Sin is not like a tumour that can be cut out, leaving the rest of us intact. Sin is more like a genetic defect that is replicated in every strand of our DNA and that cannot be removed without us being fundamentally reconstructed. Sin is so deeply wedded into us that it cannot be removed without the removal of the whole 'self' and putting on a new 'self' – a new self in the image of Jesus. It is not that we lose our identity in that process, but rather our very selves need to be completely transformed to be free from sin and evil.

But how has God achieved this 'putting off the body of the flesh'? Earlier in Colossians Paul writes:

> And you, who once were alienated and hostile in mind, doing evil deeds, he has now reconciled in *his body of flesh* by his death, in order to present you holy and blameless and above reproach before him ... (Col. 1:21-22 ESV) [emphasis added].

Paul says that the alienation, hostility and evil deeds that pervaded the Colossians have been dealt with through Jesus putting off His body of flesh in His death. The goal of Christ's death was both reconciliation (the restoration of our relationship with God) and also blamelessness. But remember that blamelessness is the promise and goal of circumcision. Paul now says that the goal and promise of circumcision is fulfilled in Jesus. Jesus will present them blameless at the last day. The means by which He will do that is through the reconciliation He has achieved in '*his* body of flesh'.

Paul is using different language here to describe the same transformation that he mentions later when refers to the Colossians 'putting off the old self' and 'putting on the new'. But the key point is that *their* putting off the body of flesh has come through Jesus putting off *His* body of flesh. The Colossians share in all that Jesus has done. They share in His death – they have been buried with Him. They share in His life – they have been raised with Him and have been made alive with Him. They have been reconciled through His death and one day He will present them blameless before His Father.[37]

In other words, the Colossians have received all that circumcision foreshadowed and promised. They have received it by receiving Christ, the promised seed to whom circumcision pointed. That is the circumcision they have received. That is the circumcision of Christ. It is the receipt of the realities to which circumcision had always pointed through Jesus' own death and resurrection. The Colossians have put off their sinful humanity and identity through Jesus crucifying His humanity in their place and they have put on a new blameless humanity and identity in Jesus through sharing in His resurrection from the dead. It is, as Paul says in Galatians, that because they belong to Christ, 'you are Abraham's seed, and heirs according to the promise' (Gal. 3:29). Paul's apparently strange introduction of circumcision into his argument here makes perfect sense.

Paul wanted the Colossians to understand that if nothing less is required than the end of our old self and the start of a new self, it is sheer folly to look for that in rituals and commandments. The only place it can be found is in the person and work of Jesus – Abraham's promised descendant.

Our desire to find new kinds of rituals to 'enhance' our Christian life seems to know no bounds. Often it stems from a desire to feel like we're really doing something or to give us a tangible sense that we're growing. But no amount of sins written down on a piece of paper and symbolically buried in the earth will reconcile you with God. No candle-lighting ritual will remake you in the image of Christ. No amount of furious flag waving will energise you to live for Christ. And no amount of well-meaning rules and regulations you devise to keep you from sin will make you a new person. In fact, not even baptism itself (even though it's important) can kill sin and make you a new person. The only thing that can kill off your old self and make you a new person is being united with Jesus.

For sure, there are useful rules that we can set for ourselves that help guard us against sin and there are practices given by God, like

---

37. Or as Paul says in Col. 2:13-15, having been forgiven, they have been made alive with Christ. This new life comes about because God has forgiven all that we have done against Him and has cancelled the debt that stood against us because of our sin. He did that through the cross. The curse meant for us, the curse demanded by God's own justice and made plain in the Old Testament law, was taken by Jesus so that being completely and utterly forgiven we might be made alive together with Him.

meeting together, singing, prayer and hearing God's Word, that energise us and spur us on in the Christian life. But when those become detached from the person and work of Jesus Christ, they become empty rules and rituals. What we need is not new rules, but Jesus. We need to ask God that we would know Jesus more, love Him more and that we would no longer live but that He would live in us.

Connecting Baptism and Circumcision

But what is the connection then between circumcision and baptism? Although when we first meet baptism it's not clear how it could possibly relate to circumcision, we've seen through the last two chapters that the two are often linked. John the Baptist links them, Paul links them in Galatians, and here in Colossians Paul links them most clearly of all. As I said before, the question is not *whether* there is a connection. There quite obviously is a connection of some sort. Rather the question is what the *nature* of the connection is.

Paul says that all this circumcision stuff has occurred 'having been buried with him in baptism'. It could be that Paul is thinking of baptism as symbolising burial. I'll address that idea a bit more fully in chapter 8. But as I've tried to show when we looked at Romans, it makes much more sense to understand that baptism identifies with a death rather than symbolises death itself. Baptism does not reflect death per se, it reflects the cleansing that comes through identifying with an already achieved death. In that way, baptism is about the very thing that runs all the way through this passage in Colossians – Christ. It is about identification with Jesus – identification with His death, but also identification with His resurrection, with His divine fullness, and with every other aspect of His person and work. But more than that, it is about identification with Jesus as the fulfilment of the promise signified in circumcision.

Now that Jesus has come, those who have received Him have been joined with all that was promised in circumcision and that Jesus has finally accomplished. That is, they have been circumcised with a circumcision made without hands. They now share in all that God had promised through Abraham's seed. So if you've linked up with Jesus by faith, then you're united with Him by the Holy Spirit, and, though you may not know it, you're circumcised! Circumcised in the sense that you've received and are receiving all that God promised through Abraham's descendant. It is not only that your heart has been circumcised; that is, you believe the promise and wait expectantly in humble repentance and faith. Rather, your whole being has been circumcised – in Christ, you have now received (and are continuing to receive) the forgiveness and renewal that God had promised would come through Abraham's seed.

The link with circumcision, then, is quite natural. Circumcision was the sign of a community of people gathered around the promised seed of Abraham who was to come, while baptism is the sign of a community gathered around a Messiah who has come. Baptism points to the same reality as circumcision but from the other direction. The seed has come, and baptism now looks back to Jesus, the long-awaited Messiah.[38]

The connection between baptism and circumcision, then, is not that one pictures the old covenant and the other pictures the new. Not really. They both point to the gospel of Jesus Christ. Nor is the idea that baptism is the fulfilment of circumcision.[39] Christ is the fulfilment of circumcision, and both circumcision and baptism point to Christ, though from different directions. The connection and distinction between circumcision and baptism is that circumcision looked expectantly forward to the coming of Jesus, while baptism looks back to the Jesus who has fulfilled all that God has promised.

The Meaning of Baptism

When people think of baptism, they often think covenant, or death and resurrection, or maybe profession of faith. But that's not the main way that baptism language is deployed in the New Testament. In fact, baptism has a great Old Testament pedigree both in cleansing and circumcision. Baptism is a sign of the cleansing that God promised in the Old Testament which has now been fulfilled

---

38. As John Calvin wrote, 'the former foreshadowed Christ promised while he was as yet awaited; the latter attest him as already given and revealed' (Calvin, *Institutes*, 4.14.20).

39. As John Meade rightly points out (Meade, 'Circumcision of the Flesh,' 153). However, Meade, in my view, has misunderstood circumcision and heart circumcision and hence their relationship to baptism. Circumcision is not a *type* of heart circumcision. Circumcision is the sign of a promise that finds its fulfilment in Jesus. Heart circumcision is a *metaphor* used to describe accepting that promise in one's heart. In other words, the relationship is not one of type and anti-type but, for physical circumcision, of sign and reality (that is, circumcision did not foreshadow the thing to which it pointed in the same way that, say, King David foreshadowed King Jesus), and then, for circumcision of the heart, of sign and metaphor.

in the promised descendant of Abraham, Jesus Christ. When John the Baptist began his ministry of baptism, he was indicating that God's promise was about to become a reality in Jesus, the one who would wash people with the Holy Spirit but also with fire.

In other words, baptism is chiefly about Jesus. Just as circumcision looked ahead to the Messiah who was to come, baptism looks back to the Messiah who has come.[40] Just as circumcision was a sign of expectation of the promised seed of Abraham, baptism is a sign that God has finally acted in the person and work of Jesus Christ.

But baptism is not only about Jesus, it's also about our need to identify with Him and take hold of Him. It's about our need to put on Jesus, by faith, like we put on a pair of new clothes. It's about our need to link up with the One better than Noah and appeal to God that we might participate in all that He has achieved in the life, death and resurrection of Jesus. But baptism also affirms God's promise that if we do connect up with Jesus by faith, then God really will rescue us from our sin and clean us up to be like Jesus.

Just like when you work in the garden and get filthy, you need a shower before you can come inside. In the same way, you and I are dirty because of the sin that lives in us and we need to be cleaned up. But we need something that goes deeper than just the outside. God offers us that in Jesus. He offers us forgiveness and cleansing through the Spirit who comes to us through Jesus' death and resurrection. That need and that provision is what baptism signifies.

---

40. Zacharias Ursinus, for instance, also makes this point: 'Circumcision promised grace on account of the Messiah which was to come; baptism on account of the Messiah already come.' (Zacharias Ursinus, *The Commentary of Dr Zacharias Ursinus on the Heidelberg Catechism*, trans. G. W. Williard, 4th ed. (Cincinnati: Elm Street, 1888), 376).

7. Who Should be Baptised?

I started this book by saying that baptism is about far more than who should be baptised and how. I've tried to show over the last few chapters that baptism is a picture of the gospel – that God is making a blameless and holy people for Himself through the promised Messiah, Jesus. Just as circumcision looked forward to the Messiah through whom God would make for Himself a blameless people, baptism looks back to the Messiah who has come, Jesus Christ.

To my mind that is the most important thing to say about baptism. Nevertheless, that still doesn't tell us who should be baptised. Should it be the babies of those in the Christian community or should it only be believing adults? Nor does it tell us what the sign should look like – sprinkling or immersion? Those are still important questions, even simply at a practical level, although Christians disagree about the answers.

But before we get to that, it's helpful to put on the table that what I'm about to say you may very well disagree with. To be honest, I really wish that wasn't the case. I wish that I could convince you. After all, I think what I'm about to outline is sensible and persuasive. To my mind it is the best reconstruction of the biblical evidence. But having thought about this for a long time and talked about it with lots of people, I'm not silly enough (anymore!) to think that it will persuade everyone, least of all rusted-on supporters of *either* position.

At one level I can live with that. There are numerous people I respect immensely who love Jesus but who don't share my view. And that's okay because what matters most is that baptism is about

Jesus and connecting up with Him. It's trusting in Him that saves you, not baptism itself. You might have all the boxes ticked in your arguments for the who and how of baptism, but if you haven't linked up with Jesus by entrusting yourself to Him then it's all for nothing.

That said, in this chapter we'll be looking at the 'who' question, since that's probably the most difficult. I'll start by laying out two of the most common positions before explaining my own view. Then in the next chapter we'll think about the 'how' of baptism.

The Two Main Options for Who

In beginning to think about who should be baptised, it helps to lay out what the options are and to try to understand the arguments for why people hold the position they do. Obviously, the amount written on all sides, defending what they think, is enormous. So, summarising it all is nearly impossible. Instead, the aim is to sketch out what the two key sides of the debate argue. I will use the descriptions given by two common theology books. For the believer's baptism view, I'll refer to Wayne Grudem.[1] He seems a good choice because his textbook on theology is a bestseller and lots of people have probably come across it or will come across it at some point. For the infant baptism view, I'll refer to Louis Berkhof.[2] His book, though much older than Grudem's, is also a classic. It's a sensible choice because he's the person with whom Grudem chiefly interacts. Although throughout this chapter I'll refer to the 'believer's baptism' side and the 'infant baptism' side, I am not claiming to describe every view on these two sides. Rather, I am dealing with representative views based largely on those two books.[3]

Believer's Baptism

The Baptist or 'believer's baptism' view[4] is that:

1. Wayne Grudem, *Systematic Theology: An Introduction to Biblical Doctrine* (Grand Rapids: Zondervan, 2004).

2. Louis Berkhof, *Systematic Theology* (Edinburgh: Banner of Truth, 1958).

3. Two helpful books for understanding some of the key views are David F. Wright, ed., *Baptism: Three Views* (Downers Grove: InterVarsity, 2009) and John H. Armstrong and Paul E. Engle, eds., *Understanding Four Views on Baptism*, Counterpoints (Grand Rapids: Zondervan, 2007).

4. Sometimes also called the 'credo-baptist' view. The term 'credo' comes from Latin and means 'to believe'.

only those who have themselves believed in Christ (or, more precisely, those who have given reasonable evidence of believing in Christ) should be baptized. This is because baptism, which is a *symbol of beginning the Christian life* should only be given to those who have *in fact* begun the Christian life[5] [emphasis added].

One of the reasons for this view is that many of the New Testament accounts of baptism seem to refer to people who have believed the message about Jesus.[6] There are numerous examples in the book of Acts:

> *Those who accepted his message* were baptized, and about three thousand were added to their number that day (Acts 2:41) [emphasis added].
>
> *But when they believed Philip* as he proclaimed the good news of the kingdom of God and the name of Jesus Christ, they were baptized, both men and women (Acts 8:12) [emphasis added].
>
> While Peter was still speaking these words, the Holy Spirit came *on all who heard the message*. ... Then Peter said, 'Surely no one can stand in the way of their being baptized with water. They have received the Holy Spirit just as we have' (Acts 10:44-48) [emphasis added].
>
> One of those listening was a woman from the city of Thyatira named Lydia, a dealer in purple cloth. She was a worshiper of God. *The Lord opened her heart to respond to Paul's message.* When she and the members of her household were baptized, she invited us to her home (Acts 16:14-15) [emphasis added].
>
> Then they spoke the word of the Lord to him and to all the others in his house. ... [T]hen immediately he and all his household were baptized. The jailer brought them into his house and set a meal before them; he was filled with joy because *he had come to believe in God* – he and his whole household (Acts 16:32-34) [emphasis added].

Not only so, but the New Testament also gives no irrefutable evidence (it is argued) that infants were ever baptised.[7]

---

5. Grudem, *Theology*, 969-70 (emphasis original).

6. We saw too in the previous chapter that John's baptism ministry was also connected with the call to repentance and faith.

7. Grudem writes, 'of all the examples of 'household baptisms' in the New Testament, the only one that does not have some indication of household faith as well

The second reason relates to the apparent certainty of some of the statements regarding those who had received baptism. So, Paul says:

> for *all of you* who were baptized into Christ have clothed yourselves with Christ (Gal. 3:27) [emphasis added].
>
> Or don't you know that *all of us* who were baptized into Christ Jesus were baptized into his death? (Rom. 6:3) [emphasis added].
>
> having been buried with him in baptism, in [whom] you were also raised with him through your faith in the working of God, who raised him from the dead (Col. 2:12).

These passages seem to assume that those who have been baptised have also experienced some kind of spiritual reality. While Grudem concedes that some infants may be regenerate or born again, he thinks it is unreasonable to say that all of those who have been baptised have been buried with Christ in baptism.[8] Thus, if you baptise infants, instead of baptism symbolising that 'inward regeneration has occurred', at best it symbolises a 'probable [or really only a possible] future regeneration'. Driving the point home, Grudem says:

> The New Testament never views baptism as something that symbolizes a probable future regeneration. The New Testament authors do not say, 'Can anyone forbid water for baptizing those who will probably someday be saved?' (cf. Acts 10:47), or, 'As many of you as were baptized into Christ will probably someday put on Christ' (cf. Gal. 3:27), or 'Do you not know that all of us who have been baptized into Christ Jesus will probably someday be baptized into his death?' (cf. Rom. 6:3). This is simply not the way the New Testament speaks of baptism.[9]

On the surface, these observations seem quite persuasive. But there are some hidden problems.

---

is Acts 16:14-15 .... The text simply does not contain any information about whether there were infants in her household or not. It is ambiguous and certainly not weighty evidence for infant baptism. It must be considered inconclusive in itself.' (Grudem, *Theology*, 978). Many would also argue that historical evidence suggests that the baptism of infants was a late development, occurring in the centuries after the New Testament. See, for example, Ferguson, *Baptism*, 856-57.

8. Grudem, *Theology*, 971.

9. Grudem, *Theology*, 979.

In the first place, the pattern of baptism in Acts may not be as clear cut as it seems. The most troubling example is that of Lydia (Acts 16). She was the one listening to Paul in the marketplace. She was the one whose heart the Lord opened to receive the message. The passage only tells us about Lydia's faith: God opened her heart and she invited the apostles saying, 'if you consider me [not us] a believer' (Acts 16:15). And yet, her whole household was baptised. A household was not simply the immediate family. Her household would have included slaves and servants and possibly children (if she had any, but we can't say whether she did or not).

But that raises even more challenging questions, because we're not just talking about children but slaves and servants too. How are they swept up in the faith of their master? Lydia hears the gospel and it has ramifications for her whole working household. That has implications, not simply for those who hold to believer's baptism, but for those who hold to infant baptism too. We'll come to that a bit later.

Second, the absolute statements about those who have been baptised cause problems for those who only baptise believers as much as they do for those who baptise children. That is, even when an adult is baptised after a profession of faith, all we can ever really say is, 'This is a symbol of a probable regeneration.' Or, 'Can anyone stand in the way of their being baptised with water? They have probably received the Holy Spirit just as we have.' Or, 'As many of you as were baptised have probably put on Christ'. Or, 'Do you not know that all of us who have been baptised into Christ Jesus have probably been baptised into His death?' We cannot ever know for sure whether that person has truly been born again and sealed by the Holy Spirit.[10] As we saw in the last chapter, the absolute statements about baptism found in the New Testament are not about the effect of baptism in and of itself but how baptism symbolises identification with Christ. They are about what baptism

---

10. Some people would reject that assertion, not least the Catholic Church. It holds that a person is regenerated by the act of baptism itself. The Catholic Catechism states, 'This sacrament is also called "the washing of regeneration and renewal by the Holy Spirit," for it signifies *and actually brings about* the birth of water and the Spirit without which no one "can enter the kingdom of God."' (see http://www.vatican.va/archive/ENG0015/__P3H.HTM [emphasis added]). But that gives a significance to baptism that the New Testament simply does not appear to give. For more detail, see Grudem, *Theology*, 971-75.

means rather than what it achieves. Those realities signified in baptism only come to fruition when a person takes hold in their heart of Christ Himself.[11]

So while believer's baptism superficially seems like the most straightforward option, I'm not convinced it makes the most sense of the biblical material.

Infant Baptism

As with believer's baptism, the reasons that people hold to infant baptism are various. But perhaps the most prominent and the most vigorously defended is what is described as the 'covenantal infant baptism' view.[12]

At the heart of the covenantal infant baptism view is the idea that there is essentially one 'covenant of grace' and so one mode in which God operates in both Old and New Testaments. There is the same mediator – Jesus (1 Tim. 2:5); the same condition – faith (Gen. 15:6; Rom. 4:3); and the same blessings – justification, regeneration and eternal life.[13] Although there are two different signs (circumcision in the Old Testament and baptism in the New Testament), they represent the same spiritual realities – in this view, 'the cutting [or washing] away of sin and a change of heart'.[14] The conclusion drawn from that essential unity is that if children were 'part of the covenant' and received the sign of the covenant in the Old Testament (i.e. circumcision) they should receive the sign in the New Testament also (i.e. baptism).[15]

In addition to seeing the underlying unity between the Old Testament and the New Testament, the covenantal infant baptism view also highlights God's continuing interest in children across both Testaments. Certainly, God's covenant with Abraham included blessings for children:

---

11. See especially the discussions in the last chapter on Galatians 3 and 1 Peter 3.

12. This view is held in Presbyterian and Reformed denominations especially, but not exclusively. The Anglican Michael Green, for instance, advocated this view in Michael Green, *Baptism: Its Purpose, Practice and Power* (1987; reprint, Oxford: Monarch, 2017).

13. Berkhof, *Systematic Theology*, 633.

14. Berkhof, *Systematic Theology*, 634.

15. See, for instance, Berkhof, *Systematic Theology*, 632-34 or Michael Horton, *The Christian Faith: A Systematic Theology for Pilgrims on the Way* (Grand Rapids: Zondervan, 2011), 794-98.

> *... to you and your descendants* I will give all these
> lands and will confirm the oath I swore to your father
> Abraham. I will make your descendants as numerous as
> the stars in the sky and will give them all these lands,
> and through your offspring all nations on earth will be
> blessed ... (Gen. 26:3-4) [emphasis added].

And throughout the Old Testament children formed part of the
spiritual life of the community:[16]

> These are the commands, decrees and laws the LORD your
> God directed me to teach you to observe in the land that
> you are crossing the Jordan to possess, so that *you, your
> children and their children after them* may fear the LORD
> your God as long as you live by keeping all his decrees and
> commands that I give you, and so that you may enjoy long
> life (Deut. 6:1-2) [emphasis added].
>
> These commandments that I give you today are to be
> on your hearts. *Impress them on your children.* Talk about
> them when you sit at home and when you walk along the
> road, when you lie down and when you get up. Tie them as
> symbols on your hands and bind them on your foreheads.
> Write them on the doorframes of your houses and on your
> gates (Deut. 6:6-9) [emphasis added].
>
> There was not a word of all that Moses had commanded
> that Joshua did not read to *the whole assembly of Israel,
> including the women and children*, and the foreigners who
> lived among them (Josh. 8:35) [emphasis added].
>
> *All the men of Judah, with their wives and children and
> little ones*, stood there before the LORD (2 Chron. 20:13)
> [emphasis added].
>
> Gather the people, consecrate the assembly; *bring to-
> gether the elders, gather the children, those nursing at the breast*
> (Joel 2:16) [emphasis added].

It is hard to see why that interest in children should evaporate in
the New Testament. And indeed, there is good evidence that it
continues. Jesus welcomes the little children (Luke 18:15-17) and,
on the Day of Pentecost, Peter reiterates that the blessing offered
was as much for the children of the people present as for the people
themselves and for those who weren't even there:

---

16.   E.g. John M. Frame, *Salvation Belongs to the Lord: An Introduction to Systematic
Theology* (Phillipsburg: P&R, 2006), 280-81.

The promise is for you and your children and for all who are far off – for all whom the Lord our God will call (Acts 2:39).

Moreover, the household baptisms in Acts are also highlighted as suggestive of the fact that God continues to be interested in families. Advocates of infant baptism suggest that at least some of those baptised in the households were probably infants,[17] although, as we have seen, that issue is contentious.

According to the covenantal infant baptism view, for these children to be 'in the covenant' means that they are 'heirs of the rich promises of God including a title, not only to regeneration, but also to all the blessings of justification and of the renewing and sanctifying influence of the Holy Spirit.'[18] That does not mean that every child who is baptised is saved (although it can sound an awful lot like it does!).[19] Rather, baptism is seen as an outward sign and seal of a legal 'covenant relationship'. Michael Horton writes:

> In the covenantal economy, the function of signs is not primarily to express an inner experience or wish. Nor is it primarily to refer symbolically to a state of affairs that transcends it. Rather, it is a judicial act: an obligation-assuming event in the present, entailing obligations that can obtain only in a relationship of persons.[20]

In that view, in circumcision, and hence in baptism, God makes commitments to the recipient and the recipient must assume the

---

17. For instance, Berkhof writes, 'It is entirely possible, of course, but not very probable, that none of these households contained children' (Berkhof, *Systematic Theology*, 634).

18. Berkhof, *Systematic Theology*, 639.

19. For instance, the 1662 Anglican Book of Common Prayer says, 'Seeing now, dearly beloved brethren, that this Child is regenerate and grafted into the body of Christ's Church, let us give thanks unto Almighty God for these benefits, and with one accord make our prayers unto him, that this Child may lead the rest of his life according to this beginning.' (https://www.churchofengland.org/prayer-and-worship/worship-texts-and-resources/book-common-prayer/public-baptism-infants). Michael Green writes, 'But while baptism is not automatic in its efficacy, that is still a far cry from being a mere witness or outward symbol. It is normally seen as effecting what it proclaims, the new birth of the candidate.' (Green, *Baptism*, 63). In other words, he thinks baptism doesn't always save people, but we should kind of expect that it does. I'm not convinced.

20. Horton, *Christian Faith*, 780.

obligation to trust and obey God's covenant.[21] Thus in baptism, God 'seals' His promises to the individual just as He did to Abraham when he was circumcised (Rom. 4:11). Horton asserts that circumcision did not only 'symbolize this promise but also ratify the entitlement of each recipient to it.'[22] Yet that seal and those promises are conditional: if a person 'keeps' the covenant through faith they will be saved, while if a person breaks or rejects the covenant through unbelief they will be condemned.[23]

That is why the view is described as 'covenantal', because baptism is seen as entering into a 'covenantal relationship' with God – a relationship in which God makes promises (and threats) and in which we have responsibilities. God's promise is salvation and his threat is judgment. Our responsibility is to believe in order to receive those promises, else we face judgment.[24]

But there are several problems with this view too.

First, this view misunderstands circumcision. We have seen that circumcision was not about what was true of the individual being circumcised but about God's truth in general. Not only was half the population of Israel not circumcised (the women), Paul also argues in Romans that circumcision said nothing about any particular recipient's entitlement. In fact, it was a sign of the entitlement of those who weren't even circumcised! Instead, the sign functioned at a community level. The act of circumcision was not an act of God entering into a covenant relationship with the person receiving the sign. God's covenant was with Abraham and his line of descendants culminating in Jesus, just as God's covenant was with David and his line of descendants. Circumcision was an invitation to be included in the covenant through faith.

That confusion about circumcision, however, is imported into baptism and leads to the potentially dangerous and misleading

---

21. Horton, *Christian Faith*, 779. In fact, for Horton, following Meredith Kline, circumcision and baptism are not only signs of God's grace but also signs of his judgment for those who do not believe (Horton, *Christian Faith*, 791; see also Fesko, *Word, Water, and Spirit*, 287-88).

22. Horton, *Christian Faith*, 779. That is essentially the view put forward in the Westminster Confession Faith (see article 28).

23. Thus Meredith Kline conceived of the 'new covenant' as a 'law covenant' with blessings for obedience (faith) and curses for disobedience (i.e. unbelief). See Meredith G. Kline, *By Oath Consigned: A Reinterpretation of the Covenant Signs of Circumcision and Baptism* (Grand Rapids: Eerdmans, 1968), 74-77.

24. Berkhof, *Systematic Theology*, 638.

language that describes the children of believers as 'heirs of ... regeneration'. That *sounds* a lot like they are saved by virtue of their birth even if that is not what is meant.[25] But it would be wrong to say that those who were circumcised were 'heirs of regeneration'. Indeed, the point of passages like Deuteronomy 10 and 30 is to suggest that they were not!

Second, this view misunderstands the notion of sealing. A seal is not dependent on a response but is a confirmation of a truth that cannot be broken – it is a deposit guaranteeing an eternal inheritance, not a partial guarantee pending the correct performance of certain stipulations (cf. Eph. 1:13; 4:30).[26] Moreover, this view has taken God's seal of Abraham's righteousness in the institution of circumcision and applied it to everyone. But Paul sees Abraham's circumcision as unique. His circumcision alone irrevocably sealed him as righteous-by-faith-while-uncircumcised. No other act of circumcision performed that same binding confirmation. Rather, every subsequent act looked back to what God had ratified in Abraham – that Abraham was righteous by faith, and that God offered the same righteousness-by-faith to them, if they believe.

Similarly, in the New Testament, baptism is nowhere said to seal and confirm an individual's participation in God's salvation plan. Rather, it is the Spirit's work in an individual's life that seals and guarantees their participation in salvation. That seal cannot be revoked. It is an absolute and unbreakable guarantee of God of a future inheritance (Eph. 1:13-14). If anyone was 'sealed' by baptism in the way that Abraham was 'sealed' through circumcision, it was Jesus. At His baptism, God spoke: 'This is my Son, whom I love; with him I am well pleased' (Matt. 3:17). Jesus' baptism 'sealed' or ratified His acceptance with God. And all subsequent Christian baptism looks back to Jesus' acceptance with God and affirms that if we link up with Jesus then we too are acceptable to God as His children through Christ.[27]

---

25. Another similar example is this: 'Israel included infant offspring in the promise of salvation' (Fesko, *Word, Water, and Spirit*, 358). I would rather say something like: 'In Israel the promise of salvation was *offered* to infants (in circumcision).'

26. Cf. Fesko who describes baptism as a sign and seal that points to 'both blessing and sanction' (Fesko, *Word, Water, and Spirit*, 297).

27. If baptism or circumcision can be called seals at all, it is only in sealing and confirming God's promise in general, rather than sealing and confirming God's promise to that individual. That is, each act of circumcision or baptism confirmed the

Third, it fails to reckon with what makes the new covenant actually new. As we saw earlier, God says through Jeremiah that the new covenant will not be like the old where the people turned away from God and He turned away from them (Jer. 31:32). But that is exactly what the covenantal view of baptism denies. It suggests that through baptism the recipient is brought into a 'covenantal relationship' with God whereby if they 'keep' their obligation to believe and obey God's covenant, God will bless them; but if they don't, God will turn away from them. But the New Testament asserts that belonging to the new covenant is not like that. If you have entered the new covenant through faith in Christ Jesus, you have been sealed with the Holy Spirit who guarantees our future inheritance, and you cannot be lost.[28]

Fourth, it ultimately fails to distinguish in any meaningful way between those who are baptised and those who aren't. The basic contention is that baptism brings a person into a 'covenantal relationship' with God involving His promises and their obligations such that if they believe God they will be saved, and if they reject God they will be condemned.[29] But how is that any different

---

offer of the gospel by pointing back to Abraham or Christ respectively – to Abraham in that he was justified by faith, and to Christ in that He is the object of faith.

28.   I am in agreement here with most baptists. One of their main contentions with the covenantal infant baptism view is that it gets the new covenant completely wrong in this respect. In many ways, much of the debate between both sides centres on this point (e.g. Stephen J. Wellum, 'Baptism and the Relationship between the Covenants,' in *Believer's Baptism: Sign of the New Covenant in Christ*, ed. Thomas R. Schreiner and Shawn D. Wright, NAC Studies in Bible & Theology (Nashville: B&H Academic, 2006), 137-53). Covenantal infant baptists get around this by suggesting the new covenant has been 'inaugurated' but not 'consummated' (e.g. Fesko, *Word, Water, and Spirit*, 352). Indeed, Kline rejects the 'guaranteed-promise conception of covenant'. But that makes short shrift of the way God's new covenant relationship is described in both Testaments. The new covenant is an oath-bound relationship wherein God promises to really do for the recipient what He has promised in a way not primarily dependent on the faithfulness of the individual. Entry into that covenantal relationship with God is sealed by the Holy Spirit and that gift is irrevocable. Indeed, it is the gift of the Spirit in new birth that makes the covenant irrevocable. Instead, covenantal infant baptists transfer the irrevocable nature of the new covenant to the so-called 'covenant of grace', which is a theological construct that is not specifically described in the Bible (e.g. Fesko, *Word, Water, and Spirit*, 354). In my view, they are overly dependent on parallels between the Bible and Ancient Near Eastern treaty forms (e.g. Kline, *Consigned*, 86), a relationship which is complex at best (e.g. Noel Weeks, 'The Ambiguity of Biblical 'Background,' *Westminster Theological Journal* 72 (2010): 221-25).

29.   It also reverses the way that circumcision worked. A person would be cut off if they refused to be circumcised. That is quite different from the view that sees

from the situation confronting every human being? God's offer of forgiveness and reconciliation is for the whole world, not simply for those who are baptised. So too, God's threat of judgment or salvation is for the whole world, not simply those who have received the sign of baptism. The same was true of circumcision. The women, though uncircumcised, had been offered the same promise and were under the same obligation to trust the promise. So too, Paul argues that circumcision was a sign of God's offer of salvation to the uncircumcised! And the Joshua 5 episode shows that uncircumcision of one group could even be a sign of the judgment upon those who had been circumcised.

Beyond the Impasse

But is there a way beyond the impasse? I think there might be. Strange as it might seem, I think it's possible that understanding circumcision better might help us to understand baptism better too. Some people may find that idea wholly unconvincing because they are still unconvinced there is any meaningful connection between baptism and circumcision. But the proof hopefully is in the pudding.

There is insufficient space in a book like this to examine every counterargument and every detail on every side of the baptism debate. Instead, in what follows, I will simply present three key areas where I think one or both of the two key sides listed above have made an error that has led to the impasse. The three areas are: (1) the basis of membership in God's covenant; (2) the relationship between the community and the members of the covenant; and (3) the relationship between the sign and membership within the covenant. The three are closely interconnected but it helps to distinguish them in order to come to terms with the issues. In each case, the issue is the nature of the move from the Old Testament to the New Testament. I have already tried to show in previous chapters that I think the nature of that move is from a Messiah who was promised to a Messiah who has come. The task here, however, is to understand how that affects our understanding of baptism and how it has misled both sides of the debate.

---

receiving circumcision (and hence baptism) as a 'sign and seal of judgement leading to death' for the one who doesn't believe (e.g. Horton, *Christian Faith*, 791).

The Basis of Membership in God's Covenant

The place to begin is with understanding the basis of covenant membership, or to put it another way, understanding the basis on which a person shared in the inheritance God promised to Abraham. Membership in the covenant was, and remains, based only on faith.

Sometimes people understand the move from the Old Testament to the New Testament a little bit like this: 'In the Old Testament there was a mixed community of God's people based on birth. But lots of the people in that community didn't really trust and follow God. So, when John the Baptist and Jesus turned up on the scene, they started telling people that what really mattered was faith. Baptism was the way they symbolised that. The new community that God was forming didn't depend on birth (like in the Old Testament) it depended on faith.'

Now, that might be the view on the street, but there's some pretty sophisticated scholarship that stands behind that view too. The problem, unfortunately, is that it's most likely mistaken. To illustrate, it's helpful to consider one of the leading contemporary views of how the covenants in the Bible play out in God's unfolding plan of salvation. The view is called 'progressive covenantalism' and it forms the basis of some strands of believer's baptism theology.[30]

At the heart of 'progressive covenantalism' is the idea that there has been a shift from a 'genealogical principle' (or family principle) to a 'faith' principle.[31] So Stephen Wellum writes:

> The genealogical principle of the Abrahamic covenant is reinterpreted as we move from promise to fulfilment. Under the previous covenants, the genealogical principle, that is, the relationship between the covenant mediator and his seed was *physical* (e.g. Adam, Noah, Abraham, David). But now, in Christ, under his mediation, the relationship between Christ and his seed is no longer physical but *spiritual*, which

---

30. I should say, I enormously respect some of the advocates of progressive covenantalism. I have benefitted immensely from their work. Indeed, I think I would go along with them on very many things, except the way they see the connection between baptism and circumcision.

31. E.g. Jason S. DeRouchie, 'Father of a Multitude of Nations: New Covenant Ecclesiology in OT Perspective,' in *Progressive Covenantalism: Charting a Course between Dispensational and Covenant Theologies*, ed. Stephen J. Wellum and Brent E. Parker (Nashville: B&H Academic, 2016), 34-35.

entails that the covenant sign must only be applied to those
who in fact are the *spiritual* seed of Abraham.[32]

What Wellum means is that in the Old Testament you were
included in the covenant by virtue of your birth, or perhaps through
a merely physical connection with the community (like a slave in
Abraham's house). Whereas, in the New Testament, inclusion in the
new covenant only comes through faith. Jason DeRouchie explains:

> New covenant membership is grounded solely in 'corporate
> identification' with the Messiah and is no longer assumed
> simply because of biological connection.[33]

He is absolutely right about new covenant membership – it comes
through identification with the Messiah, Jesus. The problem is that
he thinks that the Old Testament operated on a different basis. He
believes that membership in God's covenant with Abraham was
simply 'assumed' on the basis of 'biological connection'.

In fact, what is especially interesting is that both sides agree on
this point. On the infant baptism side, the argument (generally)
works a bit like this: children were part of the covenant in the Old
Testament, so they are part of the covenant in the New Testament.
On the believer's baptism side, the argument (generally) works a bit
like this: children were part of the covenant in the Old Testament,
but now the community is defined by faith not family, so children
are no longer part of the covenant; only those who have faith are
part of the covenant and hence the community. But both sides have
an incorrect view of the Old Testament.

As I've tried to show, inclusion in the blessings of God's covenant
with Abraham was never just a matter of physical or biological
connection. That was the point of the call to have a circumcised
heart. The sign of circumcision embodied and signified the hope
of a promised seed of Abraham through whom God would save a
people for Himself. But Old Testament people needed to take hold
of God's promise in their heart by faith, just as Abraham had done.
Participation in the full blessings of God's promise to Abraham
and sharing in his inheritance was always about identification
with the Messiah. It's just that in the Old Testament it was about
identification with a Messiah who was yet to come.

---

32. Wellum, 'Baptism,' 136-37.
33. DeRouchie, 'Father of a Multitude,' 36.

But even more telling is the fact that Paul is often found arguing against those who think that there is a biological or physical right to participation in God's new covenant. However, his argument is never that in the Old Testament a physical principle was at play, but now there is a spiritual principle (generally the baptist view). Nor is his argument that there was a physical principle at play and there is still a physical principle at play, and the problem is that people need to understand the promise-obligation nature of covenants (generally the infant baptist view). Rather, his argument is that *the heirs of God's promise to Abraham were always determined spiritually not physically* (e.g. Gal. 3:7; Rom. 4:11-12). To think otherwise is to misread the Old Testament as badly as some of Paul's Jewish opponents. What has changed is not that sharing in the inheritance is now based on faith, but that now we know that the Messiah is Jesus.

What confuses things a little, however, is that there was a covenant in the Old Testament where membership was physical.[34] That was God's covenant with the nation of Israel through Moses; the one made up of the law and which the New Testament calls the 'old covenant'.[35] In contrast to the covenant with Abraham (and the one with David), the covenant through Moses was made with the whole nation. With respect to that covenant, a person *was* included by physical connection. And even more confusingly, they were included through circumcision. If they were a woman, they were included not through their own circumcision but through the circumcision of all the males in their household (Exod. 12:48).[36] This, perhaps, is where some of the confusion lies.

But what was true of the covenant through Moses was not true of the other covenants. With respect to those other covenants (like the ones with Abraham and David), a person was connected by virtue of their relationship with the individual in the line of promise

---

34. It is also confused by the fact that there were physical benefits for those gathered around Abraham and his line of descendants. But more on that in the next section.

35. E.g. Heb. 8. So too, in Gal. 4:21-31 Paul contrasts the covenant with Abraham with the covenant made with the people through Moses.

36. The reason, I think, that circumcision was the means of inclusion in the covenant with Moses was because it preached the gospel of justification through faith in Abraham's seed. In other words, as a person was being incorporated into a community defined by the law, they were being reminded that the law itself does not save. Salvation is found in the blameless seed of Abraham. Tragically, many Jews completely misunderstood, and thought that it was circumcision itself that saved.

at the heart of the covenant (i.e. Abraham, Isaac, Jacob, David, Solomon, etc.).[37] For example, through God's covenant with David, a person could enjoy the blessings of that covenant by coming under the protection and loving rule of King David. In that case, the blessings were assured by God's commitment to David. In the case of the covenant with Moses, the blessings were dependent on the obedience of the *whole* nation.

Baptism and Covenant Membership

But why is understanding the nature of the move from the Old Testament to the New Testament so important? It's important because it has implications for how we understand the relationship between circumcision and baptism. For instance, if Stephen Wellum's understanding of the move from Old Testament to New Testament is wrong then his conclusion about the sign of the covenant is wrong too. His reason for restricting baptism only to those who have faith is that he sees a shift from biological and physical connection to faith. But if faith was crucial in the Old Testament too, then there is no shift. And so that shift cannot be the basis for suggesting a shift from circumcising a whole community irrespective of faith to baptising only those who believe.[38]

So too, on the other side, if children were not automatically part of God's covenant with Abraham in the Old Testament simply by virtue of their birth, then it is a mistake to say that they are also part of God's new covenant simply by virtue of their birth.[39] The

---

37. What Wellum calls the 'covenant mediator'.

38. This is a very significant point. In order for baptism to be considered a marker of those who have believed or those who are born again (even in an approximate loose sense), it must be established that such a shift between the Old and New Testament has taken place. This is problematic since the writers of the New Testament are constantly working to demonstrate that circumcision did not have such a function. It would be strange for them to work so hard to prove that of circumcision, only to hold the complete opposite to be true of baptism. Moreover, if they did hold that baptism was a sign of those who believed and hence had received the Spirit, then baptism would have provided the perfect foil for them to explain the weakness of circumcision. That is, they could very easily have argued that while circumcision did not mark who was in or out, baptism does because baptism is only given to those who repent and believe. The fact that the apostles did not argue in that way, while not conclusive, is suggestive of the fact that a shift has not taken place in the meaning of the signs.

39. Fesko, for instance, recognises the distinction between the Mosaic covenant and the Abrahamic covenant (Fesko, *Word, Water, and Spirit*, 339-42), however he fails

basis for baptising children, then, cannot be that they are members of the covenant on account of their birth. Instead, what we find in *both* the Old Testament and the New Testament is that the basis of membership in God's covenant with Abraham and sharing in the inheritance promised to Abraham was faith not family.

The Relationship between the Community and the Members of the Covenant who Inherit the Promise

The second point to understand, however, is the nature of the community. I have just tried to show that membership in the covenant with Abraham was not automatic for those who were part of the community gathered around that promise. Rather, membership was by appropriating God's promise in the heart – trusting God's promise to Abraham of a blameless seed. That means, however, that there were many in the wider community who were not genuine heirs of God's covenant promises.

Nevertheless, although membership in the covenant with Abraham was spiritual and required faith, that is not to say that no benefit came through physical connection. We saw in chapter 4 that there was a physical blessing and even a general 'spiritual' blessing that came, not just through biological connection, but even simply through being physically in and around what God was doing through Abraham and his promised heir. Abraham's family is a prime example. When God made His covenant with Abraham in Genesis 17, every single person in the household was caught up in it; some, whether they wanted to be or not. They were not automatically 'saved' by being in Abraham's house, but they experienced two significant benefits.

First, they shared in the physical aspects of God's care, protection and promise to Abraham. God had promised Abraham and his descendants a land. Those who joined themselves with the community of Abraham's descendants participated in the possession of that promise. Sometimes the physical blessing even extended to those well and truly outside the community, such as Egypt under the reign of Joseph, where the whole nation prospered because of their physical connection with the heir of Abraham.

---

to recognise that membership in the Abrahamic covenant was not based on birth. Thus he concludes, 'The promise to include children in the covenant does not fade away with the expiration of the Mosaic covenant' (Fesko, *Word, Water, and Spirit*, 355).

But while everyone attached to the community enjoyed the physical blessings of what God was doing through Abraham, only those who believed the promise (those whose hearts were circumcised) were heirs of the spiritual blessings.[40] Of course, the spiritual blessings were primary. But enjoyment of the physical blessings that came through physical connection with Abraham and his heir were an illustration that participation in God's spiritual blessings would come through spiritual connection by trust in the promise of the ultimate heir, Jesus Christ.[41]

But the second benefit received by those connected with the community gathered around God's promise to Abraham was that they lived in a context where the gospel was preached in advance. They heard it when they sat at home and when they walked by the way and it was written on the doorframes of their houses (Deut. 6:7-8). They heard about what God had promised through Abraham's heir and they had the opportunity to respond to that. Nevertheless, that did not mean the gospel was restricted to that community only. Even those who came in from outside could hear and join – people like Rahab, Ruth, and Naaman the Syrian.

In other words, in the Old Testament there was a large community gathered around God's promise to Abraham, but not everyone in the community was an heir of God's promise to Abraham. Only those who shared Abraham's faith were heirs with him of those promises. Nevertheless, those people in the community who did not have faith still shared in some of the physical blessings and even shared in some of the spiritual blessings – they had the words of God, and they had the symbols of the law pointing to the gospel, though they were not heirs of the central spiritual blessings of God's covenant with Abraham.[42]

The same is true this side of the coming of Jesus, except that, whereas in the Old Testament the community was gathered around the Messiah who was promised, the New Testament community is

---

40. Such as being an heir of the world to come (Rom. 4:13) and receiving the Spirit (Gal. 3:14).

41. See page 85ff. above.

42. Fesko comes close to this view when he makes the distinction that adults and infants are only baptised into 'visible union with Christ' or the 'visible covenant community' (Fesko, *Word, Water, and Spirit*, 323, 351). I have no problem with those expressions. The problem is that he equates both those things with membership within the covenant itself (see also note 49).

gathered around the Messiah who has come, Jesus Christ. The New Testament calls that community 'the church'. Indeed, the Greek word *ekklēsia* simply means something like 'assembly', 'gathering' or 'congregation'. It is a group of people gathered around something. It is gathered around the Messiah Jesus.[43]

But the New Testament also explains that, just as in the Old Testament, being part of the community does not make a person an heir of God's salvation promises or a 'member of the covenant'. That requires faith.[44] As a result, there are clearly people within the community who experience great blessings, but blessings that ultimately fall short of salvation. So, the writer of Hebrews refers to those who have:

> once been enlightened, who have tasted the heavenly gift, who have shared in the Holy Spirit, who have tasted the goodness of the word of God and the powers of the coming age ... (Heb. 6:4-5).

In other words, there are people who have experienced extraordinary spiritual blessings without truly being saved.

At one level that's obvious. While to be a genuine recipient requires a spiritual connection with God's promised Messiah, there are still blessings that come to people simply by being in and around God's community gathered around Jesus. If you live in and around God's people, if you turn up at church pretty regularly, or if you live in a home where the Bible is read every night after dinner, you will

---

43. In fact, the word 'church' is very similar to the terms in the Old Testament that describe the community as a 'gathering' or 'congregation' (Moisés Silva, ed., 'Ekklēsia,' in *New International Dictionary of New Testament Theology and Exegesis*, 5 vols., 2nd ed. (Grand Rapids: Zondervan, 2014), 2:135-37). Interestingly, Fesko points out that God's promise through Joel that He will pour out the Holy Spirit (Joel 2:28-29), which comes to fruition at Pentecost, is first announced to a community (*ekklēsia*) that includes men and women, and even children and nursing infants (Joel 2:16; see Fesko, *Word, Water, and Spirit*, 356). That is not to suggest that the Spirit was poured out at Pentecost on all those present, but simply to observe that the community to which Joel first declared the promise of the Spirit included children too young to grasp its significance.

44. That seems to be what Paul is talking about in Romans 9-11. It was possible to be part of physical Israel and yet not saved. Those 'branches' will be cut out. So too will Gentile branches who are unbelieving (Rom. 11:17-22). Covenantal infant baptists would no doubt want to point out that vine imagery is 'covenantal' (e.g. Gregg Strawbridge, 'The Polemics of Anabaptism from the Reformation Onward,' in *The Case for Covenantal Infant Baptism*, ed. Gregg Strawbridge (Phillipsburg: P&R, 2003), 282). I would suggest that begs the question.

have been 'enlightened' in some sense and you will have tasted the 'goodness of the word of God'. It's also true that if you live in and around what God is doing through His Spirit in His people, you will even taste something of the work of the Spirit and the powers of the coming age. That is just as true in the New Testament as in the Old Testament.

But it is also abundantly clear that the community gathered around Jesus in the New Testament is just as troubled by sin and unbelief as the community in the Old Testament was. Paul must tell the Corinthians to expel a guy who was sleeping with his mother-in-law (1 Cor. 5). Simon the sorcerer is condemned and called to repentance only a short time after he was baptised (Acts 8:9-24). The Christians addressed in the letter of Hebrews are in danger of the same kinds of sin and unbelief that led to a whole generation of Israelites missing out on entering the Promised Land (Heb. 3-4). Some people are teaching a different gospel (Gal. 1). Others are using the church and the gospel as a means of gain (1 Tim. 6:6) and taking advantage of the weak and vulnerable (2 Tim. 3:1-9). Jesus addresses numerous churches in Revelation who are caught up in false teaching, sexual immorality, idolatry and being spiritually asleep at the wheel (Rev. 2:12-3:6). The church is mixed. As Paul says:

> In a large house there are articles not only of gold and silver, but also of wood and clay; some are for special purposes and some for common use (2 Tim. 2:20).

Paul is speaking about the church.[45]

It is not that we are to remain complacent about sin and unbelief in the church. The New Testament writers call on us to address sin in the church. Jesus calls on the churches in Revelation to address the sins in the churches, otherwise He will come and destroy some

---

45. In a rather withering critique, Bonhoeffer writes, 'In a secularized church the longing for a pure, authentic, true, church-community of believers, separated from the world and prepared for battle, is very understandable; yet it is full of dangers: too easily an ideal church-community replaces the real church-community of God; too easily the pure church-community is understood as an achievement to be enacted by human beings; too easily Jesus' parables of the weeds among the wheat and of the fish net are overlooked; too easily it is forgotten that God loved the world and desires that everyone be saved; too easily a fallacious, legalistic biblicism displaces responsible theological reflection.' (Dietrich Bonhoeffer, *Conspiracy and Imprisonment:1940-1945*, ed. Mark S. Brocker, trans. Lisa E. Dahill, vol. 16 of *Dietrich Bonhoeffer Works* (Minneapolis: Fortress Press, 2006), 568).

of them. Just as in the Old Testament, unbelief and sin were to be addressed by putting people out of the community (e.g. Exod. 12:15; 30:38), so too, in the church we are to address unbelief and sin through the preaching of the gospel, the call to repentance, and where necessary, church discipline. But the point is that there are people within the visible boundaries of the church, just as there were in the Old Testament community, who are being discipled to know, love and trust God, and we do not yet know whether that discipleship and trust has really taken root yet.

Baptism and the Community

So why does all this matter? It matters because the nature of the community and the relationship between membership of the community or church and membership of the covenant is a point of serious disagreement between both sides of the debate. Fundamental to the disagreement is the view that both sides have on the nature of the church.[46]

On the infant baptism side, the argument runs something like this: the church is the community of people who belong to God's covenant. Those who belong to God's covenant/church should be baptised. Children of believers are just as much members of the covenant/church as their parents, since, just as children were members of the covenant/'church' in the Old Testament, so they are members of the covenant/church in the New Testament.[47]

On the believer's baptism side, the argument runs something like this: the church is the community of people who belong to God's covenant. Those who belong to God's covenant/church should be baptised. Whereas in the Old Testament, people were members of the covenant/'church' by birth, now only those who have faith belong to God's covenant/church.[48]

Interestingly, both sides generally hold that the church is (or at least should be) the community of people who belong to God's covenant.[49] For those who hold to infant baptism the covenant is a mixed covenant, containing believers and unbelievers, therefore the

---

46. E.g. Anyabwile and Duncan, 'Baptism and the Lord's Supper,' 238-39.

47. E.g. Heidelberg Catechism, Q&A 74.

48. E.g. Grudem, *Theology*, 976-77.

49. Fesko, for instance, simply takes for granted that church and covenant are interchangeable (e.g. Fesko, *Word, Water, and Spirit*, 354-55). For Fesko, 'church' = 'members of the covenant', but 'church/members of the covenant' ≠ 'the elect'. My

church is a mixed church. While for those who hold to believer's baptism the covenant is a pure covenant, therefore the church is a pure church. Those who hold to believer's baptism think that only believers are members of the church. Conversely, those who hold to infant baptism think that the members of the church community are more than just believers; it includes the children of believers too.

Moreover, as with membership in the covenant, both sides make their claims with a false sense of either continuity or discontinuity with the Old Testament. Once again, both sides have misunderstood the Old Testament.[50] As I've tried to show, those who belonged to the (Abrahamic) covenant in the Old Testament era and were heirs of God's promise to Abraham were not those who were born into it but those who shared Abraham's faith. Nevertheless, there was still also a broader community of people gathered around that promise who knew it and who were being taught it.

Likewise, in the New Testament era, those who belong to the covenant, and are heirs of God's promise to Abraham, are not those who are born into it but those who share Abraham's faith. Moreover, this faith is now explicitly in the person of Jesus Christ. Nevertheless, once again, there is still a broader community of people gathered around the promised heir of Abraham, Jesus. The New Testament seems to present the church as every bit as troubled by unbelief as the Old Testament community. Again, we must work against that, but it is not the pure community that some baptist theologians would like it to be. In other words, neither in the New Testament nor in the Old is the community of people gathered around the promise co-extensive with the members of the covenant (i.e. those who are heirs of God's promise to Abraham fulfilled in Jesus).

That distinction is profoundly helpful in practice. First, it recognises the extraordinary privileges that belong to those born into the church community while guarding against the misplaced idea that belonging to the community equals salvation. The children of believers are undeniably privileged. They grow up being discipled in that church community by their parents, Sunday school teachers, youth leaders, pastors and friends to know, love and trust Jesus. They

point is that 'members of the covenant' = 'the elect', but 'church' ≠ 'members of the covenant/the elect' (see Fesko, *Word, Water, and Spirit*, 351).

50.   Interestingly, the Baptists are right on the nature of the new covenant, but wrong on the nature of the church, while the infant Baptists are wrong on the nature of the new covenant, but right on the nature of the church.

get to hear the gospel day in and day out for years. They even share somehow in the powerful work of God's Spirit in and among His people. Nevertheless, exposure to those privileges does not equate to salvation. That requires faith.[51] So as they grow we need to look for evidence of fruit. Where there is no fruit, we need to challenge them to repent and believe in Jesus.[52]

Second, it recognises the real way in which communities are formed and operate. For instance, Wayne Grudem writes:

> The means of entrance into the church is *voluntary, spiritual, and internal*. One becomes a member of the true church by being *born again* and by having *saving faith* not by physical birth.[53]

But it is here that the believer's baptism view takes on an element of unreality. At one level Grudem is right: entrance into the invisible, *true* church of God consisting only of believers is on the basis of faith alone. But at another level the first sentence is quite misleading. Irrespective of your view on baptism, the children of parents who believe *are* brought into the community of the visible church simply by their birth. They can't help it. They didn't choose it. Moreover, they are brought up to know, love and trust Christ. At least, that's what a responsible Christian parent aims to do. Whether that child ends up really trusting in Jesus is another question. But it is undeniable that they form part of the visible church community, and they are not simply being evangelized, they are being discipled. Even if only one of their parents believes and they can't attend church every week because of the unbelieving parent, there will often be an influence from the Christian parent that is significant. I take this to be what Paul means when he says that the children of one believing parent are 'holy' (1 Cor. 7:14) – they are set apart to God and for discipleship to Him by virtue of the life and influence of their believing parent. The believer's baptism view seems to overlook the

---

51. As Beasley-Murray notes, 'Birth in a Christian home is a priceless privilege, but it is not a guarantee of inheritance in the Kingdom of God.' (Beasley-Murray, *Baptism*, 343).

52. Crucially, a proper understanding of the difference between belonging to the community and belonging to the covenant addresses the problem that the new covenant is unbreakable – you cannot be in it and then out of it. It is possible to be in the community and not be saved. But once a person has entered into the new covenant through faith in Christ and been sealed with the Holy Spirit, that gift is irrevocable.

53. Grudem, *Theology*, 977.

simple fact that a community is not formed by signs but by physical connections. That is, whether you like it or not, the people that you allow to continually hang around with you, do all the same things as you do and participate in the general life of the church *are* part of the community. Sure, you might not let them be baptised and might not let them participate in the Lord's Supper, but they do everything else. You let them come to church, be part of a growth group, sing the songs of the community, contribute to the life of the community. That's why when Paul tells the Corinthians to deal with an immoral and unbelieving member, he tells them not even to eat with them. By that, he doesn't simply mean, don't let them have Lord's Supper. He means, don't let them be part of your community life. That is, it's not simply what you say about them that matters ('you're not part of this community'), what matters is the shared life in which you let them participate. But once we accept that membership of the visible church does not necessarily imply membership of the covenant, it becomes far less problematic to say that children belong to the church, as they so obviously do in practice.

It is important to understand that what has changed between the Old and New Testament is not the nature of the community, but the object around which it is formed. The Old Testament community was formed around a Messiah who was to come but who was unknown. The church is formed around Jesus.[54] Belonging to the community did not mean being an heir of the promise. It still doesn't. The community was, and remains, mixed with believers and unbelievers. Children continue to be born apart from their will or choice into a community where the gospel is preached and people are being discipled to know and love Jesus. People who only appear to have genuine faith continue to join themselves to the Christian community. There continue to be people within the Christian community who show no evidence of faith who need to be put out of the community. Those things have not changed. What has changed is that the community is now gathered around Jesus.

---

54. That is both what makes the church the true heirs of Abraham while at the same time distinct from ethnic Israel. The church are the true heirs of Abraham because they are gathered around the heir and king promised to Abraham. But it is distinct from Israel because the nation of Israel as a political and biological entity has not given its allegiance to Jesus. By refusing to acknowledge Jesus as the promised Messiah and seed of Abraham and by continuing to wait for someone else, the nation of Israel is no longer gathered around God's promise. As such, they have suddenly found themselves outside God's community.

What the Sign of Baptism Means

There is, however, one last piece of the puzzle that needs to be slotted into place. That is, what the sign actually means. We've seen that the basis of covenant membership is faith. That was true in both the Old Testament and the New Testament. We've also seen that the community of people gathered around the promise was bigger than just those who were heirs of the promise. The community included believers and unbelievers. But what does that mean in terms of who gets the sign and who doesn't?

Interestingly, both sides agree on some of the basic principles. To illustrate, guess on which side the person who wrote the following falls:

> The *sign* of this covenant (the outward, physical symbol of inclusion in the covenant) varies between the Old Testament and the New Testament. In the Old Testament the outward sign of beginning the covenant relationship was circumcision. In the new covenant, the sign of beginning a covenant relationship is baptism ....[55]

That is a statement with which many covenantal infant baptism people would readily agree. But it's actually written by someone who holds to believer's baptism.

Strikingly, both sides would agree that circumcision marked out a person as a member of the covenant. And both sides would agree that baptism marks out a person as a member of the covenant. Where they differ is that those who hold to believer's baptism say that only those who have expressed faith are members of the new covenant, so only they should receive the sign of baptism. While those who hold to infant baptism say that believers and their children are members of the new covenant, so both parents and their children should receive the sign of baptism. But, again, both sides share a wrong view of circumcision, and hence presumably, a wrong view of baptism.

I have tried to show that circumcision was not a sign of membership in God's covenant with Abraham, rather it was a sign of what the promise was and a sign of membership in the community where that promise was known, taught, and, in general, believed. It was a sign not merely to the recipient but to the whole community and to the world beyond of God's promise to redeem the world

---

55. Grudem, *Theology*, 520.

through a descendant of Abraham. And it was an invitation to those who received it and those who witnessed it to receive in their hearts the truth that it signified.

So what does that mean for baptism? I think it means the following.[56]

First, it means that baptism is not a sign of who is in the covenant or out of it, nor who is an heir of the covenant or who is not. It doesn't say that a baby is 'in the covenant'. Nor does it say that an adult baptised as a believer is 'in' either.

I remember once visiting an elderly man. I asked him if he had any assurance of salvation. His answer was: 'I was baptised.'[57] But as a ground of assurance, baptism is dangerously inadequate. If the apostle Paul had been in the room, he might have simply quoted Philippians 3 or Romans 2. After all, it's faith in Jesus that is the ground of our hope. But the problem is more widespread than that one man. I've met numerous parents whose children were baptised but then later in life wandered away from the faith. Many of those parents cling desperately to the 'promises God made to their child in baptism.' But the only promise God has made to their children is the same promise He has made to the whole world: if you repent and believe in Jesus, you will be saved.

However, the problem is not only on one side. Jonathan Leeman worries that people hand out the 'Hello. I'm a Christian' name tag of baptism far too easily. He levels that accusation not only against those who hold to infant baptism but also against those who hold to believer's baptism yet baptise people too quickly. The result, he suggests, is nominalism. People think they're a Christian just because they've been baptised when maybe they aren't.

---

56. There is a significant assumption here, which is that what is true of circumcision can be applied to baptism. As I have pointed out above, that is actually the view of some people on both sides. The difference between the two sides lies in their views of the covenant and church, not so much their views of the relationship between the *function* of circumcision and baptism. Nevertheless, I have tried to show throughout this book that baptism and circumcision are connected. We have seen numerous places where that is the case, not just Colossians 2. Moreover, I have tried to show the biblical-theological continuities and discontinuities between the two – one looks forward and the other back. Finally, I have also tried to show that the meaning of baptism and circumcision when studied independently also share significant resonances, which also suggests their connection and relationship.

57. He was baptised as a baby. But the problem would be the same if he had been baptised as an adult.

Leeman highlights the 'pastoral dilemma of when to affirm they are Christians'. Is it, he asks:

> When they ask me why Jesus had to die at age 4 and appear very sad after my explanation? When they first profess at age 6? When they profess again at age 8 *and really seem to mean it?* However you answer that question, we're dealing in matters of subjective assessment, whether you're a Baptist or a Presbyterian.[58]

His answer is that you wait until you can be pretty sure. But that, I would suggest, is the wrong way of looking at the issue.

The problem is not simply handing out baptism too readily. The problem is turning baptism into a nametag when it's really just a brochure. To see baptism as an 'I'm a Christian name tag' is to misunderstand baptism in the same way that the Jews misunderstood circumcision. The Jews saw circumcision as a kind of boundary marker. But Paul steadfastly refuses to make baptism the new boundary marker of who is in and who is out.

So long as baptism is seen as a stamp that a person is really a Christian it will lead to nominalism, irrespective of whether one practices infant or believer's baptism. As long as people think that baptism is a marker of whether they are 'in' or not, they will end up examining the wrong thing to work out where they stand with God. They need to examine the reality of their faith in Jesus, not their past act of baptism.

Second, then, instead of being a sign of in and out, or of a person's faith, baptism is a sign of what the promise is.[59] Just as

---

58. Jonathan Leeman, 'Guest Post: Jonathan Leeman on Baptism and a Theology of Children,' *What You Think Matters*, July 2, 2015, https://thinktheology.co.uk/blog/article/guest_post_jonathan_leeman_on_baptism_and_a_theology_of_children.

59. There is one other reason that I think baptising children is a great picture of the gospel. That is, it does convey quite explicitly that we are born sinners and born in need of God's grace. It is not simply that as we go on, we chalk up sins that need to be forgiven, but as David says, we are sinful from the time of our conception on (Ps. 51:5). Baptising babies communicates that need very strongly. Additionally, it also communicates the fact that salvation is completely and utterly a work of God. It is something that God must do and that we must receive. But the initial move of salvation comes from Him, not us. When He comes to us, we are as helpless as little children. Unless He intervenes, we cannot even respond to His offer of grace in Jesus (John 6:44). It must be said, that is a theological argument and not an explicitly biblical one. It is an argument based on the attractiveness of an idea, and so it is relatively weak and should only cautiously be embraced. Nevertheless, I think it has merit.

circumcision was not a sign of faith but an invitation to faith, so baptism is not a sign of faith but an invitation to it. Baptism is a sign to the community as a whole and to all those looking on that through faith in Jesus we can be washed clean by God and made fit for His new creation, and baptism calls us to receive that promise by faith.[60] Baptism expresses God's missional heart. Like circumcision, it is a sign of God's great gospel plan to save all who turn to Him in faith. It is an offer of the gospel as much to the recipient as it is to those who are looking on.[61] And it is an assurance that whoever receives that promise by faith will be washed clean through the Spirit who both unites us with and comes through Jesus' death and resurrection.[62] Each act of baptism, then, points to the centre— Jesus—rather than defining the boundaries of who is and who

---

60. That is reflected in Calvin's view of the sacraments. He writes, 'It is common to all sacraments to have the word of God annexed to them, by which he testifies that he is propitious to us, and calls us to the hope of salvation; yea, a sacrament is nothing else than a visible word, or sculpture and image of that grace of God, which the word more fully illustrates. If, then, there is a mutual relation between the word and faith; it follows, that the proposed end and use of sacraments is to help, promote and confirm faith.' (John Calvin, *Commentary on the First Book of Moses Called Genesis*, trans. John King (Bellingham: Logos Bible Software, 2010), 1:451-52). There is a long (and furious) debate about whether baptism (and the Lord's Supper) are *bare* signs or are somehow more than that. To some degree, it depends what is meant by that distinction. At one level, yes, they are bare signs in that they do not achieve anything in and of themselves. But at another level, they are not bare signs, since through the Spirit's power they achieve God's sovereign purpose, testifying to the gospel and strengthening faith. In the same way, we might say that God's words in the Bible are 'mere words' in that they do not of themselves achieve anything. They can be read, known, spoken, memorised and recited, all to no avail. But, when empowered by the Holy Spirit, they achieve God's purpose, either of giving life or condemning people's rebellion.

61. Baptism, then, is a 'means of grace' much like God's Word is: it offers and communicates the gospel, and empowered by the Spirit, achieves God's purpose in those who hear it.

62. A number of confessional statements from the Reformation era describe baptism (and Lord's Supper) as 'seals' (e.g. Heidelberg Catechism, Q&A 66). They seem to mean by that the same thing as I am saying here: they confirm and ratify the truth of God's gospel promises to all who believe. On occasion, however, some seem to go a little bit further and suggest that the individual themselves is sealed (e.g. The Westminster Confession of Faith, chap. 28). In my view, this is based on a misreading of Romans 4:11 (discussed earlier). While Abraham himself was sealed in his circumcision, others were not. Rather, subsequent acts of circumcision looked back to what God had ratified as true in the case of Abraham. Moreover, the language of 'seal' in the New Testament is largely used to describe the Holy Spirit sealing individual believers to ratify their possession of the eternal inheritance. For that reason, to avoid confusion with the biblical text, I prefer to avoid using the word seal, and simply say that baptism 'reaffirms' the truth of God's gospel promise.

isn't 'in'. It offers and confirms the gospel promise, not only to the individual being baptised, but all those present. As Calvin wrote:

> Therefore, let it be regarded as a settled principle that the sacraments have the same office as the Word of God: to offer and set forth Christ to us, and in him the treasures of heavenly grace. But they avail and profit nothing unless received in faith.[63]

Nevertheless, although baptism points to the person and work of Jesus, it is also a Trinitarian act. Baptism symbolises the cleansing work of God, by the Holy Spirit who is sent by the Father and the Son (John 14:26; 15:26). Moreover, the Spirit comes to us through Jesus, who Himself was sent by the Father. More particularly, the Spirit comes to us through Jesus' death and resurrection and unites us with that same death and resurrection. And that cleansing work of Spirit and Son makes us to be children of God (John 1:12). Thus, we are baptised into the promise from the Father, through the Son and by the Holy Spirit. So, although baptism can be summarised as baptism in the name of Jesus (Acts 2:38; 8:16; 10:48; 19:5), it is properly and more fully, baptism in the name of the Father, Son and Holy Spirit (Matt. 28:19).

Third, baptism is a call to repentance and radical obedience grounded in God's promise. In the same way that circumcision simultaneously called people to and promised obedience, baptism also calls us to and promises us obedience. Baptism is a call to blamelessness, righteousness and cleansing. It is a call to 'live as a disciple, to die to sin and to live to righteousness, and to suffer for the gospel.'[64] Nevertheless, that call is anchored in God's grace. Baptism calls us to pursue and receive the grace of forgiveness, cleansing and obedience through faith in Christ Jesus, with whom we are united by the Holy Spirit. That complete cleansing from the ongoing presence of sin will not be perfected until Jesus returns to gather His people. Nevertheless, it is already beginning to work its way out now in a changed life through the Holy Spirit.

Fourth, baptism marks out the community where the promise is known, proclaimed and, in general, believed.[65] We have seen

---

63. Calvin, *Institutes*, 4.14.17.

64. Peter Adam, personal correspondence.

65. Cf. Grudem who says that baptism ought only to be given to those who 'give evidence of membership in the church', by which he means faith. (Grudem, *Theology*, 977).

how circumcision functioned as a community-level sign rather than an individual sign. And there is some evidence from the New Testament that baptism too is a community-level sign. For instance, Paul says in 1 Corinthians 10:

> For I do not want you to be ignorant of the fact, brothers and sisters, that our ancestors were all under the cloud and that they all passed through the sea. They were all baptized into Moses in the cloud and in the sea. They all ate the same spiritual food and drank the same spiritual drink; for they drank from the spiritual rock that accompanied them, and that rock was Christ (1 Cor. 10:1-4).

What Paul says here is a little obscure. But his basic point is that the people of God's Old Testament community experienced something of the blessings of Christ even though Christ had not been fully revealed and had not yet accomplished His definitive work in His life, death and resurrection. In particular, Paul says 'they were all baptized'. To be sure, they were all baptised into Moses, not Christ. But Paul is drawing an equivalence between Israel's experience and the experience of the Corinthians. That's clear because he goes on to draw application from the Old Testament people's experience for the Corinthians:

> Now these things occurred as examples to keep us from setting our hearts on evil things as they did (1 Cor. 10:5-6).

The direction of Paul's argument is this: 'They experienced something of the blessings of Jesus, but you have even more. Don't copy their mistake and abandon Jesus for sin.' Implicit in that comparison is the idea that just as all from that community were baptised into Moses, so too, all from the Corinthian church community were baptised into Jesus. But Paul sees that, as in the Old Testament, there are some within the New Testament community who are in danger of abandoning Christ or going after sin. In Paul's thinking, then, baptism did not and does not mark out who is saved and who isn't, but who is part of the community of God's people. In the New Testament, as much as in the Old Testament, baptism marks out the community where Jesus is known, not the individuals who are saved.

That understanding makes considerable sense of the pattern of household baptism we see in the book of Acts (Acts 11:48; 16:15, 33; 18:8). As noted above, Lydia's whole household (slaves and all) were baptised when she herself believed.[66] So too, Paul says that he baptised the household of Stephanus (1 Cor. 1:16).

That seems strangely reminiscent of the events of Genesis 17 where, as well as Abraham's children being circumcised, any male in his household community was also circumcised, including his male servants and their male children. We also see that modelled in other places in the Old Testament with respect to circumcision. Whole households (not just a biological family) would join the community of believers through all the males in their household being circumcised. So, God says to Moses:

> A foreigner residing among you who wants to celebrate the LORD's Passover must have all the males in his household circumcised; then he may take part like one born in the land. No uncircumcised male may eat it (Exod. 12:48).

Ben Witherington notes:

> Household inclusion in the church may not always have involved the faith commitment of every household member. In the Greco-Roman world the head of the household usually determined the household's religion, and servants may have followed suit out of loyalty to their master.[67]

To us that might seem like a complete sham. How could we baptise people who make no profession of faith? But it's only a problem if we fail to understand how the sign was working. If baptism is a sign

---

66. Interestingly, Calvin also sees the household as going far beyond one's own children. He writes, 'surely, all the godly ought to have this desire, to have those who are under them to be partakers of the same faith. For he is unworthy to be numbered among the children of God, and to be a ruler over others, whosoever is desirous to reign and rule in his own house over his wife, children, servants, and maids, and will cause them to give no place to Christ. Therefore, let every one of the faithful study to govern and order his house so that it may be an image of the Church. I grant that Lydia had not in her hand the hearts of all those which were of her household, that she might turn unto Christ whomsoever she would; but the Lord did bless her godly desire, so that she had all her household obedient. The godly (as we have already said) must endeavour, with might and main, to drive from their houses all manner of superstition; secondly, that they have not profane families, but that they keep them under the fear of the Lord.' (John Calvin, *Commentary upon the Acts of the Apostles*, trans. Henry Beveridge, 2 vols. (Bellingham: Logos Bible Software, 2010), 2:104-105).

67. Ben Witherington III, *The Acts of the Apostles: A Socio-Rhetorical Commentary* (Grand Rapids: Eerdmans, 1998), 493. Similarly, David Peterson notes that household baptism reflected the 'Jewish practice of incorporating *families* as proselytes [recruits or disciples] through baptism.' (Peterson, *Acts*, 461 [emphasis added]).

of who is 'in'/saved, then baptising a household of servants (not to mention children) is highly problematic. If baptism merely marks out the household as a place where the gospel is known and taught, then it isn't problematic at all.

That may also explain why people seem to be baptised so quickly in the New Testament. On the day of Pentecost some 3,000 people were baptised. There was no time for testing out the genuineness of people's profession of faith. They were simply baptised. That pattern seems to continue. When Philip shares the gospel with the Ethiopian eunuch, the eunuch is baptised immediately (Acts 8:35-38). If baptism is a nametag of who is in and who is out, it is crucial, as Jonathan Leeman says, to make sure we have it right. But if baptism is merely a sign for people who belong to the community where people are hearing the gospel and being discipled in knowing Jesus, it can be administered quickly.

Baptism, like circumcision, is not a sign of who is 'in' or 'out', saved or not saved, it is a sign of what the promise is – that through faith in Jesus we can be forgiven and cleaned up. But baptism is also a sign of membership in the community where that promise is known, taught, and, in general, believed.[68]

But finally, baptism is an appeal to God for the promises symbolised by it. As we have seen, Peter says that baptism is an 'appeal to God for a good conscience' (1 Pet. 3:21 ESV). Importantly, Peter does not say who is praying for whom. It could be that what is in view is the person being baptised praying for themselves. But that need not be the case. There are lots of examples in the Bible of people praying for others. Daniel prayed for the forgiveness of Israel (Dan. 9). James encourages us to pray for the sins of our fellow Christians (James 5:14-16). And we're told that Jesus forgave the sins of the paralysed man because Jesus saw the faith of the four friends who carried him (Mark 2:5).[69]

---

68. Witherington writes, 'For Paul, water baptism is doubtless an initiatory rite, not a confirmation ritual, which helps explain how it was possible for Philip to baptize Samaritans before they demonstrated the presence of the Holy Spirit' (Ben Witherington III, *Troubled Waters: Rethinking the Theology of Baptism* (Waco: Baylor University Press, 2007), 90).

69. As Edwards notes, the fact that Jesus responds to their faith shouldn't surprise us, 'the Gospels preserve several instances of Jesus fulfilling the petition of one party on behalf of another' (e.g. Mark 5:21-43; 7:24-30; John 4:46-53; Matt. 8:5-13; so James R. Edwards, *The Gospel According to Mark*, Pillar New Testament Commentary (Grand Rapids: Eerdmans, 2002), 76).

In our individualistic culture we might find that idea bordering on heretical, but it is helpful to realise that we routinely pray in that way. We pray for God to show mercy to our fellow Christians. We even pray for God to show mercy to those we know who are not Christians. When we do that, we don't imagine God forgiving them without any response of faith on their part; rather, we consider that part of the package. We ask God to draw them to Himself. We know that even in repentance and faith, God must make the first move (2 Tim. 2:25-26). No one can come to Jesus unless the Father draws them, and those whom the Father draws will come (John 6:44-46).

In light of the community function of baptism, then, it is probably best to view baptism as the prayer of the community (a community that includes the individual themselves) that God would do His work of salvation in that person's life.

Baptism and Discipleship

Once we understand what has changed between the Old Testament and the New Testament, it begins to make sense that just as children were circumcised into the community gathered around the Messiah who was to come, so they also should be baptised into the community gathered around the Messiah who has come (i.e. the church). In that way, both circumcision and baptism, then, share the function of symbolising the inclusion of people in the community gathered around God's Messiah.

It needs to be acknowledged, though, that lots of people find that deeply problematic. For some, like Jonathan Leeman who was quoted above, the risk is that people will wrongly think they're Christians when they're not. So it helps to put flesh on the bones of what it looks like for a person to be baptised into the church community. The best place from which to do that is the Great Commission.

Before leaving His disciples to ascend to heaven, Jesus meets them and gives them, and the church that would be formed through them, a task. Jesus says:

> All authority in heaven and on earth has been given to me. Therefore go and make disciples of all nations, baptizing them in the name of the Father and of the Son and of the Holy Spirit, and teaching them to obey everything I have commanded you. And surely I am with you always, to the very end of the age (Matt. 28:18-20).

This commission is to make more disciples, and the method is by baptising and teaching.[70] If anything can be made of the fact that baptism is mentioned first, then the process is that first they baptise people, and then they teach them to obey Jesus in everything. They don't first teach them to obey Jesus in everything and only baptise them once they're sure they're saved. They baptise them first.[71]

In the case of someone coming to faith as an adult that makes perfect sense. They have not been following Jesus, you share the gospel with them, they're convicted of sin and the need for Jesus, they're baptised and then you continue the discipleship process. You teach them to obey Jesus' commands about how to live. You pray with them when they've done something wrong. You teach them to confess their sins and trust in God's forgiveness in Jesus. In other words, you *disciple* them. And all the time you're looking for spiritual fruit – for genuine repentance and faith and the evidence of a transformed life. You don't assume they are automatically saved just because they've been baptised. And if you see signs that they haven't really understood the gospel or aren't really living it out, you challenge them and say, 'Maybe you're not a Christian and you need to really repent and trust in Jesus.' But if you do see fruit, you grow in confidence and assurance that they truly do belong to Jesus.

In the case of a child who is born into a house where Jesus is known and followed, it is more problematic. As a godly parent (whatever your view on baptism), your aim is to teach them to trust and follow Jesus. You teach them to obey Jesus' commands about how to live, but you also pray with them when they've done something wrong. You teach them to confess their sins and trust in God's forgiveness in Jesus. In other words, you *disciple* them. And all the time you're looking for spiritual fruit – for genuine repentance and faith and the evidence

---

70. Technically, there is one verb 'make disciples' and three participles: 'go', 'baptising' and 'teaching'. It seems the most likely, based on Matthew's style and grammar that 'go' and 'make' take place together (they are 'coordinate'), while 'baptise' and 'teach' describe the way of making disciples (Ferguson, *Baptism*, 137). For that reason, it is also unlikely that 'baptising' and 'teaching' should be seen as taking place after 'make disciples' (see also Daniel B. Wallace, *Greek Grammar Beyond the Basics: An Exegetical Syntax of the New Testament* (Grand Rapids: Zondervan, 1996), 645, also 625-26).

71. See France, *Matthew*, 1115-16. The Swiss Reformer, Zwingli, made a similar point (see Ulrich Zwingli and Heinrich Bullinger, *Zwingli and Bullinger*, ed. Geoffrey W. Bromiley, Library of Christian Classics 24 (Philadelphia: Westminster Press, 1953), 141-42).

of a transformed life. You don't assume they're automatically saved. And if you see signs that they haven't really understood the gospel or aren't really living it out, you challenge them and say, 'Maybe you're not a Christian and you need to really repent and trust in Jesus.' But if you do see fruit, you grow in confidence and assurance that they truly do belong to Jesus.[72]

In other words, you treat them in precisely the same way that you would an adult who has been baptised into the community where Jesus is taught and followed. But here's the crucial question: if you treat them like you would any other disciple of Jesus, why don't you baptise them as you would any other disciple of Jesus? Why if you're doing the second part of the Great Commission—teaching them to obey Jesus—why wouldn't you do the first part – baptise them?

The reason you wouldn't do that is if baptism were a profession of personal faith or if it were a sign of who was in or out of the spiritual community of the saved. But if baptism is only a sign of what the gospel is and a sign of who is in the community where the gospel is taught and people are being discipled to know Jesus, then baptising children into that community makes perfect sense.

For instance, John Piper writes:

> We do not baptize our children according to the flesh, not because we don't love them, but because we want to preserve for them the purity and the power of the spiritual community that God ordained for the believing church of the living Christ.[73]

But while the idea is noble, it is perhaps slightly misguided. Yes, we want to maintain the purity of the church. I am deeply committed to that ideal. Nevertheless, the way we maintain the purity of the church is not by pretending that children are not members of the church when they plainly are. Rather, we maintain the purity of the church by challenging, rebuking and encouraging them as they grow to believe and live out the gospel, just as we would anyone else

---

72. As Bonhoeffer noted, while the misuse of infant baptism has led to the secularisation of the church and the separation of baptism from faith, nevertheless, historically speaking, a commitment to the baptism of believers has not renewed the church either. The solution to empty Christianity and cheap grace is not the end of infant baptism, but the proper exercise of church discipline (Bonhoeffer, *Conspiracy and Imprisonment*, 566-72).

73. Piper, 'How Do Circumcision and Baptism Correspond?'

who belongs to the church and is being discipled to follow Jesus. And in so far as it becomes evident that the gospel has not taken root in their lives, we move to counsel them and we may eventually exercise some form of church discipline.

It is important to understand, too, that the determining factor for whether children are baptised is not whether they are children of believers. The key issue is whether the children are part of a community where the gospel is taught and where they are being discipled to know Jesus. That may chiefly be the children of believers who belong to a church. But it could even include, for example, grandchildren who are brought along to church and Sunday school every Sunday by their grandparents and who are being discipled by those grandparents to know and follow Jesus. Ben Witherington puts it like this:

> Water baptism is like enrolment in school, the school of Christ. Just as parents, apart from and without the consent of their offspring, enroll their children in school, so is the case of infant baptism. In neither case is it presumed that the child being enrolled/baptized already knows and accepts what is going to be taught.
>
> On the other hand, when an adult enrolls in school, the situation changes. It is assumed that the adult enrolled under his own volition, has some knowledge of the content of the course, and has accepted the responsibilities of the course requirements. This is analogous to adult baptism since it is assumed that the adult has freely chosen baptism, has planned to or has already accepted Christ, and has expressed a desire to lead a Christian life. The new convert, like the student, has only the most rudimentary knowledge of the Christian life, the course content, but it is enough for him to make an informed choice and to commit himself to a life of learning and growing in the faith.[74]

He continues:

> Water baptism then is not a confirmation that the pilgrimage is completed or even well under way, but *it can be seen as a recognition that the journey has begun.* It is a commitment in a certain direction, and it is also a recognition that God has already begun his work in the one being baptized. ... The church will do well to recognize baptism for what it is –

---

74. Witherington III, *Troubled Waters*, 125-26.

not a graduation exercise, but the first step in the process of the Christian life, enrollment in the school of Christ[75] [emphasis added].

Imagine, for instance, a first-century household like Lydia's. A woman receives the gospel and is baptised. She goes home and asks those in her household who wants to know and serve Jesus and be discipled to follow him. Some say, yes. They're baptised. Some say, no. They aren't baptised. It's unlikely they would be cut off from the household as in the case of Abraham's household, but it would probably be made clear that they're rejecting the gospel and so cut off from God. But there might be children too. Some might be hard-hearted and say, 'No, I don't want to follow Jesus'. But others would say, 'Yes, I do want to follow Jesus.' You couldn't be sure they really meant it, but you would begin the process of discipling and then see what fruit was borne as the years went by. Others might be too young to respond, but they would still be taught to know and love Jesus and be prayed for by the church and the household. Such a scenario seems entirely plausible on the basis of the biblical evidence. What would make it unworkable in some people's minds would be their overinflated understanding of baptism.

It makes sense to me, then, to think that it is right and proper to baptise children who are born (or come later) into the community of people where they are being brought up to know and trust Jesus. That's what happened in the Old Testament and that is still what is happening in the New Testament. Being part of the church community does not make them 'saved'. But they most certainly enjoy special privileges. Nevertheless, as they grow up it is imperative to ensure that they have truly grasped the gospel. If they haven't, that *must* be made clear to them and they must be called to live according to the gospel they've heard. Their ongoing place as a member of the church community, and more importantly, their salvation, depends on the evidence of a living faith.

So, Which Is It, Infants or Believers?

The simple answer to who should be baptised is that we should baptise disciples. We should baptise those who have begun the journey of discipleship, whether that's because they were born

---

75. Witherington III, *Troubled Waters*, 126.

into that journey, or whether it's because they chose to take it on later in life.

I think it's important to reiterate that these issues are hard. There are people whom I love who disagree with me, but I still love them, even if they're not convinced. I am certainly under no illusions that everyone who reads this chapter will be absolutely persuaded.

It also needs to be said that I don't think the arguments in this chapter are iron-clad. That is, I don't believe we can have the same level of certainty about the recipients of baptism as we do, say, with the nature of what Jesus accomplished on the cross. Some doctrines in the Bible are much clearer than others. That said, I do regard the position I have outlined here as the one that makes the most sense of the biblical evidence.

My basic contention is that understanding the Old Testament better helps us to understand baptism too. Unintentionally, both sides, to some degree, have transferred their misunderstanding of circumcision to baptism. Baptism is not a sign of who is an heir of God's promises in Jesus and who isn't, but a sign of what the gospel is – a sign that through Jesus we can be forgiven and cleansed to be fit for God. Baptism is a call to receive that promise through repentance and faith, and baptism is a sign that broadly marks out the community where that gospel is preached, taught, lived and believed.

One of the most encouraging moments in my life was a few years ago when one of the couples in my church spoke at the baptism of their baby girl. It's our practice to give parents the option of saying something. I'd prepared words as well to say to explain what baptism signifies but they captured the meaning so well that in the end I said nothing more. In that moment they proclaimed the gospel to us – that each of us is born in sin and in need of the sovereign work of God through his Son Jesus Christ, and they called upon God to act. This is what they said,[76]

> We are bringing our daughter Eliza Grace to be baptised today. ... Eliza means consecrated or pledged to God.
> We had this in mind when we gave her this name. We know that Eliza belongs to God. We want to dedicate her to him. We have been praying that she will one day make her own mind up to commit her life to God.

---

76.   I have lightly edited this for style.

Grace is a familiar girl's name and one that expresses a key idea for us as Christians. Graciousness is a dominant characteristic of our God. We rely on his generosity in everything. We want Grace to shape Eliza's life.

That is why we want to have her baptised today.

We know that baptising her isn't going to make her a Christian. Sometimes I wish it were that easy! But this water isn't special in any way. It just came out of the tap in the kitchen.

And I know Karl certainly hasn't got any special powers to somehow turn Eliza into a Christian. Knowing Karl he'll probably avoid holding her at all! [ouch!]

But by baptising her we are acknowledging that something else needs to happen in Eliza's life. Something only God can do. She's only just been born, but we know that she needs to be born again. Baptism is a picture of this. Unfortunately for her she has been born to two sinful parents and has inherited the same sinful heart that we have. She looks all cute and innocent at the moment, but I know that one day Eliza is going to tell her Dad a lie. She will disobey us. She will be selfish and unkind to others. Worst of all she will be at odds with her creator God.

She needs to be washed clean by God and given a new heart from him and this is what we believe the water to be a picture of. We're kind of acting out a prayer that God would do this for Eliza.

We also are making a promise and commitment as her church family that we will endeavour to teach, and encourage and lead little Eliza to know, love and follow Jesus her Saviour and Lord and that we will never do anything to hinder this.

8. How Should Baptism Be Done?

Immersion or Sprinkling?

In the last chapter we considered the question of who should be baptised. I tried to show why I think it's right for children in the church community to be baptised. In many ways, that is the most complicated and contentious issue. In this chapter we're turning to consider the issue of how baptism should be done.

The reason that the 'how' of baptism is less contested is because one side insists on their view while the other side is largely indifferent. That is, on one side there are those who maintain that baptism *ought* to be administered by a person being fully immersed, while on the other side people say that how baptism is done doesn't really matter so long as there's water.[1]

The idea that baptism ought to be by immersion is attractive. It's grounded in the death and resurrection imagery found in Romans 6 and Colossians 2 where Paul says that we were 'buried with him in/through baptism' in order that we might also be raised with Him. The idea is that baptism symbolises participating in Jesus' death and resurrection in our place. As a person goes down under the water it represents their death and burial with Jesus and as they come up out of the water it represents their resurrection with Jesus.

---

1. Typically, immersion is linked with believer's baptism and sprinkling with infant baptism. I suspect the practicalities of baptising a baby by immersion have some impact on that!

There are other arguments that people muster for the view that baptism ought to be by immersion. They point out that John baptised in a river and people 'went down' to him and that Jesus 'came up' out of the water when He was baptised. And they argue that the word 'baptise' itself means 'to dip'. But the theological argument is grounded in the death and resurrection symbolism.[2]

However, while it is appealing to think of baptism in that way, there are several reasons why I think that although baptism *can* be by immersion, immersion is not at the heart of the imagery of baptism.

Caution is Required

In the first place, caution is required when thinking about what baptism signifies. There is an important difference between the ideas that are connected with baptism and what the act itself symbolises. Again, circumcision provides a good example (wouldn't you know it!).

In Colossians 2, Paul says that Christians have been 'circumcised by Christ' in that they have put off the 'body of flesh'. As a result, many have understood that the core idea that circumcision signified is 'cutting off' our sinful natures. John Calvin wrote:

> For the Jews, circumcision was the symbol by which they were admonished that whatever comes forth from man's seed, that is, the whole nature of mankind, is corrupt and needs pruning.[3]

But the Old Testament background of circumcision suggests that is not what was signified at all. Circumcision was about God's promise to provide a seed of Abraham through whom He would make a people for Himself who are holy and blameless. The *result* of that is, of course, the stripping off of people's sinful natures. But that does not lie at the heart of the symbolism. It needs to be recognised that the same may be possible with baptism too. It *may* be that baptism is connected with death and resurrection while not necessarily symbolising that as such.

Another reason to be cautious is that our imagery of burial is not necessarily the same as that of first century Jews. For us, burial involves being put in the ground and 'buried' under the earth. For Jewish people 'burial' referred to being put in an above ground

---

2. E.g. Grudem, *Theology*, 967-69; Beasley-Murray, *Baptism*, 133; Ferguson, *Baptism*, 157, 160.

3. Calvin, *Institutes*, 4.14.21.

cave.[4] So when Lazarus was raised from the dead he came *out* not *up* (John 11:44).[5] Indeed, in Ancient Greek the term 'bury' (*thaptō*) has quite a broad meaning, ranging from burial to cremation to simply holding a funeral.[6] A better translation might be the more ambiguous expression, 'lay to rest'. In other words, the down and up of immersion in water that seems to symbolise so well the kind of burial practised in modern western cultures would not have seemed quite so fitting to the people of Jesus' day.

Baptise Can Simply Mean Wash

So how can we tell what baptism symbolises? It helps to think a little about what the word itself means.

The word 'baptise' (*baptizō*) is used a few times in the Greek translation of the Old Testament that was floating around in Jesus' day.[7] In response to Elisha's command to wash and cleanse himself, Naaman bathes in the river (2 Kings 5:14). In some ancient Jewish literature, people bathe in a spring (Judith 12:7) or wash after contact with a dead body (Sirach 34:30).[8] So too, there is a related 'baptism' word (*baptō*) that usually refers to dipping something in a liquid of some kind, such as dipping hyssop in blood to paint the doorframes of the houses during the Passover (Exod. 12:22), or a priest dipping a finger in blood during a sacrifice (Lev. 4:6), or dipping and leaving an unclean item in water to cleanse it (Lev. 11:32). It can also refer to Nebuchadnezzar being 'drenched' with the dew of heaven.[9]

So too, in the New Testament that related 'baptism' word (*baptō*) clearly just means something like 'dip' rather than completely

---

4.   Moisés Silva, ed., 'Thaptō, Etc.,' in *New International Dictionary of New Testament Theology and Exegesis*, 5 vols., 2nd ed. (Grand Rapids: Zondervan, 2014), 2:415-18.

5.   Jesus, too, was buried in a cave not under the earth. The related noun, *taphos*, in the NT refers to cave tombs such as Jesus' tomb (Matt. 27:61, 64, 66; 28:1), the whitewashed tombs of the Pharisees (Matt. 23:27, 29), or the throat as a tomb/cave (Rom. 3:13).

6.   Silva, 'Thaptō, Etc,' 2:415-16; Franco Montanari, 'Thaptō,' in *The Brill Dictionary of Ancient Greek*, ed. Madeleine Goh and Chad Schroeder (Leiden: Brill, 2015).

7.   Otherwise known as the Septuagint or LXX.

8.   Judith and Sirach are Jewish works from the period between the end of the Old Testament and the beginning of the New Testament. Like many other ancient works, they can give us broader insight into the historical setting of the Bible and also into the meaning of words found in the Bible.

9.   According to Theodotion's version of Dan. 4:33 and 5:21. See Moisés Silva, ed., 'Baptō, Etc,' in *New International Dictionary of New Testament Theology and Exegesis*, 5 vols., 2nd ed. (Grand Rapids: Zondervan, 2014), 1:460.

submerge something. Jesus says that the person who dips his hand in the dish with Him will betray Him (John 13:26). In one of his parables, Jesus speaks about Lazarus dipping the end of his finger in water (Luke 16:24). And in Revelation, Jesus' robe has been dipped in blood (Rev. 19:13). Did Judas dip the bread all the way under the liquid in the bowl? That would have been quite messy! Or is the point that Lazarus must completely submerge his entire finger in the water? Or that Jesus' blood was completely submerged in blood?

But there are also several places in the New Testament where the term 'baptise' (*baptizō*) simply means 'wash'. For instance, Mark explains that the Pharisees:

> When they come from the marketplace they do not eat unless they **wash**. And they observe many other traditions, such as the **washing** of cups, pitchers and kettles (Mark 7:4).

The same is true in Luke 11, except there Jesus also links baptism with cleansing:

> But the Pharisee was surprised when he noticed that Jesus did not first **wash** before the meal. Then the Lord said to him, 'Now then, you Pharisees clean the outside of the cup and dish, but inside you are full of greed and wickedness' (Luke 11:38-39).

Similarly, as we've seen, the writer of Hebrews describes the Old Testament cleansing rituals as 'baptisms' (Heb. 9:10). It is striking that those rituals are described using the term 'baptisms' since very few of those rituals were done specifically through immersion. Most of them involved washing, more generally, or sometimes merely sprinkling. Nevertheless, we should probably not think of those ceremonies as involving only a few droplets of water, rather they would have used enough water to actually cleanse people and things.

Again, there is some evidence that 'immersion' does not necessarily imply 'submersion'.[10] The evidence from first and second century A.D. Judaism is that the hand washing rituals were practiced through pouring water into the hands rather than submerging

---

10. See Clement F. Rogers, 'How Did the Jews Baptize?,' *Journal of Theological Studies* 12 (1911): 437-45, Clement F. Rogers, 'How Did the Jews Baptize?,' *Journal of Theological Studies* 13 (1912): 411-14 and the response by I. Abrahams, 'How Did the Jews Baptize?,' *Journal of Theological Studies* 12 (1911): 609-12.

the hands into water.[11] Similarly, although it is not described as a baptism, we have evidence from the Dead Sea Scrolls that one of the ways that a person was cleansed was by he and the priest entering the water and then the priest sprinkling the water for cleansing over him.[12] So too, the first-century Jewish philosopher Philo describes the regular Jewish cleansing rituals as 'sprinkling' and 'pouring' with water from the sea, rivers, and fountains. In the case of the sea and rivers, he seems to envisage people standing in them and sprinkling or maybe splashing themselves with water.[13]

Later in the history of the church, in the fourth century, Gregory of Nyssa could write that baptism ought to involve a threefold immersion. But remarkably the 'immersion'; he has in mind is not submersion but rather pouring water three times over the person being baptised.[14]

Moreover, when Jesus refers to the Spirit in John 7:38, He uses the expression 'living water'. 'Living water' typically referred to water that was flowing rather than stagnant. Similarly, in John 4:14, Jesus promises a 'spring of water welling up to eternal life.' As we saw, Jesus drew that imagery from Ezekiel and the river flowing out from the presence of God to restore the whole world. If that imagery forms the basis of baptism, then pouring would form a better symbol than submerging.[15]

11.　Isidore Singer, ed., 'Ablution,' *The Jewish Encyclopedia: A Descriptive Record of the History, Religion, Literature, and Customs of the Jewish People from the Earliest Times to the Present Day* (New York; London: Funk & Wagnalls, 1901-1906), Alfred Edersheim, *The Life and Times of Jesus the Messiah*, 8th ed. (New York: Longmans, Green, and Co., 1896), 2:11-13.

12.　See 4Q277. The fragmentary 4Q414 13, also mentions bathing and sprinkling. For a discussion of cleansing in the Dead Sea Scrolls see, Lawrence, *Washing in Water*, chap. 4.

13.　That must be so, since only in the case of the water from 'fountains' is a pitcher used to capture the water and then pour it onto the person. How else does one sprinkle themselves with water from the sea and a river without the use of a vessel except by splashing themselves while standing in or near it? See Philo, *Spec. Laws*, 1.262.

14.　Gregory of Nyssa, *Great Catechism*, ch. 35. According to Gregory of Nyssa, the water poured over them takes the place of earth being poured over them in their burial. Two interesting points arise from that. First, how our imagery of what burial looks like affects the way we interpret the language of 'being buried with him'. And second, how Gregory has assumed that burial takes place through being covered in earth; a practice that was foreign to the Judaism of the first century.

15.　The early Christian document, the Didache, permits pouring water over a person's head as a mode of baptism, though it seems to prefer baptism using 'living

Finally, the language that is often used in the New Testament with regards to baptism of 'going down into the water' and 'coming up out of the water', does not necessarily imply immersion either (e.g. Matt. 3:16; Mark 1:10; Acts 3:38-39). Not least because in Acts 8, *both* Philip and the Eunuch are said to go down into the water and to come back up again.[16] It's hardly likely that Philip submerged himself at the same time as he submerged the Ethiopian. Rather, the point is that they both went down to stand in the water and they both came back out of it. How the baptism took place when they were standing there, whether by submersion or pouring, Luke does not think is important enough to mention.

We should probably understand, then, that 'baptism' or 'immersion' can be achieved through pouring and sprinkling; that is, it is being 'covered' or drenched in water.[17]

The idea that stands behind immersing, drenching, bathing and sprinkling is washing and cleansing. That washing can take place in all manner of ways. It might be washing by sprinkling water with hyssop and wool. It might be washing from going down into a lake. It might be washing using a bowl and a facecloth (if such things existed!). Nevertheless, the key idea seems to be washing.[18]

There Are Lots of Metaphors Bound Up with Baptism

It should also be noted that there are lots of metaphors bound up with baptism, not simply death and resurrection. Paul links baptism with putting on Jesus like putting on a new set of clothes

---

water' than other water. It also oddly prefers cold water to warm water, though both are permissible (Didache 7.1-3). One can only guess at the reasons for preferring warm water. Early Jewish sources also display a complicated hierarchy of various kinds of water that are suitable for cleansing, with 'living water' at the top of the list (m. Miqva'ot 1:1-8).

16. Fesko, *Word, Water, and Spirit*, 332. The same is true in the document from the early, post New Testament church, the Shepherd of Hermas (Herm. Sim. 9.16.6; see Ferguson, *Baptism*, 218).

17. This is the position taken by Ian Marshall (see note 23).

18. Even if you're unpersuaded by the evidence here about the general meaning of *baptizō* and remain convinced that baptism ought to be by full submersion, for the reasons outlined in the next two sections I think it is unlikely that full submersion symbolises burial. Instead, submersion still should be taken as a sign of washing and cleansing.

(Gal. 3:26).[19] He links it with circumcision as a sign of sharing in all that was promised to Abraham and his promised descendant, Jesus (Col. 2:11-12). Peter associates baptism with the imagery of Noah and his family surviving the flood (1 Pet. 3:20-21). And Ananias relates it to washing (Acts 22:16). Most often baptism is connected with the work of the Spirit (Matt. 3:11; Mark 1:8; Luke 3:16; John 1:33; Acts 2:38; 10:47; 11:16; 1 Cor. 12:13).

Of course, Paul also connects baptism with death and burial (Rom. 6:3-4; Col. 2:12); so, too, does Jesus (Mark 10:39). But to say they are connected is not necessarily to say that baptism *symbolises* death and burial. Why should that metaphor take precedence over the others? As we saw in the last chapter, the stress lands not on baptism as a picture of death and resurrection, rather baptism signifies the cleansing available through the sacrificial and atoning death of Jesus. Just as in the Old Testament, the water mixed with ashes or blood did not symbolise death and burial, but rather symbolised cleansing whose power came through the substitutionary death of another.

Indeed, as Beasley-Murray astutely observes, when Jesus connects His death with baptism (Mark 10:38; Luke 12:50) it is 'His death which is likened to a baptism, not His baptism which is likened to a death.'[20] That is, Jesus views His death as an act of cleansing, not His baptism as a symbolic death.

Moreover, the meaning which John gives to his baptism is significant here too. John's baptism clearly had no reference to death and resurrection.[21] How could it? That was simply not on the table for first-century Jews. The symbolism of John's baptism was rooted in cleansing, washing and identification with the coming Messiah. If death and resurrection were included in the meaning of Christian baptism, they had to be invested later. But the adjustment to John's baptism that we see in Acts 19 is not with respect to its symbolic meaning. Paul does not say to the disciples of John in Ephesus,

---

19.   Some incorporated that imagery into baptism, requiring that baptism should be performed naked. E.g. Cyril of Jerusalem, *Lectures on the Mysteries*, 20.2-4. See Ferguson, *Baptism*, 124.

20.   Beasley-Murray, *Baptism*, 76.

21.   As Beasley-Murray notes, 'there is no intimation that John interpreted his baptism in terms of death and resurrection; not a hint is given of his preaching that he had ever heard of such a view of baptism.' (Beasley-Murray, *Baptism*, 41, see also p. 54). Ferguson, too, holds that John's baptism symbolised cleansing rather than death and resurrection (Ferguson, *Baptism*, 157).

'Don't you realise that baptism is about being buried in baptism and rising to new life.' He says, in effect, 'Don't you realise that God's cleansing work symbolised in baptism is by the Spirit who comes through the Messiah, and that Messiah is Jesus of Nazareth.' That is not to say that cleansing is not connected with death and resurrection. Of course, it is. But it is simply to point out that death and resurrection are not the meaning of the *symbolism* of baptism.

The Dominant Theological Idea is Cleansing

What we've found as we've worked through the Old and New Testament background for baptism is that the key idea is not death and resurrection but cleansing.[22] The complicated cleansing rituals of the Old Testament foreshadowed a day when God would cleanse His people with more than just water. David longed for the day when God would wash him with more than just hyssop. Malachi foresaw a time when God would clean His people up even with fire and laundry soap.

When first-century Jewish people heard John talking about Jesus baptising with the Spirit, they presumably would have understood that in terms of the Old Testament metaphors that described God's future promise to give the Spirit to His people. But the kind of language which is used in the Old Testament for the giving of the Spirit is 'pouring'. For example:

> For I will *pour water* on the thirsty land, and streams on the dry ground; I will *pour out my Spirit* on your offspring, and my blessing on your descendants (Isa. 44:3) [emphasis added].
>
> I will no longer hide my face from them, for I will *pour out my Spirit* on the people of Israel, declares the Sovereign Lord (Ezek. 39:29) [emphasis added].
>
> And afterward, I will *pour out my Spirit* on all people. Your sons and daughters will prophesy, your old men will dream dreams, your young men will see visions. Even on my servants, both men and women, I will *pour out my Spirit* in those days (Joel 2:28-29) [emphasis added].

---

22. As Beasley-Murray notes, 'Cleansing is the primary meaning of baptism in all religious groups that have practised it' (Beasley-Murray, *Baptism*, 103).

As R. T. France points out, the Spirit is not easily conceived of as a pool or river into which one is submerged. Rather the kind of 'liquid metaphor' associated with the Spirit in the Old Testament is pouring.[23] So too, the key Old Testament promise in Ezekiel 36 is that God will 'sprinkle' His people with water (Ezek. 36:25). What unites these various passages is not the mode by which water is dispensed but the idea that, through the Spirit, God will clean people up just like water does.

Of course, it might be possible to argue that the Old Testament used the language of sprinkling and washing but that baptism shows that now God cleans us even more thoroughly – we're submerged not just sprinkled! The great problem with that idea is that those great Old Testament promises of God's new work in the Spirit are specifically using the language of pouring to refer to the future New Testament event rather than an existing Old Testament reality. In other words, the greater event *is* a pouring rather than a submersion. When theses promises are fulfilled on the Day of Pentecost, Peter again uses the language of the Holy Spirit being 'poured out' (Acts 2:33; also Acts 2:17, quoting Joel 2:28).[24]

Moreover, in other places in the New Testament, the great work of the Spirit brought about through Jesus continues to be described in the language of washing rather than immersion. As we have seen, Jesus describes the work of the Spirit as a spring welling up within (John 4:14; John 7:38). So too, Paul speaks about the Corinthians who have been 'washed' (1 Cor. 6:11) and God's great plan in Ephesians is to 'wash' His church (Eph. 5:26). In Titus, it is the *washing* of rebirth and renewal (Titus 3:5). Ian Marshall suggests, then, that the best translation of John's statement about baptism may be something like, 'I have drenched you with water, but He will drench you with the Holy Spirit', or 'I have cleansed/purified you with water, but He will cleanse/purify you with the Holy Spirit.'[25]

---

23. R. T. France, *The Gospel of Mark: A Commentary on the Greek Text*, New International Greek Testament Commentary (Grand Rapids: Eerdmans, 2002), 72. Marshall makes the same point. He also highlights that in 1 Corinthians 10:2 Paul says that the Israelites were 'baptised' in the cloud and in the sea during the Exodus. While being baptised/submerged in the sea would make sense, being submerged in the cloud would not, certainly not in any down and up sense which is so pivotal to the immersion view of baptism. Instead, Marshall suggests the proper meaning of baptism is 'being drenched in a liquid poured out from above' (I. Howard Marshall, 'Meaning of the Verb "to Baptize,"' *Evangelical Quarterly* 45 (1973): 132, 137).

24. Fesko, *Word, Water, and Spirit*, 331.

25. Marshall, 'Meaning of the Verb "to Baptize,"' 139.

Of course, theologically speaking, we can absolutely say that the way that God cleans us up is by the Spirit uniting us with Jesus in His death and resurrection. That is so important. Nevertheless, it does not seem to be the case that the act of baptism itself is supposed to symbolise death and resurrection by people going under water and coming up again. The dominant imagery is washing or cleansing rather than death and resurrection.[26]

So, Which Is It, Sprinkling or Immersion?

So how should people be baptised? The answer is: it doesn't matter. Baptism is a picture of what the gospel is about: God cleaning His people up through the death and resurrection of the Messiah, Jesus. It's not directly a picture of death and resurrection, although it's true that those ideas are connected. Fundamentally, baptism is a picture of the cleaning up that God does through Jesus and the Spirit, but that picture can happen through sprinkling, pouring and immersion.[27]

---

26.   Grudem specifically rejects the idea that the primary imagery of baptism is cleansing, though he acknowledges that it is certainly part of the picture. He rests his argument largely on Romans 6 and Colossians 2 (see Grudem, *Theology*, 969). But the weight of the evidence from both the Old and New Testaments suggest that cleansing is the primary idea. The number of cleansing references far outweighs those two passages where baptism is connected with death and resurrection.

27.   That said, if someone feels deeply convicted that they must be submerged to signify sharing in the death of Jesus, it seems hard to fathom how that could be unhelpful.

9. Washed by God

I began this book by saying that baptism is about so much more than the questions of who should be baptised and how it should be done, and I want to finish by reaffirming that. Tied up in baptism is a picture of what the gospel message really is.

The problem, as we've seen, is that you and I are born as sinners and rebels against God. It's not that we're sinners because we sin, but we sin because we're sinners – wedded into our very nature is the seed of rebellion against God. In order to be reconciled to God, then, not only does the offence of our sin need to be forgiven, we ourselves need to be cleaned up too.

Understanding our need for deep cleansing helps us to communicate the gospel more clearly in our present age. Our society typically presents us with two opposite choices: either we hide what we feel and 'deny ourselves'; or we embrace our deepest desires and 'be who we are'. In that climate, the gospel is reduced to 'God accepts you as you are and leaves you as you are'. But the true biblical gospel presents us with a third way: we can admit what we feel and desire and we can trust that God won't reject us but will rescue us from those feelings and desires. When we come to God through Jesus, God both forgives us for our sins and sinfulness and He promises to transform us into the image of Jesus. The gospel acknowledges the terrible distortion of sin and offers forgiveness for that *and* it promises that God will not leave us as we are but will make us new creations. That transformation will not be complete until the day Jesus returns to gather His people to Himself. Nevertheless, the gospel is wonderful news, because if the sin the gospel deals with is the sin bound up with our very identity (the filth which clings to our hearts and minds), that means there is no distortion, no inner experience which is beyond the power of the cross and resurrection of Jesus.

Because baptism so clearly communicates the nature of the gospel, we shouldn't give it up or treat it with indifference. Jesus commanded us to do it (Matt. 28:19). It is His gift to help us make clear to ourselves and others what the promise of the gospel really is.[1] So, if you've begun the journey of following Jesus, I would encourage you to be baptised, or if your children have begun the journey of following Jesus, then I would encourage you to have them baptised.

Of course, the aim is not simply to understand what baptism means, but to receive that precious promise by faith. The aim is to link up with Jesus by faith and trust in all that God has promised in Him. If you haven't done that yet, please do that now. It's the most important thing you'll ever do. And if you have done that, then rejoice and share the good news with others!

---

1. 'Finally we should observe that the authority of Christian Baptism is of the weightiest order. It rests on the command of the Risen Lord after His achieving redemption and receiving authority over the entire cosmos; it is integrated with the commission to preach the good news to the world, and it is enforced by His own example at the beginning of His messianic ministry. Such a charge is too imperious to be ignored or modified. It behoves us to adhere to it and conform to it as God gives grace' (Beasley-Murray, *Baptism*, 92).

Books on Baptism

Introductory

Armstrong, John H., and Paul E. Engle, eds. *Understanding Four Views on Baptism*. Counterpoints. Grand Rapids: Zondervan, 2007.

Berkhof, Louis. *Systematic Theology*. Edinburgh: Banner of Truth, 1958.

Grudem, Wayne. *Systematic Theology: An Introduction to Biblical Doctrine*. Grand Rapids: Zondervan, 2004.

Wright, David F., ed. *Baptism: Three Views*. Downers Grove: InterVarsity, 2009.

Believer's Baptism

Beasley-Murray, George R. *Baptism in the New Testament*. 1962. Reprint, Milton Keynes: Paternoster, 2005.

Ferguson, Everett. *Baptism in the Early Church: History, Theology, and Liturgy in the First Five Centuries*. Grand Rapids: Eerdmans, 2009.

Jewett, Paul K. *Infant Baptism and the Covenant of Grace: An Appraisal of the Argument That as Infants Were Once Circumcised, so They Should Now Be Baptized*. Grand Rapids: Eerdmans, 1978.

Schreiner, Thomas R., and Shawn D. Wright, eds. *Believer's Baptism: Sign of the New Covenant in Christ*. NACSBT. Nashville: B&H, 2006.

Infant Baptism

Fesko, J. V. *Word, Water, and Spirit: A Reformed Perspective on Baptism*. Grand Rapids: Reformation Heritage, 2010.

Green, Michael. *Baptism: Its Purpose, Practice and Power*. 1987. Reprint, Oxford: Monarch, 2017.

Kline, Meredith G. *By Oath Consigned: A Reinterpretation of the Covenant Signs of Circumcision and Baptism*. Grand Rapids: Eerdmans, 1968.

Stott, John R. W, and J. Alec Motyer. *The Anglican Evangelical Doctrine of Infant Baptism*. London: Latimer Trust, 2008.

Strawbridge, Gregg, ed. *The Case for Covenantal Infant Baptism*. Phillipsburg: P&R, 2003.

Witherington III, Ben. *Troubled Waters: Rethinking the Theology of Baptism*. Waco: Baylor University Press, 2007.